SUZUKI GT750

A COMPILATION OF 4 FACTORY MANUALS

ENGINE MANUAL

SERVICE GUIDE

DISC BRAKE SERVICE MANUAL

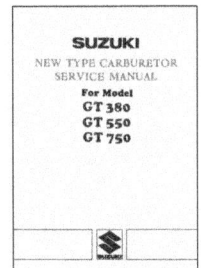

BS40 CARBURETOR MANUAL

1971

1977

A Floyd Clymer Publication - 2025 VelocePress.com

PREFACE

TRADEMARKS & COPYRIGHT

SUZUKI® is the registered trademark of the SUZUKI MOTOR CO., LTD. and this publication is not sponsored by or endorsed by the trademark owner. We recognize that some words, model names and designations, for example, mentioned herein are the property of the trademark holder. We use them for identification purposes only. This is not an official publication however; it may include non-copyright works of the trademark holder.

INTRODUCTION

Welcome to the world of digital publishing ~ the book you now hold in your hand was printed using the latest state of the art digital technology. The advent of print-on-demand has forever changed the publishing process, never has information been so accessible and it is our hope that this book serves your informational needs for years to come. If this is your first exposure to digital publishing, we hope that you are pleased with the results. Many more titles of interest to the classic automobile and motorcycle enthusiast, collector and restorer are available via our website at www.VelocePress.com. We hope that you find this title as interesting as we do.

NOTE FROM THE PUBLISHER

The information presented is true and complete to the best of our knowledge. All recommendations are made without any guarantees on the part of the author or the publisher, who also disclaim all liability incurred with the use of this information.

INFORMATION ON THE USE OF THIS PUBLICATION

This manual is an invaluable resource for those interested in performing their own maintenance. However, in today's information age we are constantly subject to changes in common practice, new technology, availability of improved materials and increased awareness of chemical toxicity. As such, it is advised that the user consult with an experienced professional prior to undertaking any procedure described herein. While every care has been taken to ensure correctness of information, it is obviously not possible to guarantee complete freedom from errors or omissions or to accept liability arising from such errors or omissions. Therefore, any individual that uses the information contained within, or elects to perform or participate in do-it-yourself repairs or modifications acknowledges that there is a risk factor involved and that the publisher or its associates cannot be held responsible for personal injury or property damage resulting from the use of the information or the outcome of such procedures.

WARNING!

One final word of advice, this publication is intended to be used as a reference guide, and when in doubt the reader should consult with a qualified technician.

www.VelocePress.com

IMPORTANT INFORMATION REGARDING PAGE NUMBERS

Each of the four manuals included in this publication have their own index. The page numbers that correspond to each individual index are printed to the bottom of each page.

The page numbers printed to the top of each page are the page numbers within the book to enable quick access to each of the four individual manuals. They are referenced below:

Book page number 1	ENGINE SERVICE MANUAL
Book page number 113	SERVICE GUIDE
Book page number 153	DISC BRAKE MANUAL
Book Page number 181	BS40 CARBURETOR MANUAL

SUZUKI SERVICE MANUAL

MODEL

GT750

ENGINE

FOREWORD

This service manual has been published as the guidance of Suzuki GT750 engine for proper service in the workshop.

This manual is constructed in sequence of Description, Specification, Operation, Trouble shooting, Removal, Inspection, Repair, Adjustment and Assembly for every chapter. In addition to these items, this manual also refers complementarily to a foundermental principle, reason for an adoption of the mechanism and its function as many as possible in order to have GT750 engine comprehended by all the mechanics.

Suzuki will be happy if this manual assists in providing prompt and well done repair work so that GT750 customers will receive reliable service.

Prepared by
SUZUKI MOTOR CO.,LTD.
Export Service Section
July, 1972
Printed in Japan

SECTION INDEX

	PAGE
1. GENERAL INFORMATION	1
2. ENGINE TUNE-UP	9
3. ENGINE	14
4. CLUTCH	33
5. TRANSMISSION	37
6. LUBRICATING SYSTEM	43
7. COOLING SYSTEM	53
8. FUEL SYSTEM	63
9. EXHAUST SYSTEM	72
10. ENGINE ELECTRICAL SYSTEM	74

1. GENERAL INFORMATION

	Page
GENERAL DESCRIPTION	2
GENERAL SPECIFICATION	3
PERFORMANCE CURVES	5
DIMENSIONS	6
SPECIAL TOOLS	7
GAUGE & SERVICE MATERIALS	8

2. ENGINE TUNE-UP

ENGINE TUNE-UP	9

GENERAL DESCRIPTION

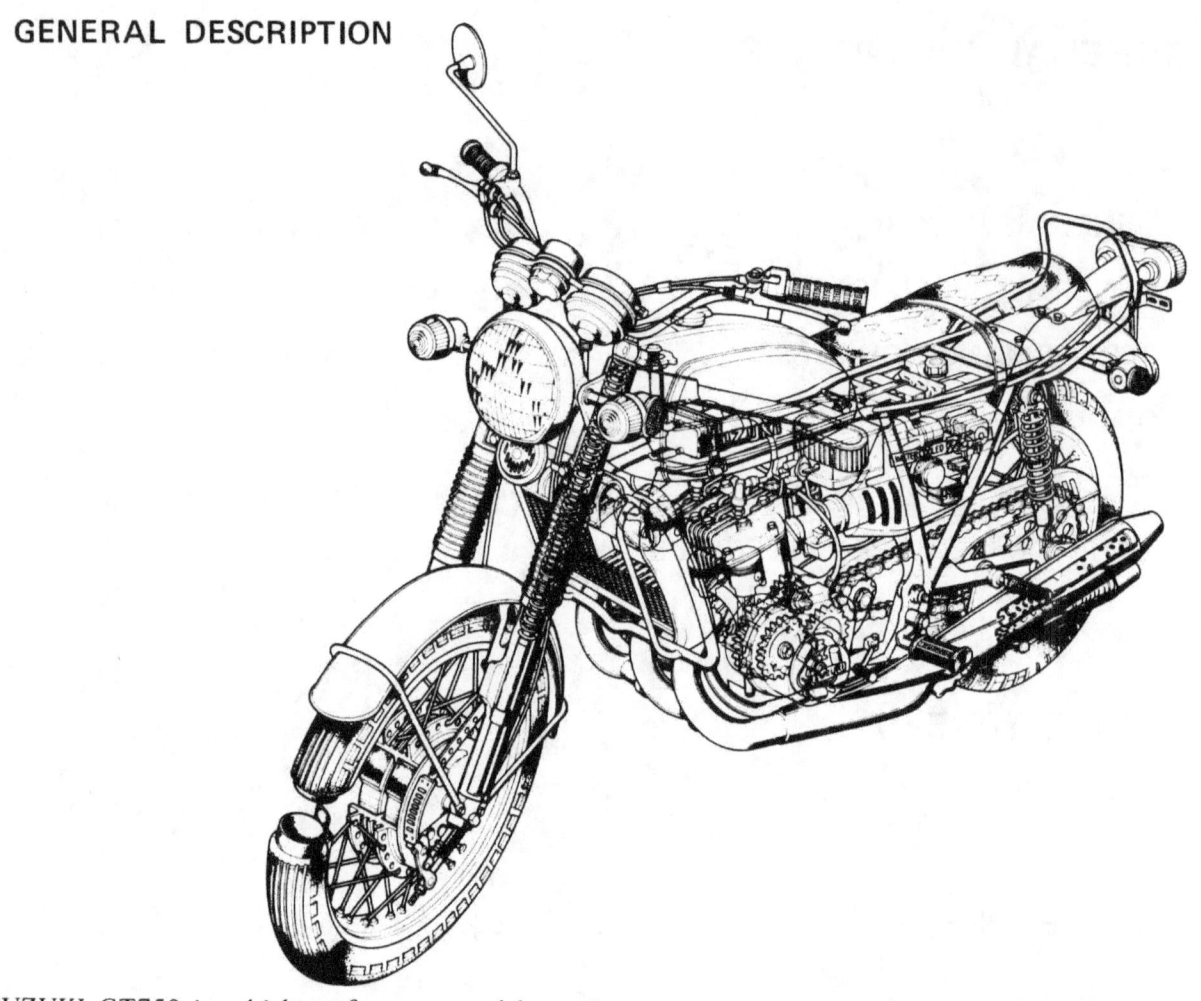

SUZUKI GT750 is a high performance and large size sporty type motorcycle equipped with advanced new mechanisms which are to be described below.

This two-cycle engine has a three-cylinder construction of piston valve type having the total displacement of $738 cm^3$ (45.0 cu in). In order to improve the cooling efficiency and at the same time to display its full power, the engine adopts a water cooling system. On the other hand, to reduce the weight of engine for motorcycle application, the material for main components, such as cylinder block, cylinder head uses aluminum alloys.

A three big bore carburetor system (VM32 SC) is adopted, with each carburetor being used for each cylinder. This arrangement has made it possible to feed always an optimal mixture gas to combustion chambers over a wide range of engine speed, from low to high speed ranges. The exhaust pipe connects three exhaust mufflers with exhaust coupler tubes. Such a newly developed intake and exhaust gas system has given the engine a well balanced highly tuned performance.

The engine driven metering oil pump supplies oil to required locations of cylinders and crank shaft, as is so often the case as in SUZUKI CCI System. In the past, oil supplied returned to crank chamber was exhausting white smoke from exhaust muffler. To avoid this, a new mechanism called SRIS (SUZUKI Recycle Injection System) has been adopted in this machine.

An aluminum corrugated type radiator is adopted in the cooling system for weight reduction. The system is of the sealed pressure type. Combined with the use of "year's round anti-freeze & summer coolant", this system needs no additional supply of water except in the case of unusual leak. A motor driven cooling fan is installed, which operates whenever the water temperature rises due to unusually severe operation conditions of engine.

GENERAL SPECIFICATION

Dimensions and Weight	
Overall length	2215 mm (87.2 in)
Overall width	865 mm (34.0 in)
Overall height	1125 mm (44.3 in)
Wheelbase	1470 mm (57.8 in)
Ground clearance	140 mm (5.5 in)
Tires front	3.25–19 in 4PR
rear	4.00–18 in 4PR
Dry weight	214 kg (482 lb)
Performance	
Maximum speed	184–192 kph (115–120 mph)
Acceleration (0–400 m)	12.6 sec.
Braking distance	1.4 m (46.0 ft) @ 50 kph (30.0 mph)
Engine	
Type	2-cycle, water cooled, piston valve engine
Dimensions (L x W x H)	607 x 499 x 445 mm (26.3 x 19.7 x 17.5 in)
Weight	84 kg (38.2 lb)
Cylinder	Sleeved, aluminum, three
Bore x stroke	70 x 64 mm (2.76 x 2.52 in)
Piston displacement	738cc (45.0 cu-in)
Corrected compression ratio	6.7 : 1
Maximum horse power	67 hp/6,500 rpm
Maximum torque	7.7 kgm/(55.7 lb-ft)/5,500 rpm
Starter	Electric and kick
Cooling System	
Type	Water cooled, pressure forced circulation
Radiator	Corrugated fin and tube pressure type
Water pump	6 brade impeller centrifugal type
Thermostat	Wax pellet element type
Cooling solution capacity	4.5 ltr (1.2/1.0 gal, US/Imp)
Fuel System	
Carburetor	VM32SC, three
Air cleaner	Resin-processed, paper filter
Fuel tank capacity	17 ltr (4.5/3.7 gal, US/Imp)

Lubrication System	
Engine	SUZUKI CCI
Gear box	Oil bath 2.2 ltr (4.7/3.9 pt, US/Imp)
Oil tank capacity	1.8 ltr (3.8/3.2 pt, US/Imp)

Ignition System	
Ignition system	Battery
Ignition timing	24° (R.L 3.63, C3.42 mm) B.T.D.C.
Spark plugs	NGK B-7ES or Nippon Denso W22ES

Transmission System		
Clutch		wet multi-disc
Gear box		5-speed constant mesh
Gear shifting		Left foot, lever operated return change
Primary reduction ratio (gear)		1.673 : 1 (82/49)
Final reduction ratio (chain)		3.133 : 1 (47/15)
Gear ratios	low	2.846 : 1 (37/13)
	second	1.736 : 1 (33/19)
	third	1.363 : 1 (30/22)
	fourth	1.125 : 1 (27/24)
	top	0.923 : 1 (24/26)
Overall reduction ratios		
	low	14.92 : 1
	second	9.09 : 1
	third	7.14 : 1
	fourth	5.89 : 1
	top	4.48 : 1

Suspension	
Front suspension	Telescopic fork with hydraulic damper
Rear suspension	Swinging arm with hydraulic damper

Steering	
Steering angle	40° (right & left)
Caster	63°
Trail	95 mm (3.74 in)
Turning radius	2.6 m (8.5 ft)

Brakes	
Front brake	Mechanical, 2 panel 4 leading shoes
Rear brake	Mechanical, leading trading shoes

Electrical Equipment	
Generator	Alternator 12V 280W
Starter	12V 500W
Cooling fan	12V 27.6W
Battery	12V 14AH
Head Lamp	12V 50/40W
Tail/brake lamp	12V 8/23W
Neutral indicator lamp	12V 1.5W
Turn signal indicator lamp	12V 1.5W
Speedometer lamp	12V 3W
Tachometer lamp	12V 3W
Turn signal lamp	12V 23W
Fuse	20A
Water temperature gauge	12V 2W

SPECIFICATIONS SUBJECT TO CHANGE WITHOUT NOTICE.

You may find some slight differences between your motorcycle and this service guide.
This is because of differences of traffic regulations in different countries.

PERFORMANCE CURVES

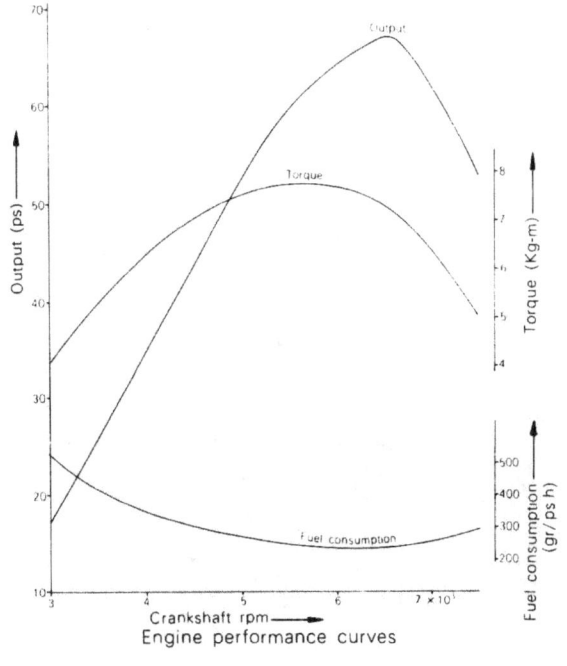

Engine performance curves

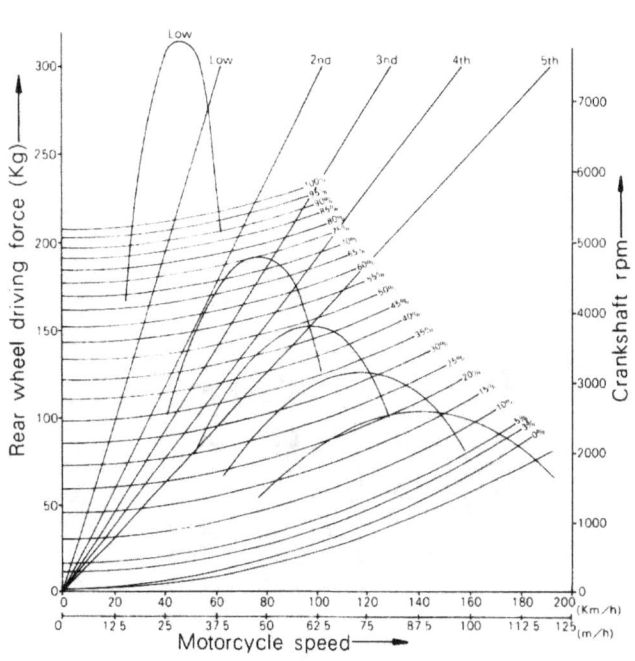

Motorcycle speed

DIMENSIONS

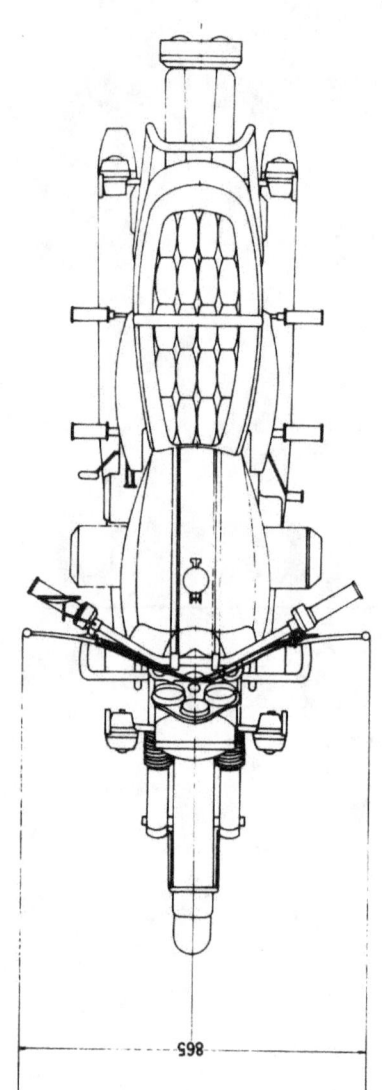
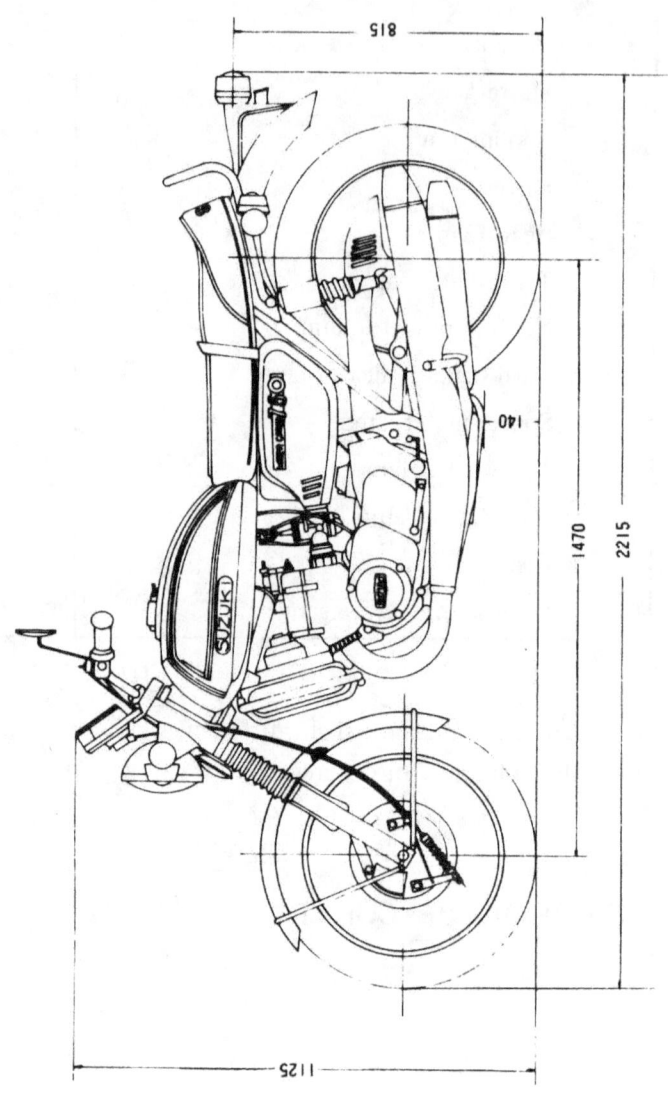
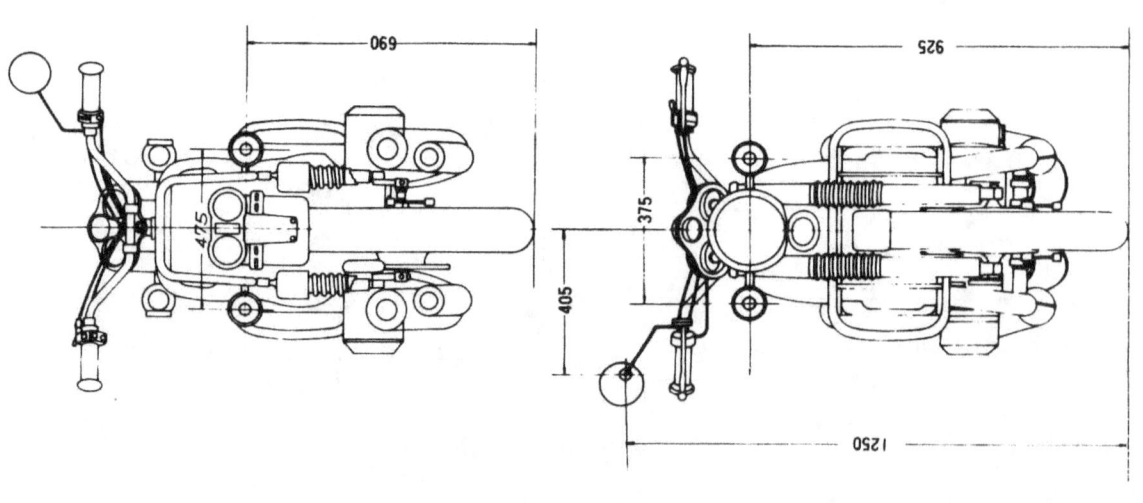

SPECIAL TOOLS

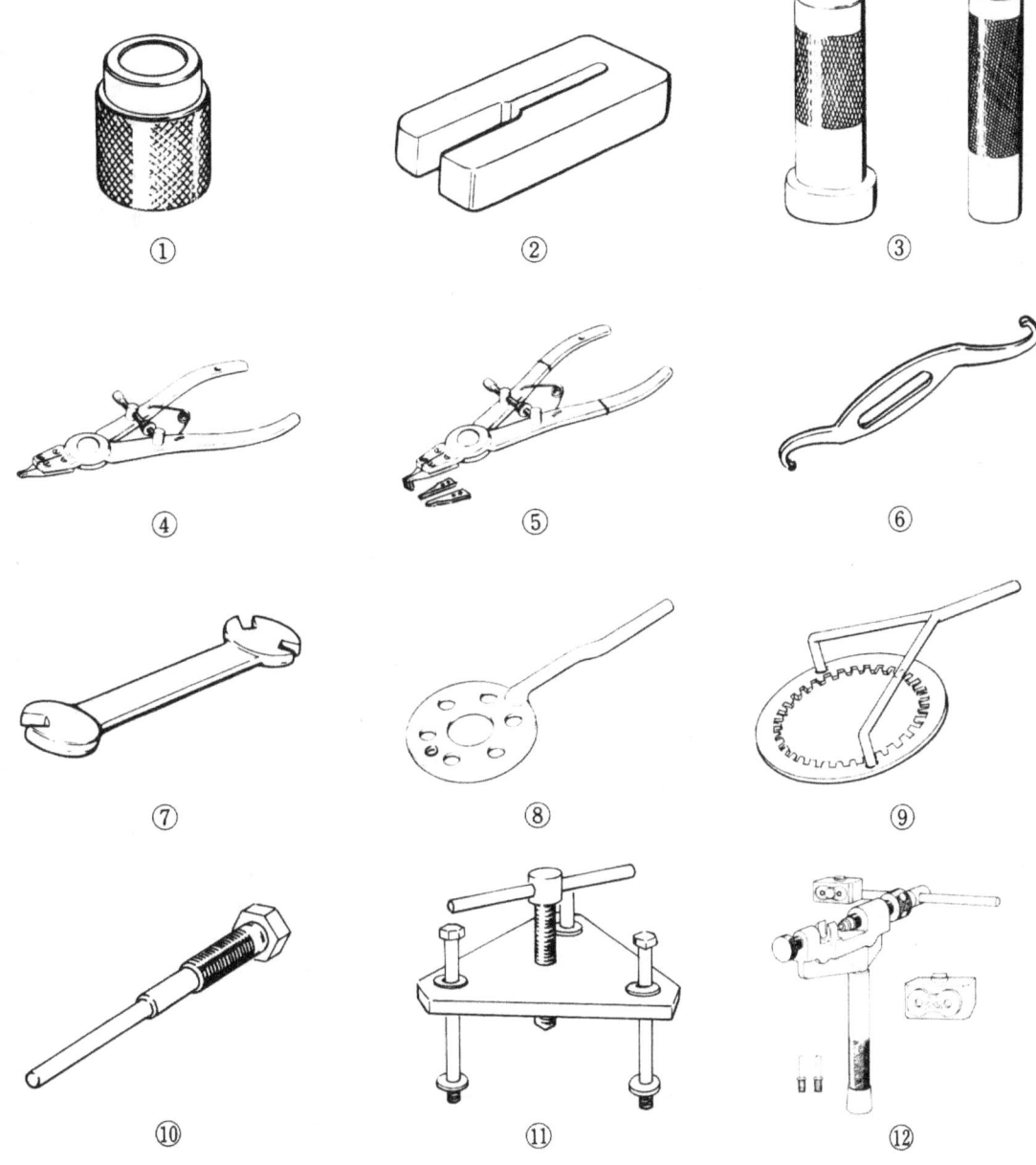

Ref. No.	TOOL No.	Name
1	09940 - 53110	Front fork oil seal installing tool
2	09910 - 20113	Piston holder
3	09913 - 70122	Bearing & oil seal installing tool (Big)
	09913 - 80110	″ ″ ″ (Small)
4	09920 - 70111	Snap ring opener (Small)
	09920 - 70120	″ ″ (Big)
5	09900 - 06103	Snap ring remover
6	09940 - 10122	Steering stem lock nut wrench
7	09940 - 60112	Spoke nipple wrench
8	09920 - 40111	Starter clutch holder
9	09920 - 53110	Clutch sleeve hub holder
10	09930 - 33110	Rotor remover
11	09920 - 13110	Starter clutch remover
12	09900 - 21802	Chain joint tool

GAUGE & SERVICE MATERIALS

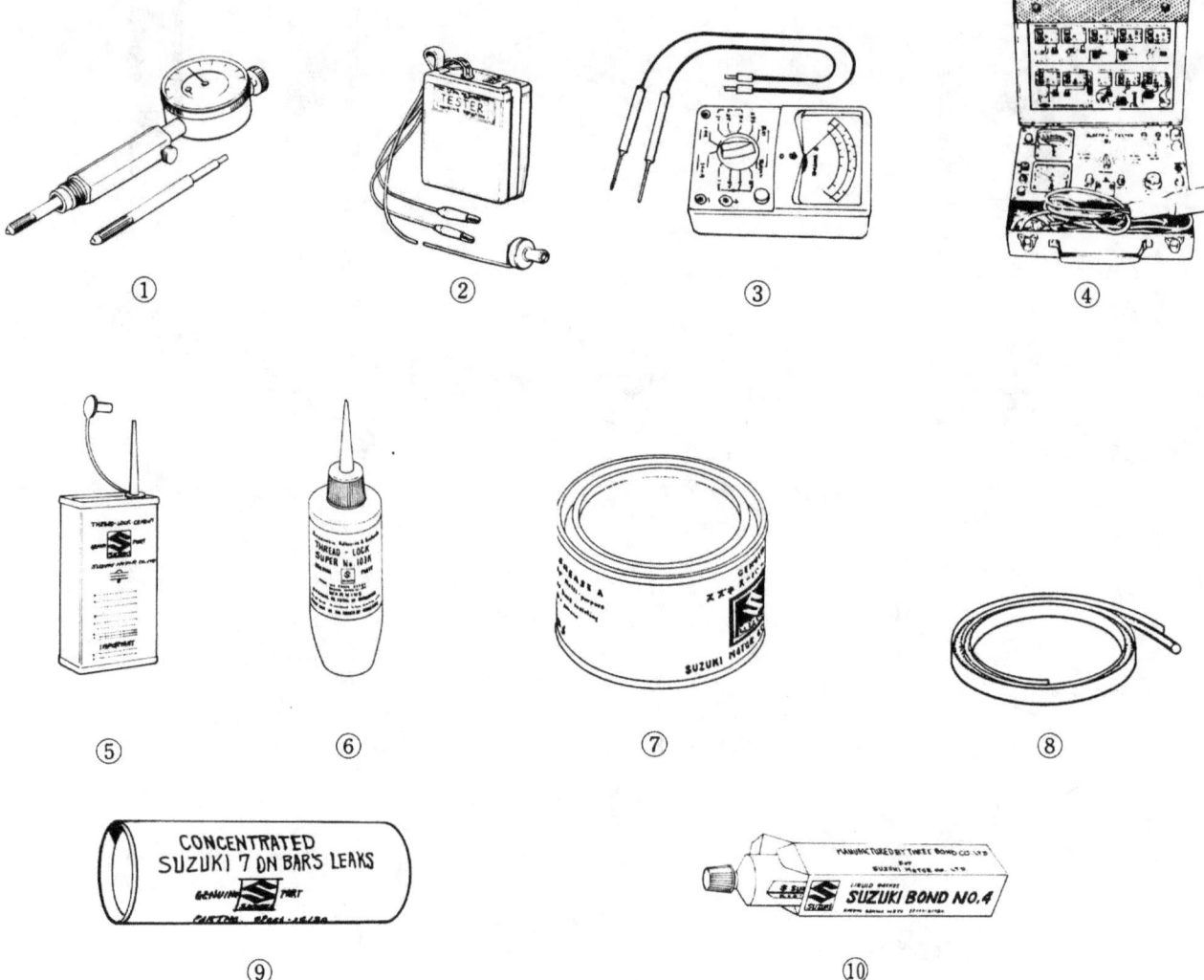

Ref. No.	Part No.	Name	Applied for
1	09931 - 00111	Timing gauge	
2	09900 - 27002	Timing tester	
3	09900 - 25001	Pocket tester	
4	09900 - 28101	Electro tester	
5	99000 - 32040	Thread lock cement	1. Starter clutch hub set screw 2. Gear shifting cam guide set 3. Paul lifter set screw 4. Kick starter guide set screw 5. Gear shifting cam stopper plate set screw 6. Gear shifting arm stopper 7. Starter clutch nut
6	99000 - 32030	Suzuki lock super 103Q	Second drive gear
7	99000 - 25020	Suzuki super grease C	
8	14219 - 31000	Exhaust coupler seal	Exhaust coupler tube
9	99000 - 24130	Suzuki 7 on Bar's Leaks	Cooling system
10	99000 - 31030	Suzuki bond No.4	Crankcase

2. ENGINE TUNE-UP

Periodical inspection and maintenance are essential to maintain the best performance from engine as originally designed.

If any deficiency is encountered during operation of the motorcycle, it must be diagnosed immediately, and proper care should be taken by tuning up the engine.

The engine of GT750 incorporates a great number of new system and equipments which can only be taken care with special knowledge and proper care.
The procedures described in the following orders should be carefully studied to accomplish the correct engine tune-up.

Inspection & Adjustment

Battery

1. Check level of the electrolyte in the battery cells. The electrolyte should be at the level line on the battery case.
   If necessary, replenish the battery with distilled water.

2. The specific gravity of a full charged battery should be 1.260–1.280 at 20°C (68°F).
   When the battery specific gravity decreases less than 1.220, the battery should be changed. If the difference between each cell is more than 0.025 reading after fully charged, the battery should be inspected and replaced if necessary.

3. Check the battery terminals, clean and tighten if necessary.
   Check the battery case for cracks or other damages, and replace if necessary.

4. Check the battery breather pipe if its end is opened or clogged.

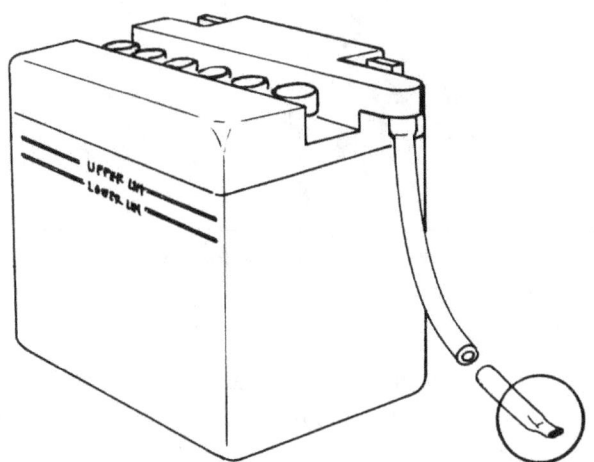

Fig. 2–1   Battery breather pipe

Engine oil (CCI oil) & Oil pump

1. Check the engine oil level in the oil tank. If the oil level is found below the oil level inspection eye, replenish SUZUKI CCI OIL or non-diluent (non-self mixing type) Two Stroke Oil with around SAE 30 wt.

Fig. 2–2   Oil level inspection eye

2. Check to see if air is present in the oil pump and pipe. Expel air if it is.
   For expelling air in the oil pump and pipe, refer to "Inspection & Repair" of OIL PUMP on page 50.

3. Adjust the oil pump lever ① with the cable adjuster ② so that the aligning marks ③ align when the punch mark ④ on the throttle valve comes on upper end of the hole on the carburetor body as the throttle grip gradually winds up. See Fig. 2–3.

Fig. 2-3 Adjusting oil pump lever

Cooling System

1. Check the cooling system for leaks, weak hoses, loose hose clamps and correct coolant level. If the cooling solution level is under the level plate inside the inlet pipe when cool, replenish with distilled water.

2. Check the coolant for deterioration. Check if the transmission oil or gasoline is present in the coolant.

3. When refilling, use GOLDEN CRUISER 1200 Anti-freeze & Summer Coolant tested and guaranteed by Suzuki or equivalents in the market.
GOLDEN CRUISER 1200 Anti-freeze & Summer Coolant is "year around" Ethylene-Glycol solution and serves approximately 2 years or 3,500 km (2,000 miles).
See page 60 for details.

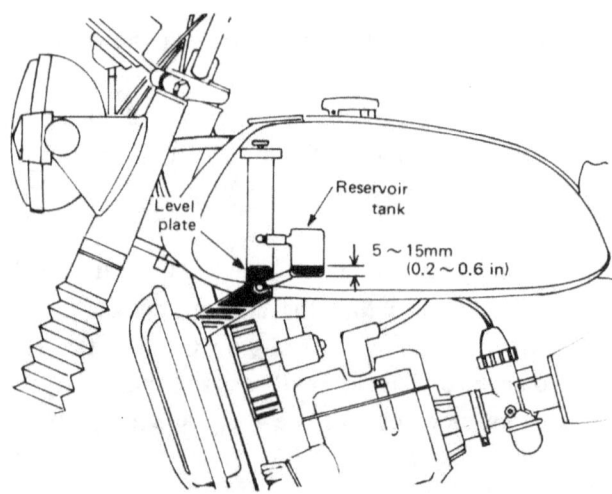

Fig. 2-4 Cooling solution level

Air cleaner

1. Clean the cleaner element with compressed air. Replace the element if damaged or excessively dirty.

2. Check to see if the cleaner is assembled properly after servicing.

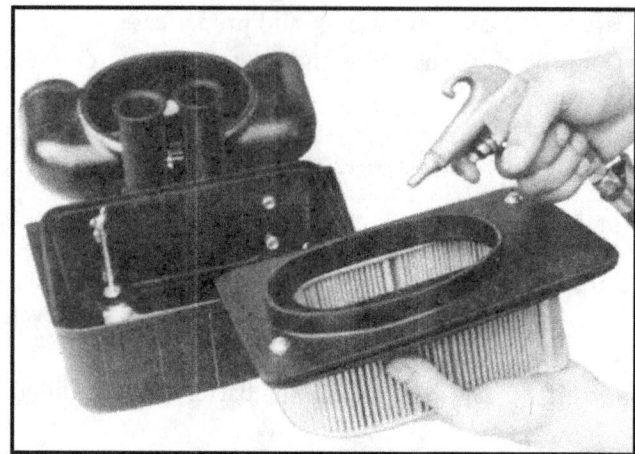

Fig. 2-5 Cleaning air cleaner

Fuel cock

1. Check the fuel cock for clogging, and check to see if the diaphregm ① works properly.

2. Clean the fuel cock filter ②, and replace if necessary.

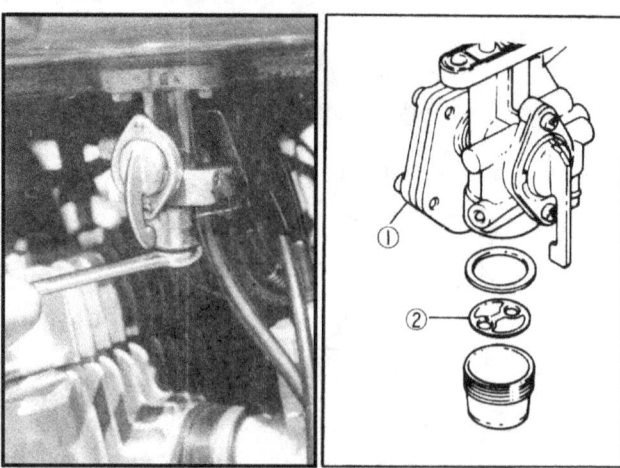

Fig. 2-6 Checking fuel cock

Spark plug

1. Inspect each plug individually for badly worn electrodes, glazed, broken or blistered porcelain, and replace the plug/s as necessary.

2. Clean the spark plugs throughly using a sand blast cleaner.

3. Inspect each plug for heat range. If excessive carbon deposits are observed on the insulator tip, replace with a hot range type spark plugs. If the plugs show burning white or rapid electrode wear, replace with a cold range type spark plugs.

4. Check the spark plug gap. The specified gap is 0.7–0.8 mm (0.027–0.031 in) for NGK and 0.6–0.7 mm (0.024–0.027 in) for ND makes.

Ignition timing

1. Adjust ignition timing with the timing gauge in accordance with the following table keeping in mind that the gauge stroke is not uniform because of the difference in inclination of spark plug hole at each cylinder.

Fig. 2–7 Adjusting ignition timing

Standard ignition timing : 24°±2 (B T.D.C.)

2. Adjust also contact point gap to have 0.35 mm (0.014 in) at maximum opening.

Fig. 2–8 Checking contact point gap

3. Check the contact points for wear or flatness of points surface.
   Check for defective condenser.

Carburetor

Adjust the carburetor in the following methods.
1. Turn the cable adjuster ① on the top of the carburetor to have a play of 2–3 mm (0.08–0.09 in) between the cable and cable adjuster.

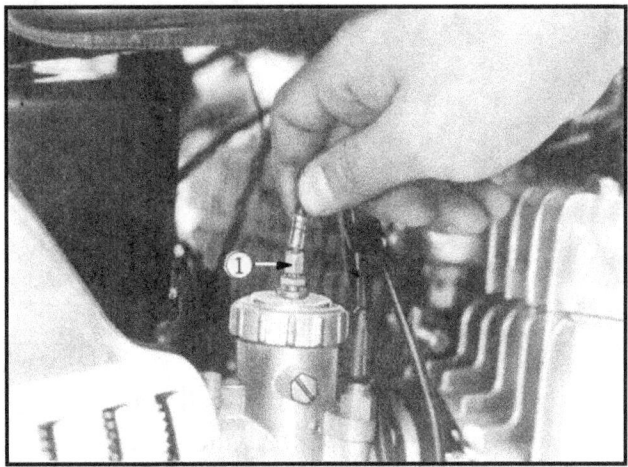

Fig. 2–9 Adjusting cable play

Crank angle (B.T.D.C.)		22°	23°	24°	25°	26°
Piston distance from B.T.D.C. mm (in)	R & L	3.20 (0.126)	3.35 (0.134)	3.64 (0.143)	3.94 (0.155)	4.25 (0.167)
	C	2.88 (0.113)	3.15 (0.124)	3.42 (0.136)	3.72 (0.146)	3.99 (0.157)

R & L : Right and left cylinder
C   : Center cylinder

2. Removing aligning hole plug ① from mixing chamber body of each carburetor, then adjust three carburetors by turning the cable adjuster so that a punch mark ② on the side of throttle valve comes on upper surface of the hole with the throttle grip gradually wound up.

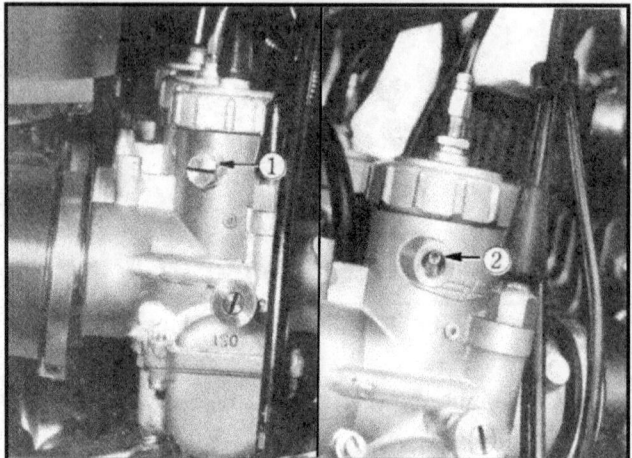

Fig. 2–10 Coordinating three carburetor

3. Screw pilot air adjusting screw of each carburetor all the way in and back it out 1½ turns.

Fig. 2–11 Adjusting pilot air adjusting screw

4. Start the engine and after sufficient warm-up adjust idling speed with the throttle stop screw. Idling adjustment is made with each cylinder actuated one by one by so turning the related throttle valve stop screw as to have a tachometer reading of 1,000 rpm in each case.

Caution: In the case one cylinder firing, the related throttle valve stop screw should be screwed into a considerable extent to keep running.

Fig. 2–12 Adjusting throttle valve stop screw

5. After adjusting the carburetor so that each cylinder has a speed of 1,000 rpm independently, equally turn the throttle stop screw of three carburetors backward to set an idling speed at 1,000 rpm with three cylinders firing.

6. Finally turn the throttle cable adjuster under throttle grip to have a play of 0.5–1 mm (0.02–0.04 in) on the throttle cable.

Transmission oil

1. Check for transmission oil level by removing the oil level screw ①.

Fig. 2–13 Oil level screw

2. Replenish 20W/40 oil of superior quality if oil does not come out of the level screw hole when standing the motorcycle on its center stand.

3. Pour 2200 cc (0.58/0.48 gal US/Imp.) of transmission oil when changing oil.

Clutch

Check the clutch system for play by the following sequence.

1. Remove the clutch adjusting cap and the gasket from the clutch cover. Check for axial play of clutch release shaft ① when the release arm ② is at the lowest position, and adjust the play by loosening the release shaft double nuts ③ to be approximately 0.2 mm and tighten it again firmly.

Fig. 2-14   Adjusting clutch

2. Adjust the clutch cable adjusters ④, ⑤ both at the clutch cover and the clutch lever to have ample play in the clutch cable.

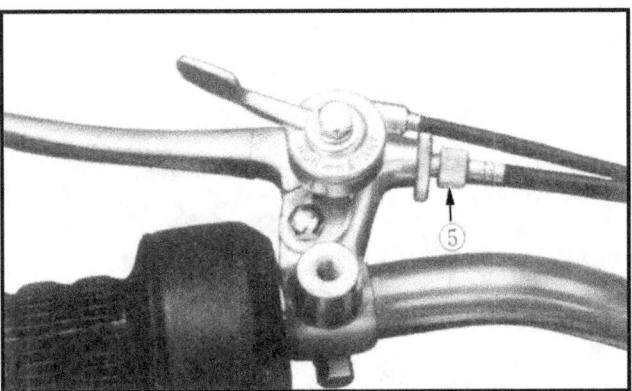

Fig. 2-15   Adjusting clutch cable adjuster

3. ENGINE

	Page
DESCRIPTION	14
TROUBLE SHOOTING	15
ON FRAME SERVICE	20
Cylinder Head	20
Cylinder	20
Piston	21
Starter Clutch	21
Alternator	21
Clutch	21
Starting Motor	22
MAJOR SERVICE	22
Removal	22
Disassembly	23
Inspection & Repair	25
Cylinder Head	25
Cylinder & Piston	25
Piston Ring	28
Crankshaft, Connecting Rod & Bearing	29
Assembly	30

DESCRIPTION

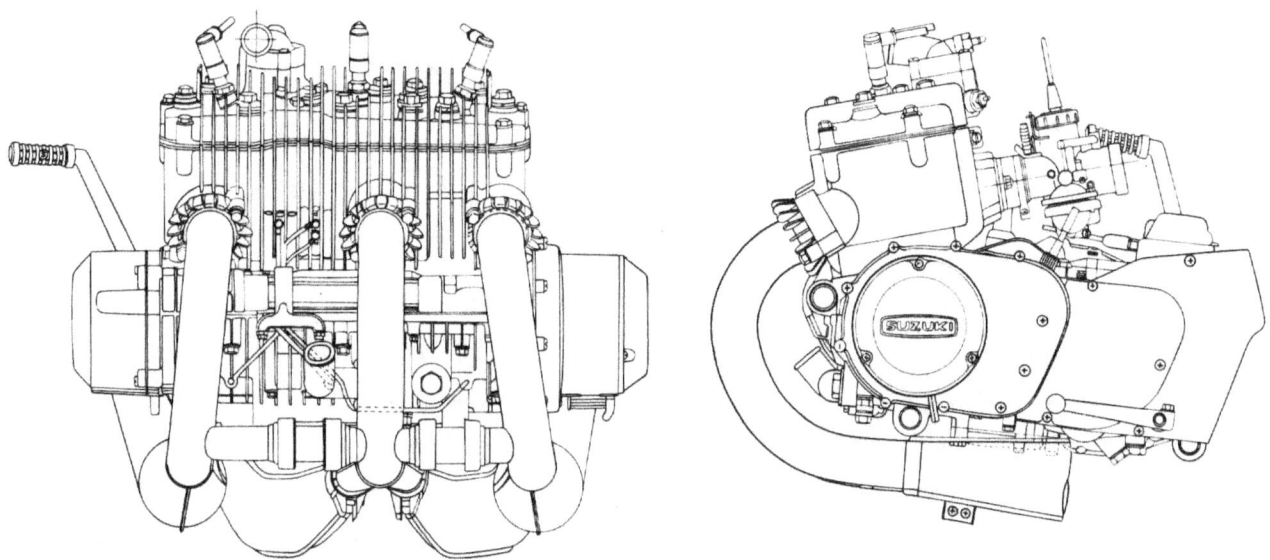

Fig. 3-1 Front and side view of GT750 engine

GT750 Engine is a water cooled, two cycle engine, and has a three-cylinder structure having piston valves. The cylinder head, made of aluminum alloy for weight reduction and high rate of heat radiation, has a dome type combustion chamber. The cylinder block is a one-piece cast structure with the coolant passages used for the cooling over the entire length of cylinder, and the block is made of an aluminum alloy with cast-in cylinder liners.

A fully counter-balanced 120° crankshaft is supported with four main bearings. Piston is also made of a light alloy and two keystone rings are fitted.

TROUBLE SHOOTING

Symptoms & Probable Causes	Remedies

Hard Starting

1. Defective fuel system
    a. Defective starter system — Repair (Refer to page 65)
    b. Defective diaphragm cock — Clean or replace (Refer to page 10)
    c. Dirty or clogged carburetor — Disassemble and clean
    d. Loose carburetor mounting clamps — Tighten clamps
    e. Leaking or clogging fuel passage — Clean or replace
    f. Clogged fuel tank cap — Repair or replace

2. Incorrect ignition system
    a. Burnt contact point/s — Replace point/s
    b. Incorrect point gap — Adjust gap (Refer to page 92)
    c. Incorrect spark plug gap — Adjust gap (Refer to page 93)
    d. Incorrect ignition timing — Adjust timing (Refer to page 94)
    e. Loose or defective spark plug/s and high tension cord/s — Tighten or replace
    f. Defective ignition coil — Replace coil
    g. Defective condenser/s — Replace condenser/s
    h. Wet spark plug/s — Clean or replace plug/s (Refer to page 93)

3. Engine
    a. Worn pistons, piston rings & cylinders — Replace pistons, piston rings, and bore cylinders (Refer to page 26)
    b. Worn crankshaft oil seal — Replace oil seal
    c. Loose cylinder head — Tighten nuts (Refer to page 32)

4. Defective electric system
    a. Defective starter motor — Repair (Refer to page 80)
    b. Discharged battery — Charge battery
    c. Defective battery — Replace
    d. Defective starter clutch — Repair or replace (Refer to page 78)

Symptoms & Probable Causes	Remedies
Low Power or Loss of Power	
1. Low compression	
a. Cylinder head gasket leaking	Replace gasket
b. Piston ring stuck or defective	Replace ring/s
c. Worn piston ring/s or cylinder/s	Replace piston/s, ring/s and bore cylinder/s (Refer to page 26~29)
d. Worn or defective crankshaft oil seal/s	Replace oil seal/s
2. Incorrect ignition system	
a. Incorrect ignition timing	Adjust timing (Refer to page 94)
b. Defective spark plug/s	Clean or replace
c. Defective contact point/s	Repair or replace
d. Defective condenser/s	Replace condenser/s
3. Insufficient fuel	
a. Clogged or maladjusted carburetor	Disassemble, clean & adjust (Refer to page 68)
b. Clogged diaphragm cock	Repair or replace (Refer to page 71)
c. Clogged fuel pipe/s	Clean pipe/s
4. Insufficient air intake	
a. Restricted air cleaner	Clean or replace element (Refer to page 10)
5. Overheating	
a. Insufficient cooling solution	Replenish (Refer to page 61)
b. Defective thermostat	Replace thermostat (Refer to page 57)
c. Worn or damaged water pump	Replace pump
d. Clogged or leaky radiator	Flush, repair or replace (Refer to page 55)
e. Incorrect ignition timing	Adjust timing (Refer to page 94)
f. Faulty cooling fan	Repair or replace
g. Clogged cooling system passage	Clean
h. Low grade engine oil	Change with proper oil
i. Clogged or obstructed radiator fins	Clean

| Symptoms & Probable Causes | Remedies |

Popping, Spitting & Detonation

1. Ignition system
    a. Incorrect ignition timing — Adjust timing (Refer to page 94)
    b. Loose wire and high tension cord — Check connection
    c. Defective spark plug — Clean or replace
    d. Incorrect heat range spark plug — Clean or replace (Refer to page 95)
    e. Defective ignition coil and condenser — Replace
    f. Burnt contact points — Dress or replace (Refer to page 92)

2. Air-fuel mixture
    a. Lean mixture — Clean and adjust carburetor (Refer to page 68)
    b. Dirty carburetor — Clean carburetor
    c. Clogged fuel pipe and cock — Clean or replace
    d. Incorrect float level — Adjust (Refer to page 70)
    e. Water in carburetor — Clean and check fuel tank
    f. Loose carburetor mounting nut — Tighten

3. Cylinder head
    a. Excessive carbon deposit — Remove carbon
    b. Clogged water passage in cylinder head — Clean water passage
    c. Defective cylinder head gasket — Replace gasket

Rough Engine Idling

1. Fuel system
    a. Unbalanced carburetor idling adjustment — Adjust and synchronize each carburetor (Refer to page 69)
    b. Incorrect float level — Adjust (Refer to page 70)
    c. Incorrect throttle wire play — Adjust wire play (Refer to page 70)

2. Engine
    a. Worn crankshaft oil seal — Overhaul engine and replace
    b. Incorrect ignition timing — Adjust (Refer to page 94)
    c. Defective cylinder gasket — Replace
    d. Wet spark plug — Clean or replace

Symptoms & Probable Causes	Remedies

Engine Misfires at Accelerating

1. Fuel system
   a. Water in fuel or clogged carburetor jets — Disassemble and clean carburetor
   b. Clogged fuel pipe or cock — Clean or replace
   c. Defective fuel cock diaphragm — Replace fuel cock
2. Ignition system
   a. Defective spark plug & incorrect gap — Replace & adjust (Refer to page 93)
   b. Defective high tension cord — Replace
   c. Burnt or defective contact point & condenser — Replace
   d. Defective ignition coil — Replace
   e. Incorrect ignition timing — Adjust (Refer to page 94)
3. Engine
   a. Worn crankshaft oil seal — Overhaul engine and replace
   b. Defective cylinder head gasket — Replace

Engine Noise

Tracing the noise source of engine is a very difficult matter even for a skilled engineer. Naturally it seems impossible to specify the procedure to trace the source of engine noise. The best way would be to rely upon the judgement of a skilled man.
In the following we will describe a tracing procedure through which you might be able to trace the noise source more systematically to some extent.

In case of grinding and dragging noise:

1. When the clutch is off, the character of noise changes.
   a. Defective clutch system or too much play in clutch system — Adjust or replace (Refer to page 36)
   b. Defective transmission gear system — Check or replace
   c. Defective transmission bearing — Check or replace

Symptoms & Probable Causes	Remedies

2. The character of noise never changes whether clutch is on and off.
   a. Defective crankshaft bearing — Replace
   b. Defective pump system — Check or replace
   c. Defective starter clutch — Check or replace
   d. Faulty ignition system — Check or replace
   e. Failure in power train except clutch system — Check and repair

In case of knocking or slopping noise:

1. Noise is generated over all the speed range.
   a. Scored piston onto cylinder — Hone cylinder and replace piston
   b. Worn piston pin — Replace

2. Noise is generated during the engine deceleration from high speed range.
   a. Excessively worn piston — Replace
   b. Worn connecting rod bearing — Replace

In case of rustling noise during idling:

1. Insufficient oil in transmission case — Check
2. Insufficient lubrication for contact breaker cam etc. — Check
3. Check if the noise comes from the water pump located under engine case.

Irregular clicking noise:

1. Markedly worn piston ring — Replace
2. Broken piston rings — Replace
3. Piston ring caught at cylinder port — Grind off edge of port

Excessive Oil Consumption

1. Oil leak
   a. Loose oil pipe & connector — Repair or tight
   b. Loose check valve gasket — Tight or replace
   c. Loose oil pump fitting screw — Tight

2. Oil pump
   a. Incorrect oil pump adjustment — Adjust control lever (Refer to page 10)
   b. Clogged check valve — Replace

ON FRAME SERVICE

The following maintenance procedure can be performed without dismounting engine from the frame.

Cylinder Head

Removal

1. Drain cooling system by loosening the water drain plug ①.

Fig. 3-2 Water drain plug

2. Disconnect fuel hose and fuel cock, and then fuel tank can be removed.

3. Disconnect radiator inlet hose.

Fig. 3-3 Radiator inlet hose

4. Loosen water by-pass hose clamp.

5. Loosen cylinder head fitting bolts diagonally as shown in illustration to dismount the cylinder head.

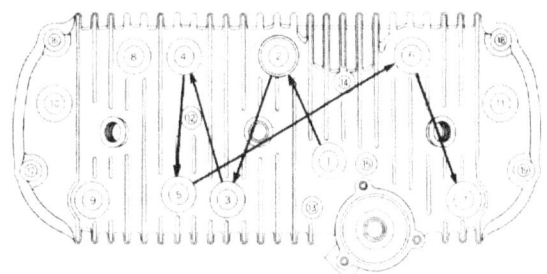

Fig. 3-4 Tightening order of cylinder head bolts

Cylinder

Removal

1. After removing cylinder head, loosen exhaust pipe clamps.

2. Loosen the carburetor fitting clamps and then remove carburetors.

3. Remove SRIS (SUZUKI Recycle Injection System) pipes ① from cylinder.

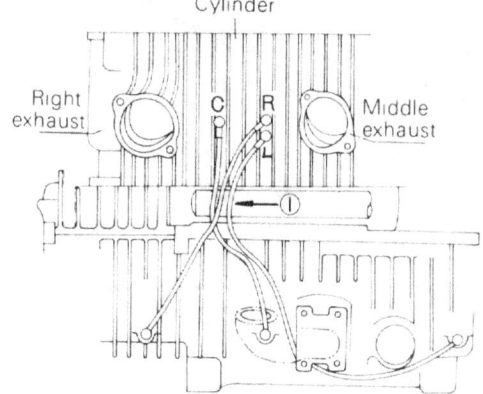

Fig. 3-5 SRIS pipes

4. Lift up cylinder after loosening cylinder set nut.

Fig. 3-6 Cylinder set nut

Piston

Removal

1. After removal of cylinder, remove piston pin circlips from piston pin hole placing waste cloth over crankcase preventing circlips from dropping into crankchamber.

2. Pull out piston pin, and then take off piston.

Starter Clutch

Removal

1. Remove starter clutch cover ①.

Fig. 3-7 Removing clutch cover

2. Remove water pump drive gear.

3. Take off starter clutch assembly using the Starter Clutch Remover ① (09920-53110) and Starter Clutch Holder ② (09920-40111).

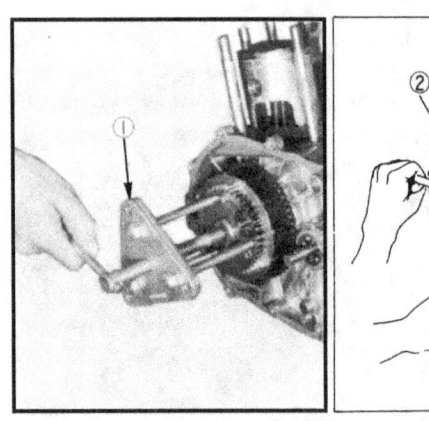 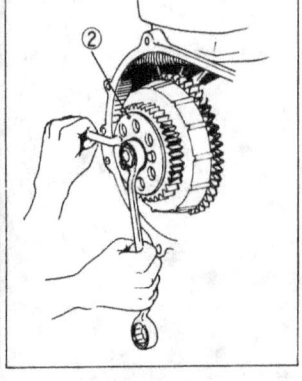

Fig. 3-8 Taking off starter clutch

Alternator

Removal

1. Remove alternator cover.

2. Take off brush holder ① holding it firmly with hands, keeping in mind that brushes may jump out of holder and accordingly wires may be cut off.

3. Remove starter ②.

Fig. 3-9 Removing alternator brush

4. Remove rotor ① by using Rotor Remover ② (09930-33110).

Fig. 3-10 Removing alternator rotor

Clutch

Removal

1. Remove clutch inspection cap and loosen clutch release shaft nuts ①, and then take off clutch lever ②.

2. Remove clutch cover ③.

Fig. 3-11 Removing clutch cover

3. Remove clutch pressure disk ① and release shaft ②.

Fig. 3-12 Removing clutch disk

4. Remove clutch sleeve hub nut using Clutch Sleeve Hub Holder (09920-53110). Subsequent to the removal of clutch plates and sleeve hub, take off primary driven gear spacer ① and bushing ② by drawing with bolts ③, then remove the primary driven gear by sliding it backward.

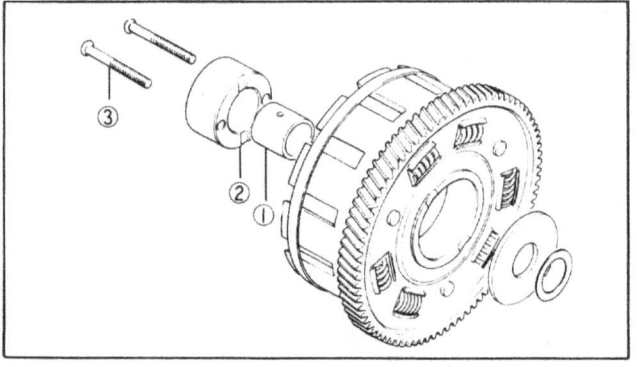

Fig. 3-13 Removing primary driven gear spacer and bushing

Starting Motor

Removal

1. Remove cylinder block.

2. Remove by-pass hose and starting motor cover.

3. Take off by-pass hose union ① and then draw starter motor backward.

Fig. 3-14 Taking off by-pass hose union

MAJOR SERVICE

Removal

1. Drain the cooling system. See page 20.

2. Disconnect the starting motor wire from the battery terminal.

3. Disconnect the fuel pipes and unhook the fuel tank setting band ①, then remove the fuel tank by sliding it backward.

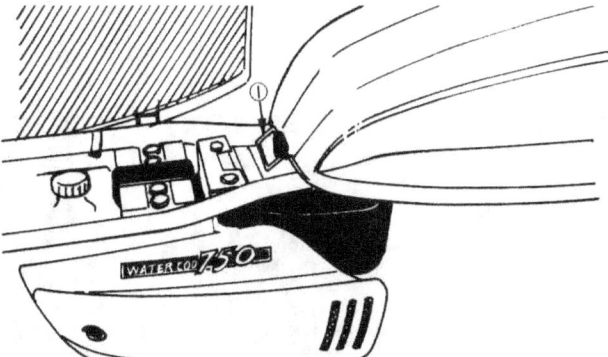

Fig. 3-15 Unhooking fuel tank setting band

4. Disconnect the radiator inlet hose. See Fig. 3-3.

5. Remove the cooling fan with its bracket.

Fig. 3-16 Removing cooling fan

6. Loosen the exhaust pipe clamp set bolts and rear foot rests, then remove the mufflers ① and coupler tubes ②.

Fig. 3-17 Exhaust pipes & coupler tubes

7. Remove the frame left cover, and disconnect the alternator and the contact breaker couplers ①, ② from the coupler bracket, and also disconnect the starting motor lead ③ from the starter switch relay and the engine ground wire from the frame.

Fig. 3-18 Electric parts holder

8. Remove the air cleaner by loosening set bolts ① and carburetor clamps.

Fig. 3-19 Loosening air cleaner set bolts

9. Remove the left foot rest and gear shifting lever, and then remove the engine sprocket ① with the drive chain on it.

Fig. 3-20 Removing engine sprocket

10. Disconnect the clutch, oil pump, carburetor and tachometer cable.

11. Remove the right foot rest and brake pedal.

12. Remove the engine mounting bolts and mounting plates, then remove the engine from frame.

Disassembly

1. Drain the transmission oil.

2. Remove the contact breaker assembly by unscrewing three set screws.

Fig. 3–21 Contact breaker assembly

3. Remove the starter clutch cover, and the water pump drive gear ① and starter idle gear ②, then remove the starter clutch with the Starter Clutch Remover (09920–53110). See page 21.

4. Extract the tachometer driven gear ③ with the sleeve on it, after loosening the set bolt ④.

Fig. 3–22 Removing water pump driving parts

5. Remove the gear shifting switch ① and drive shaft oil seal retainer ②.

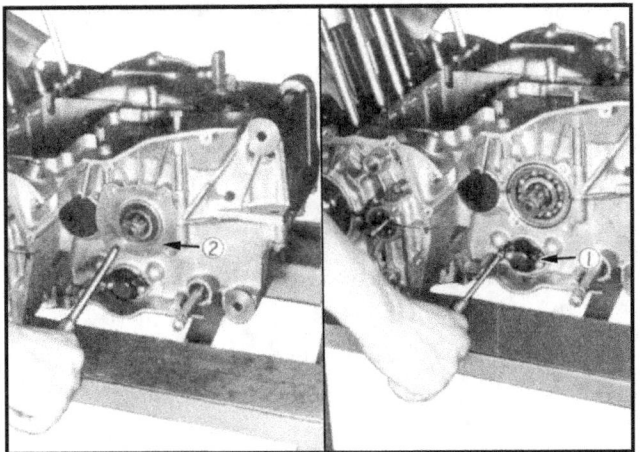

Fig. 3–23 Removing gear shifting switch and oil seal retainer

6. Remove the alternator housing assembly, and the rotor with the Rotor Remover (09930–33110). See Fig. 3–10.

7. Remove the by-pass hose from cylinder head, and loosen the cylinder head bolts in criss-cross style, and remove the cylinder head. See page 20.

8. Remove the SRIS (SUZUKI Recycle Injection System) oil hoses from the cylinder and crankcase, and remove the cylinder by loosening the cylinder fitting nut at the lower part of cylinder block. See page 20.

9. Remove the piston pin circlips, and piston pins and remove pistons.

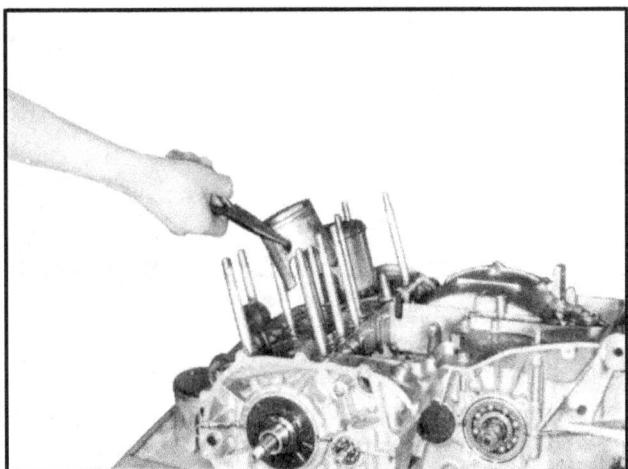

Fig. 3–24 Removing piston pin circlip

10. Remove the starting motor cover ①, and the water pump by-pass hose union (Fig.3–14), and slide the starting motor backwards to remove it.

Fig. 3–25 Removing starting motor

11. Remove the oil pump cover, the oil pump and oil pipe comp..

12. Remove the clutch adjusting cap, then loosen and remove the clutch release shaft fitting nuts to take off the clutch release arm.
    Remove the clutch cover, and the clutch pressure disk by removing six bolts, then take out the drive and driven plates.
    Remove the clutch sleeve hub with the Clutch Sleeve Hub Holder (09920-53110). See page 21.

Fig. 3-26   Removing clutch cover

Remove the primary driven gear assembly after pulling out the primary driven gear bushing with two bolts screwed into it. See page 22.
Remove the transmission oil reservoir plate which is located on crankcase inside the clutch chamber.

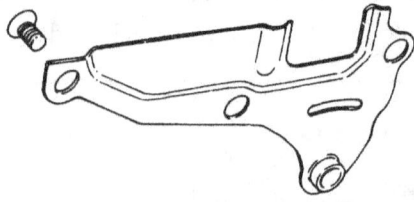

Fig. 3-27   Transmission oil reservoir

13. Remove the kick starter shaft spring guide, and the spring and its holder.

14. Loosen the crankcase fitting bolts in the reverse order of relieved (casted) numbers on the crankcase, and remove them all to open the crankcase.

15. Remove the shafts and gears.

Inspection & Repair

Clean out all disassembled engine parts completely, before starting the inspection and repair work. All locations with water leakage and defects should be checked carefully beforehand. Don't mix or change the originally mated parts of the pistons, piston rings and bearings.

Cylinder Head

1. Remove carbon deposits in combustion chamber with scraper or wire brush. Due care should be taken not to scratch the parting surface of cylinder head.

2. Check for any cracks in the head casting, also check for scratches or nicks on the parting surface. Replace the head, if necessary.

3. Check the flatness of parting surface using a feeler gauge ①. If warpage or distortion exceeding 0.04 mm (0.001") is found on the surface, repair the surface, or replace the cylinder head.

Note: When measuring the flatness, measure in six directions.

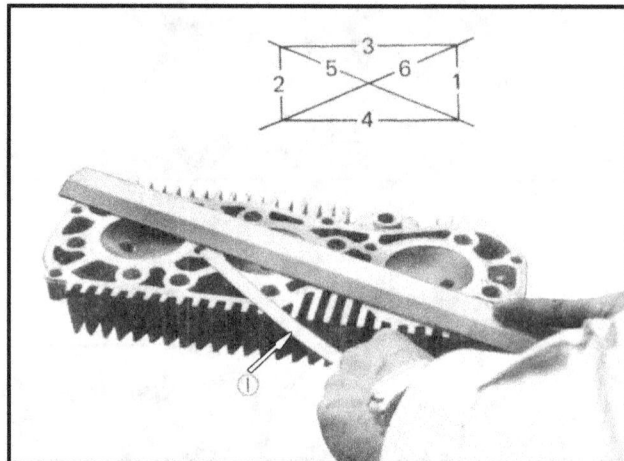

Fig. 3-28   Checking cylinder head flatness

Cylinder & Piston

1. Remove the carbon deposit in exhaust port, but ample care should be taken not to scratch the inner wall of cylinder.

2. Check any cracks in cylinder block, and then check any burrs and nicks on the parting gasket surface. Use special apparatus observe the minor defects, since they may not be found visually. The block should be pneumatically tested with the air pressure of 3 kg/cm², and it is acceptable if no leakage is found out.

3. Measure the cylinder block surface flatness on the gasket side in the same way as the cylinder head. If its warpage exceeds 0.05 mm (0.002") in magnitude, scrape off the surface or replace the block itself.

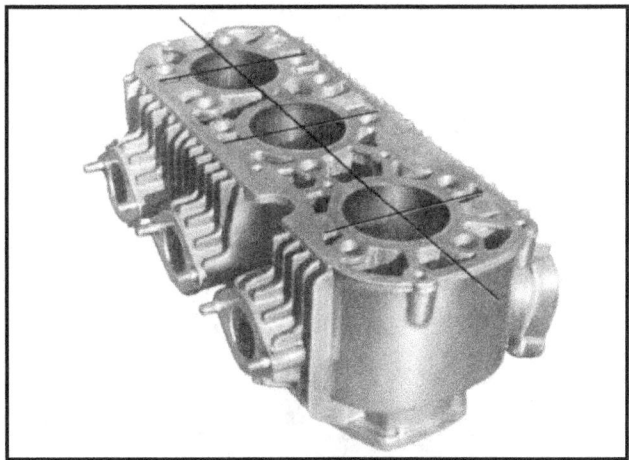

Fig. 3-31   Directions to be measured

Fig. 3-29   Checking cylinder block flatness

4. Measure the out of roundness and taper wear of the cylinder bore with the cylinder gauge. Cylinder bore should be measured at upper, middle and lower points of the bore surface in both lateral and transverse directions with respect to the cylinder block center line as shown in the figure.

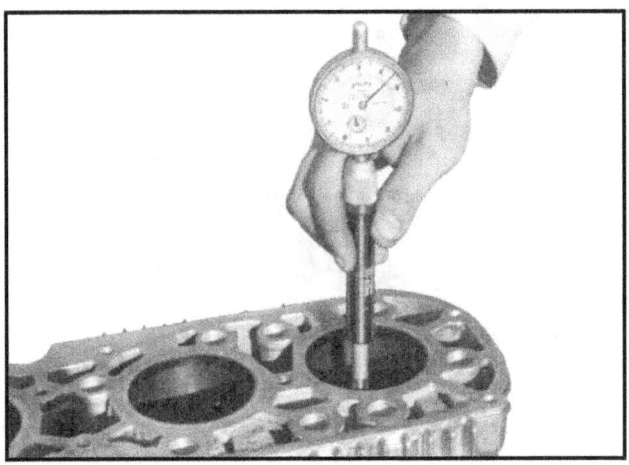

Fig. 3-30   Measuring cylinder bore for wear

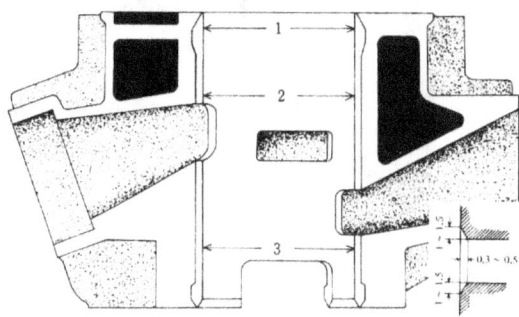

Fig. 3-32   Positions to be measured

If differences between the maximum and minimum bore diameters measured exceed 0.07 mm (0.0018"), rebore and polish off the cylinder by honing.

Cylinder bore (Standard):
    70.000~70.015 mm (2.7559~2.7565")
Wear & taper limit: 0.07 mm (0.0018")

If reboring is needed, measure the bore diameter at the location of maximum wear, and then select oversize pistons. The amount of reboring needed should be determined by the diameter of oversize pistons used, and the cylinder bore clearance.

Piston diameter:
  STD: 69.950~69.965 mm (2.7539~2.7545")
  O/S 0.5:
      70.450~70.465 mm (2.7736~2.7742")
  O/S 1.0:
      70.950~70.965 mm (2.7933~2.7939")
Piston bore clearance (Standard):
    0.045~0.055 mm (0.0018~0.0022")

Note: When reboring, both intake and exhaust ports are to be chamfered as shown in Fig. 3-32.

Piston diameter should be measured always normal to the piston pin center line and at 32 mm (1.26") above the lowest end.

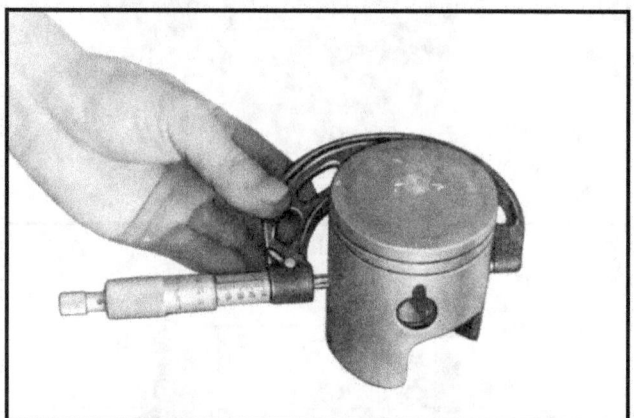

Fig. 3-33 Measuring piston diameter

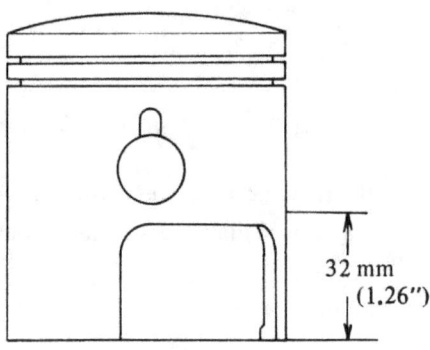

Fig. 3-34 Measuring point

Necessity of determining measuring points of piston and cylinder bore diameters

Reasons for having measuring points of both piston and cylinder bore diameters fixed are as follows:

(1) As shown in Fig. 3-32, the cylinder has inlet, scavenging, and exhaust ports bored on the cylinder surface. When a piston is subjected to reciprocating motion cylinder wall, amount of wear of cylinder is always larger in the neighborhood of the port, resulting in a kettle type elliptic shape when magnified. On the other hand, near the top position, the wall is exposed to higher temperatures and pressures from combustion gas which contribute to accelerated wear of the cylinder. Naturally, the roundness and cylindricalness of the cylinder become needed and are to be measured at the top, middle, and bottom positions in both parallel and normal directions to the cylinder axis. This is needed to represent the shape of piston cylinder correctly.

(2) As shown in Fig. 3-35, piston has a taper in longitudinal direction and has an elliptic cross section. During engine operation, the piston is heated and expands. As the wall thickness increases, so does the expansion rate of piston. This taper is needed to obtain a true cylindrical form with roundness during engine operation, by machining as shown in the drawing.

I: Distance from the skirt bottom 32 mm (1.26")
II: Diameter at 90 to the pin boss
III: Diameter parallel with pin boss

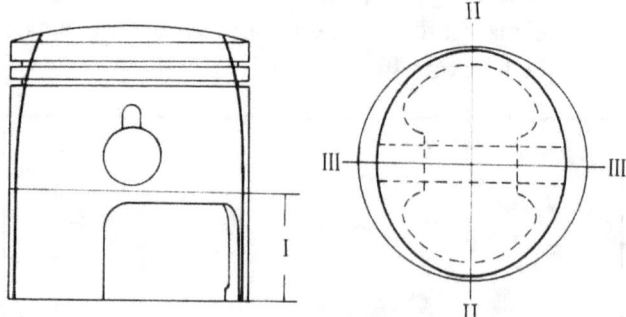

Fig. 3-35 Piston's out-of-round & tapering

5. Measure the clearance between cylinder and piston using piston feeler gauge.

To measure the piston clearance, insert a feeler gauge into the cylinder bore, then insert the piston top into the bore with the feeler gauge fixed at 90° to the piston pin axis. Then pull out the gauge: this can be done more accurately using a spring scale. The allowable limit of tension force should be between 1 and 2 kg (2.2~4.4 lb).

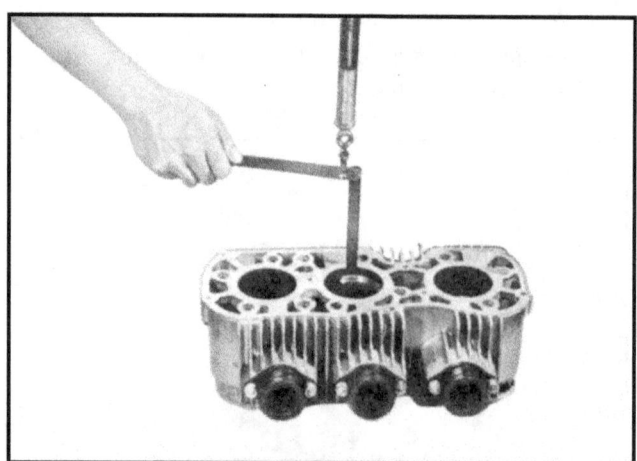

Fig. 3-36 Measuring cylinder clearance

If the piston clearance exceeds 0.070 mm (0.0018″), the cylinder should be rebored, or else the piston must be replaced.

Note: Two kinds of piston are available: Be carefull not to confuse each piston. (Refer to "Assembly" item.)

6. Examine piston pin boss and piston ring groove carefully for any abnormal wear, burrs or cracks. Check the piston side wall for any trace of sticking or scratches. If damaged excessively, replace the piston. If the damage is slight, polish it with #400 emery sand paper. As piston rings are paired with piston, replace both, if necessary.

Fig. 3-37 Polishing piston surface

Piston Ring

1. Check piston ring for any defects such as abnormal wear, etc.. To check the ring wear, insert piston ring into the cylinder bore from bottom to check the end gap of the ring. Replace the piston ring if the ring gap exceeds 0.7 mm (0.027″).

   Piston ring end gap (Standard):
   0.15~0.35 mm (0.006~0.014″)

Note: When checking the piston ring in the cylinder bore, insert it with the piston to settle it horizontally in the bore.

Fig. 3-38 Checking piston ring end gap

If only the rings are to be replaced without boring the cylinder, be sure to measure the ring end gap at the lower position of the cylinder bore where the amount of wear is expected to be a minimum.

2. Measure the side clearance of piston ring. Same key-stone type rings are used for top and second rings. Its periphery is machined like a barrel shape. Consequently, any piston ring trouble is quite rare. Piston groove wear may occur, which must be spotted.

   Standard value of ring side clearance:
   0.030~0.095 mm (0.001~0.004″)

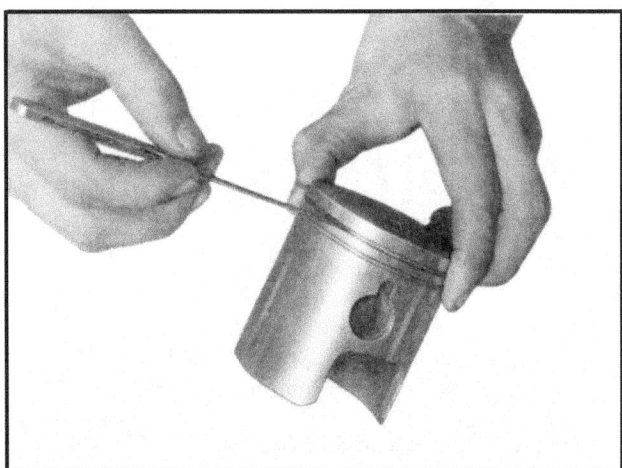

Fig. 3-39 Measuring piston ring side clearance

✱ The benefits of the key stone type rings ✱

The function of piston ring is to seal off the explosive gas preventing it blowing through cylinder and piston. To do this, the rings should be adhered onto the cylinder wall tightly, floating on the piston. But after long hours of operation, the carbon deposit as the product of incomplete combustion tends to accumulate in ring grooves, causing sticking of ring, resulting in poor sealing. The keystone ring in effect clears off the carbon deposit in grooves due to the tapered surface during reciprocating motion of piston.

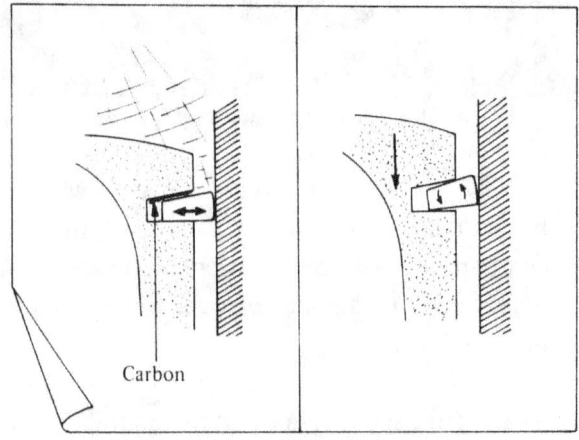

Fig. 3-40 Function of piston ring

The external barrel-like shape of the ring is effective for preventing the ring edge from contacting the cylinder wall or cylinder port edge, thus ring noise, oil film breakage, piston seizure, and excessive wear can be avoided. Very thin and wide rings are used, which is effective in reducing the tension. So it now becomes possible to prevent cylinder wall scuffing, and at the same time to reduce the friction power.

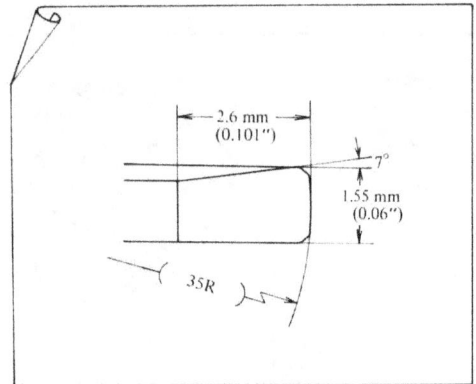

Fig. 3-41 Piston ring dimension

Crankshaft, Connecting Rod & Bearing

Crankshaft is assembled by press fitting. It is supported to crankcase by four main bearings. Both big and small end bearings in the connecting rod are of needle roller type having cages, resulting in extended engine life and reduced power loss.

1. Check the amount of bend and twist of connecting rod; the bent or twisted rod may cause abnormal wear in piston or cylinder or result in piston seizure.

2. Check the wear amount of small end bearing of connecting rod. Insert the bearing and piston pin in the small end and examine the play. If the play exceeds 0.05 mm (0.002″), replace the rod.

3. Check the amount of wear in connecting rod big end bearing. Measure the play at the end of connecting rod as shown in the figure. Replace the rod when the play exceed 3 mm (0.018″).
   Standard value of play at the end of connecting rod: 0.5~0.8 mm (0.02~0.03″)
   Standard value of play for connecting rod big end thrust: 0.2~0.6 mm (0.008~0.023″)

(Note) Check for abnormal wear or burn in connecting rod big end thrust washer.

Fig. 3-42 Checking con-rod big end wear

4. Check for wear or creep of big end bearing. Turn bearing outer race, and check if the turning is smooth or if clicking noise is generated. Then check for the axial play of each bearing.

5. Check the bending of crankshaft. Mount crankshaft at both ends on V block, measure the run-out at crank web section or bearing with dial indicator. Half of this D.I.R. value is the bend of crankshaft. If the D.I.R. exceeds 0.08 mm (0.003"), replace or repair the shaft. Depending on the reading of indicator, correct the shaft hammering on the protruded side of the shaft to reduce the amount of bend using a copper hammer.

Fig. 3-43   Checking crankshaft bending

6. Check for the wear of oil seals and the damage of seal lips.
   If the sealing of oil lips is defective, fresh mixture may not be fully compressed resulting in hard starting and reduced power.

Note: Even when only one of the main bearing or oil seals is damaged, replace all of them as a set. Use always genuine parts, especially for bearings, because they are of special order-made.

Assembly

All rotating or sliding parts should be washed with solvent and then lubricated with engine oil before assembling. All gaskets, packings, oil seals, cotter pins and lock washers should be replaced upon assembly.
The special liquid gaskets and the adhesive cements are used to prevent the oil from leaking or to prevent the bolts and nuts from loosening.

1. Install the crankshaft assembly into the crankcase, with all the punch marks ① on the outside of crankshaft bearing aligning with the mating surface.

Note: Be careful that only the outermost right side bearing should be aligned at the backside of crankshaft, while others at the frontside.

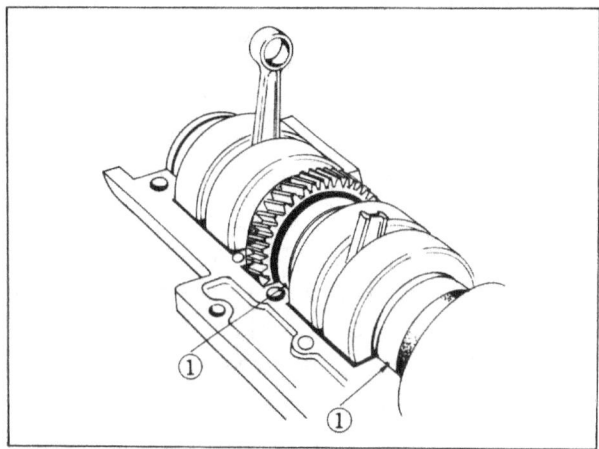

Fig. 3-44   Aligning mark on crankshaft bearing

2. Be sure to force the oil seals toward each bearing tightly except one placed between the primary gear and right crankshaft, so as not to come into contact with the crankshaft webs while running.

3. After installing the transmission gears, gear shifting mechanism and kick starter gear assembly into the lower crankcase, assemble the upper and lower crankcases with SUZUKI BOND No. 4 (99000-31030) applied on the upper mating surface.

Caution : The special attention should be paid to the following two points when assembling the crankcase.

a. Use exclusively the SUZUKI BOND No. 4 as a liquid gasket when reassembling in the market. Spread it on the upper surface thinly after cleaning the surface from dust, oil, water and other materials by swabbing with waste cloth. Wait at least 10 minutes before assembling.

b. The crankcase, 1st driven, 2nd driven and kick starter drive gears should be selection-assembled to get a optimum backlash for less noise from the transmission. Follow the instruction when replacing these parts.
Refer to chart at page 32.

∗ When replacing crankcase assembly (11304–31802)

Install the 1st driven, 2nd driven and kick starter drive gears which are supplied together with the crankcase assembly.

∗ When replacing 1st driven gear (24310–31821) and/or 2nd driven gear (24320–31822)

There are two gears in the package, one is yellow painted and the other is white painted. Check the paint color indicated on the crankcase, then choose the suitable gear according to the chart.

∗ When replacing kick starter drive gear (26240–31823)

There are two gears in the package, one is brown painted and the other is yellow painted. Check the paint color indicated on the crankcase, then choose the suitable gear according to the chart.

4. Tighten the crankcase fitting bolts in the order casted upon the crankcase outside, with specified tightening torque.
Standard specified tightening torque:
6mm bolt   60~100 kg-cm(4.34~ 7.23 lb-ft)
8mm bolt 130~230 kg-cm(9.38~16.65 lb-ft)
10mm bolt 250~400 kg-cm(18.08~28.90 lb-ft)

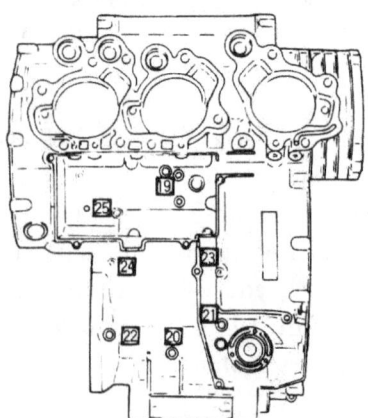

Fig. 3–45   Upper crankcase

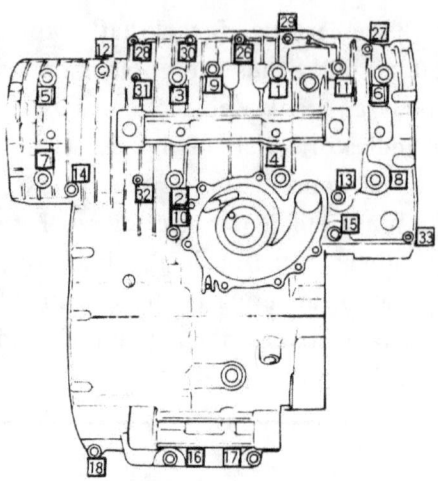

Fig. 3–46   Lower crankcase

5. The following bolts should be tighten with the clamps or special washers instead of the plane washers.

∗ The fitting bolts for No. 8, 10, 14 should be tighten with the clamps for the alternator and contact breaker cords.

∗ The fitting bolt for No. 13 should be tighten with the copper washer.

∗ The fitting bolt for No. 22 should be tighten with the engine ground lead wire clamp.

∗ The clamps connecting the alternator and contact breaker cords should be fixed with No. 6 bolt.

6. Assemble the pistons onto the connecting rod with the arrow marks on its head toward front.

Note: There are two kinds of pistons marked "R" and "L" on the head, the piston with "R" is to be right, and that with "L" is to be left and center cylinders.

7. Install the piston rings into the piston.

Caution: In case that the piston rings are not replaced with the new one when reassembling, install them in the same position as they were originally assembled.

8. Install three "O" rings in place on the front end of upper crankcase.

9. Place the new cylinder gasket on the upper crankcase, and install the cylinder block.

Caution: Make sure that the piston ring end gap has aligned with the knock pin on the piston groove.

10. Tighten the cylinder set nut.

11. Place the cylinder head on the cylinder block and tighten the bolts in the order illustrated in the figure with the specified torques.

Standard specified torque:
   8 mm bolts and nuts
       180~220 kg-cm (13.0~15.9 lb-ft)
   10 mm bolt
       300~400 kg-cm (21.7~29.0 lb-ft)

12. Connect the SRIS pipes to the check valves both on the crankcase and cylinder block.

CRANKCASE COLOUR	1ST DRIVEN GEAR	2ND DRIVEN GEAR	KICK START DRIVE GEAR
BROWN	YELLOW	YELLOW	BROWN
BLACK			
RED			
YELLOW			
BLUE	WHITE	WHITE	YELLOW
GREEN			
WHITE			
PAINTED COLOUR	PAINTED COLOUR	PAINTED COLOUR	PAINTED COLOUR

4. CLUTCH

	Page
DESCRIPTION	33
SPECIFICATIONS	34
TROUBLE SHOOTING	34
Removal & Disassembly	35
Inspection & Repair	35
Assembly & Adjustment	36

DESCRIPTION

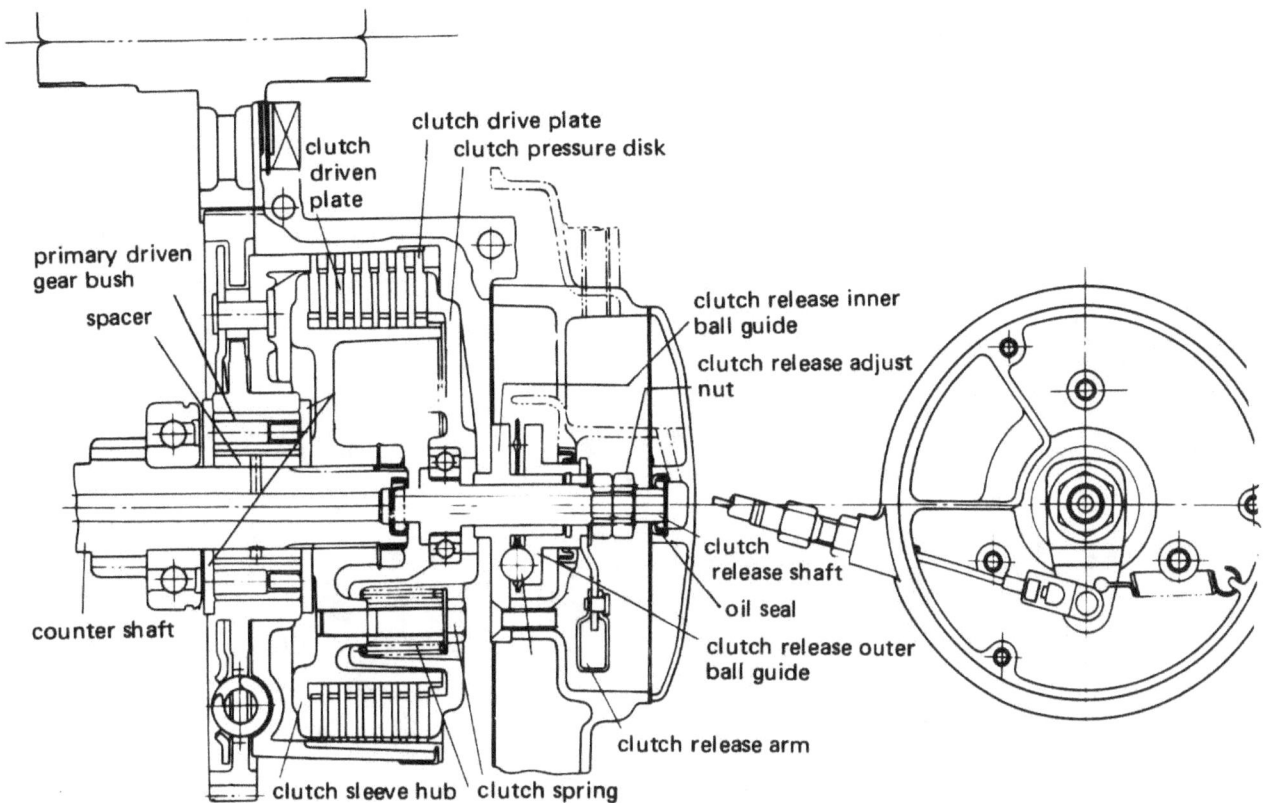

Fig. 4−1 Cross-sectional view of clutch

Large capacity multi plate wet type clutch is used in the vehicle consisting of eight large clutch cork plates, seven clutch steel plates, and six loading springs.

By operating clutch lever, clutch release mounting on the right side clutch cover moves release rod. Thus engagement or disengagement of cork with steel plate can be obtained, which lead to power on off to transmission. In the release mechanism, three balls are used to reduce the operating force of clutch lever.

The transmission oil splashed up by clutch, is sent to the inside of counter shaft through release rod, thus the lubrication of sleeve hub and bushings is attained.

Two kinds of clutch damper springs are installed in primary driven gear. They absorb abnormal driving shock torque and prevent damages of engine parts, leading to more comfortable drivability.

SPECIFICATIONS

Cork plate thickness	2.9~3.1 mm (0.114~0.122")
Steel plate thickness	1.9~2.1 mm (0.07~0.08")
Clutch spring free length	40.4 mm (1.59")
Clutch spring load	23.5 kg (51.7 lb)
Primary gear backlash	0.02~0.07 mm (0.001~0.003")
Clutch lever operation load	13.5 kg (29.7 lb)
Clutch lever free play at lever end	3 mm (0.12")

TROUBLE SHOOTING

Symptoms & Probable Causes	Remedies
Clutch slippage	
a. No play in the clutch cable	Adjust clutch cable
b. Weak or unequal clutch pressure spring/s	Replace spring/s
c. Worn cork plates	Replace plates
d. Maladjustment of clutch release mechanism	Adjust
e. Warped cork or steel plates	Replace plates
Excessive noise	
a. Excessive primary gear backlash	Replace gear
b. Worn or defective dumper spring	Replace primary driven gear
c. Excessive play in countershaft	Repair or replace
Irregular operation	
a. Worn clutch sleeve hub	Repair or replace
b. Worn or oilless clutch wire/s	Lubricate or replace
c. Defective clutch release mechanism	Repair

Removal & Disassembly

Refer to "Disassembly of Engine" at page 25.

1. Remove clutch adjusting cap and gasket.

2. Loosen clutch release shaft lock nuts with two open end wrenches and remove nuts and release arm.

3. Remove clutch cover, and take out clutch drive cork and driven steel plates one by one from the clutch housing.

4. Remove clutch sleeve hub with Clutch Sleeve Hub Holder (09920–53110).

5. Remove primary driven gear assembly after pulling out bushing with two bolts installed on it.

6. Remove transmission oil reservoir plate.

Inspection & Repair

a. Measure the wear amount of clutch drive plate.
   STD thickness: 2.9~3.1 mm (0.011~0.012")
   Wear limit: 0.2 mm (0.008")

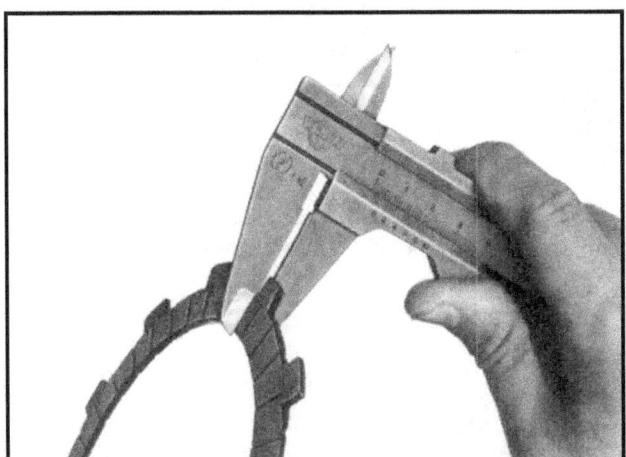

Fig. 4–2   Checking clutch drive plate for wear

b. Measure the free length of clutch spring.
   STD length: 40.4 mm (1.59")
   Spring setting limit: 1.4 mm (0.055")

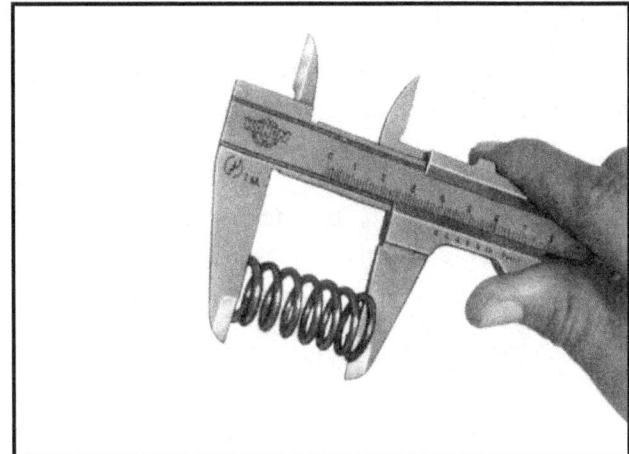

Fig. 4–3   Measuring free length of clutch spring

c. Place driven plate on surface plate, measure the clearance between them with thickness gauge. If the clearance exceeds 0.3 mm, replace the plate.

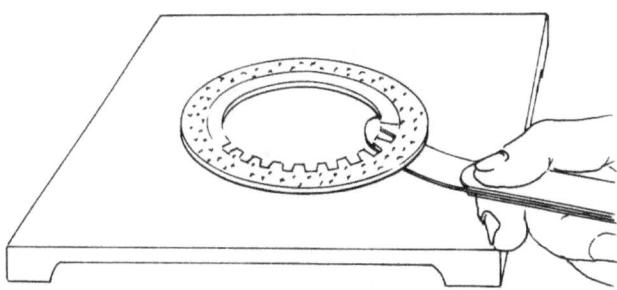

Fig. 4–4   Checking warpage of clutch driven plate

d. Check the tooth flank of sleeve hub for any crack, scratch, or uneven wear. If the amount of wear is small, repair it. If too large, replace it.

e. Check the wear amount of bearings installed in clutch pressure disk. Turn the bearing. If smooth rotation is not obtained, replace it, even if no noise is generated.

f. Check the outer and inner ball guide of clutch release mechanism for any crack or uneven wear, etc.

Assembly & Adjustment

All parts are to be cleaned out and all sliding surfaces should be lubricated by applying oil.

a. After applying thread lock cement on threads of tightening bolts, mount transmission oil reservoir plate on crankcase with bolts.

b. Insert primary driven gear bushing, spacer, and washer to counter shaft.

Caution: In inserting bush ① and washers ②, take care in aligning their direction. Some motor oil is to be applied to the inside of bushing and the outside of spacer.

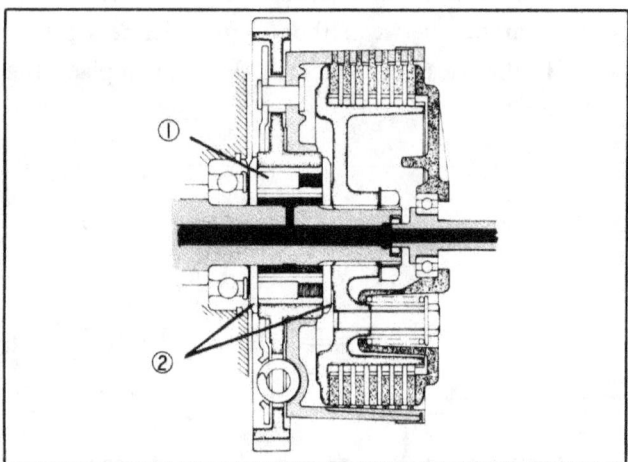

Fig. 4-5 Cross sectional view of clutch

c. Tighten clutch sleeve hub nut at specified torque of 400~550 Kg.-cm (29~40 lb.-ft).

d. Supply motor oil into the hole of clutch sleeve shaft.

e. To assemble clutch release ball guide, tighten set screw after setting the outer ball guide into the specified position as shown in Fig. 4-6.

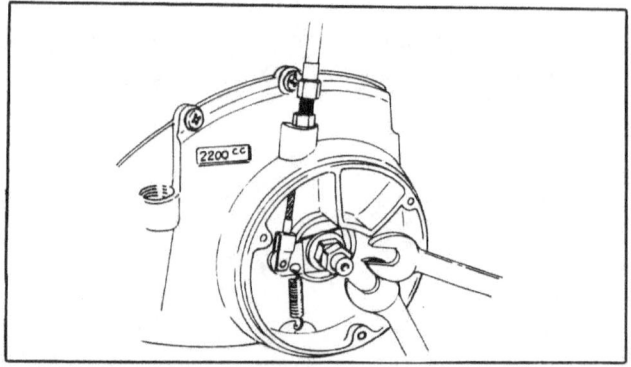

Fig. 4-6 Tightening release shaft nuts

f. Clutch should be adjusted as follows. Loosen cable adjuster Ⓐ until an ample play of clutch cable ① can be obtained. Tighten the double nuts ② by insuring an axial play of the release shaft ③ to be approximately 0.2 mm. Then, adjust the play of lever to be 3 mm at the root by adjusting the cable adjuster Ⓐ Ⓑ

Fig. 4-7 Adjusting clutch

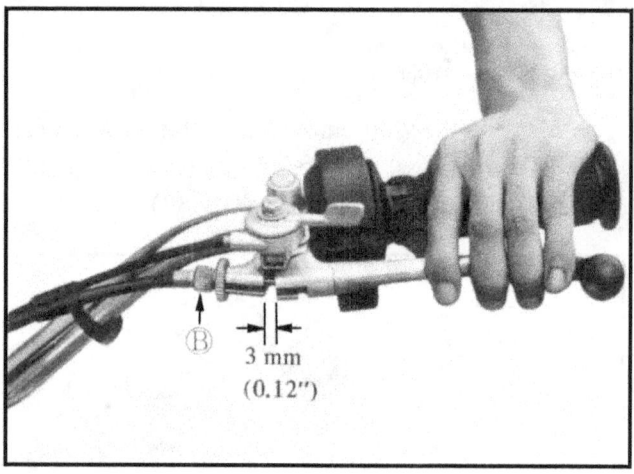

Fig. 4-8 Adjusting cable play

5. TRANSMISSION

	Page
DESCRIPTION	37
SPECIFICATIONS	37
TROUBLE SHOOTING	38
Removal & Disassembly	38
Operation	39
Inspection	40
Assembly	41

DESCRIPTION

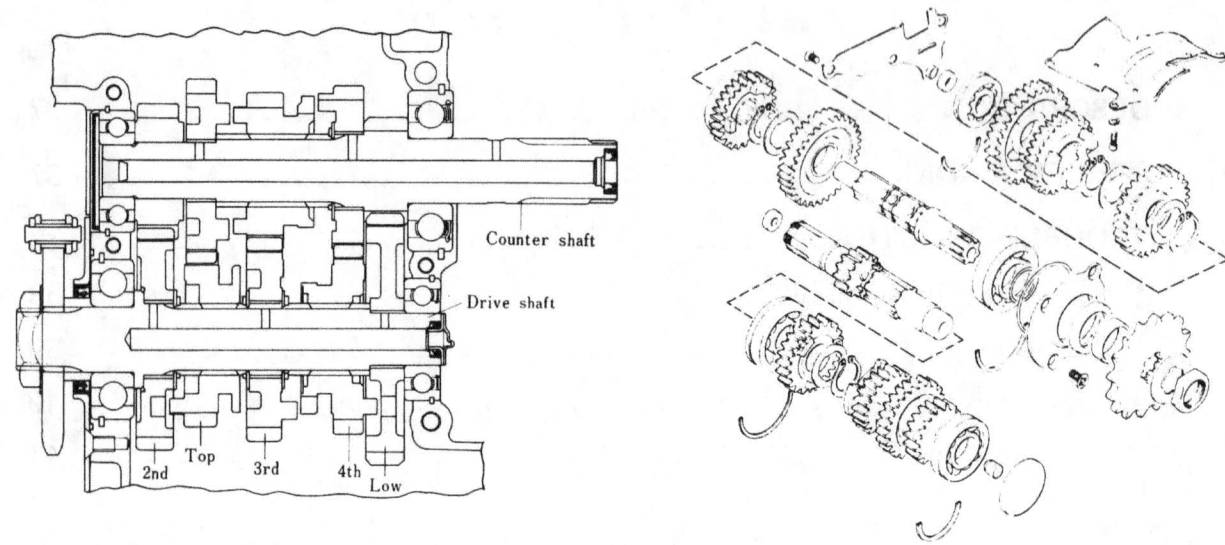

Fig. 5-1 GT750 Transmission gears

Five speed, constant mesh transmission is adopted. Gears can be shifted by select-fitting-gears through gear shifting cam and shifting fork fitted on it.

SPECIFICATIONS

Gear ratios

1st (low)	2.846 : 1 (37/13)
2nd	1.736 : 1 (33/19)
3rd	1.363 : 1 (30/20)
4th	1.125 : 1 (27/24)
5th (top)	0.923 : 1 (24/26)

Primary reduction ratio (gear)　　　1.673 : 1 (82/49)

Final reduction ratio (chain)　　　　3.133 : 1 (47/15)

Overall reduction ratios

1st (low)	14.92 : 1
2nd	9.09 : 1
3rd	7.14 : 1
4th	5.89 : 1
5th (top)	4.48 : 1

Kick gear reduction ratio　　　　　4.24 : 1

TROUBLE SHOOTING

Symptoms & Probable Causes	Remedies
Difficult gear shifting	
a. Improper clutch disengagement	Adjust clutch
b. Foreign objects on gear teeth	Repair
c. Defective or damaged gear/s	Replace gear/s
d. Inoperative gear shifting fork/s	Repair or replace
e. Improper operation of gear shifting mechanism	Repair
f. Excessive high oil viscocity	Change oil (Refer to page 12)
Gear slipping out	
a. Worn gear dog and dog hole	Replace
b. Worn yokes on gear shifting fork/s	Replace
c. Worn spline on shaft/s	Replace
Excessive gear noise	
a. Excessive gear backlash	Replace gear/s
b. Worn bearing/s	Replace bearing/s
c. Worn spline on shaft/s	Replace shaft/s
d. Improper gear oil	Change oil (Refer to page 12)

Removal & Disassembly

1. After opening crankcase, lift up both ends of counter shaft assembly and drive shaft assembly, which now enables us to remove the assembly from lower crankcase.

2. Disassembling gear shift mechanism: After pulling out gear shifting shaft ① from crankcase lower cover, remove shifting pawl lifter ② and cam guide ③. Remove shifting cam driven gear ④. Pull out neutral stopper spring holder ⑤ from the rear side of low crankcase. Take out shifting cam ⑥ and shifting fork shafts ⑦ from casing.

3. Disassembly of counter shaft: Pull out press fit 2nd driven gear by using an arbour press, then 4th driven gear can be pulled out after removal of circlip as shown in Fig. 5-1.

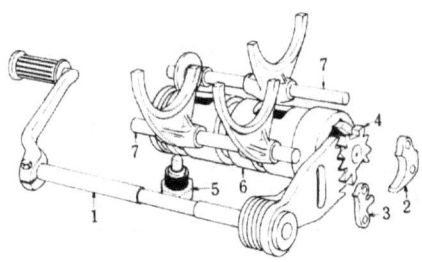

Fig. 5-2 Gear shifting mechanism

Caution: Replacement of 2nd gear is permitted only twice. After that, the counter shaft assembly is to be replaced. Otherwise, the tightening force of second gear deteriorates causing the gear to creep.

4. Drive shaft can be disassembled by removing the circlip as shown Fig. 5-1.

Operation

1. Engine power is transmitted by way of the clutch to the rear drive wheel using driving gears as shown under.

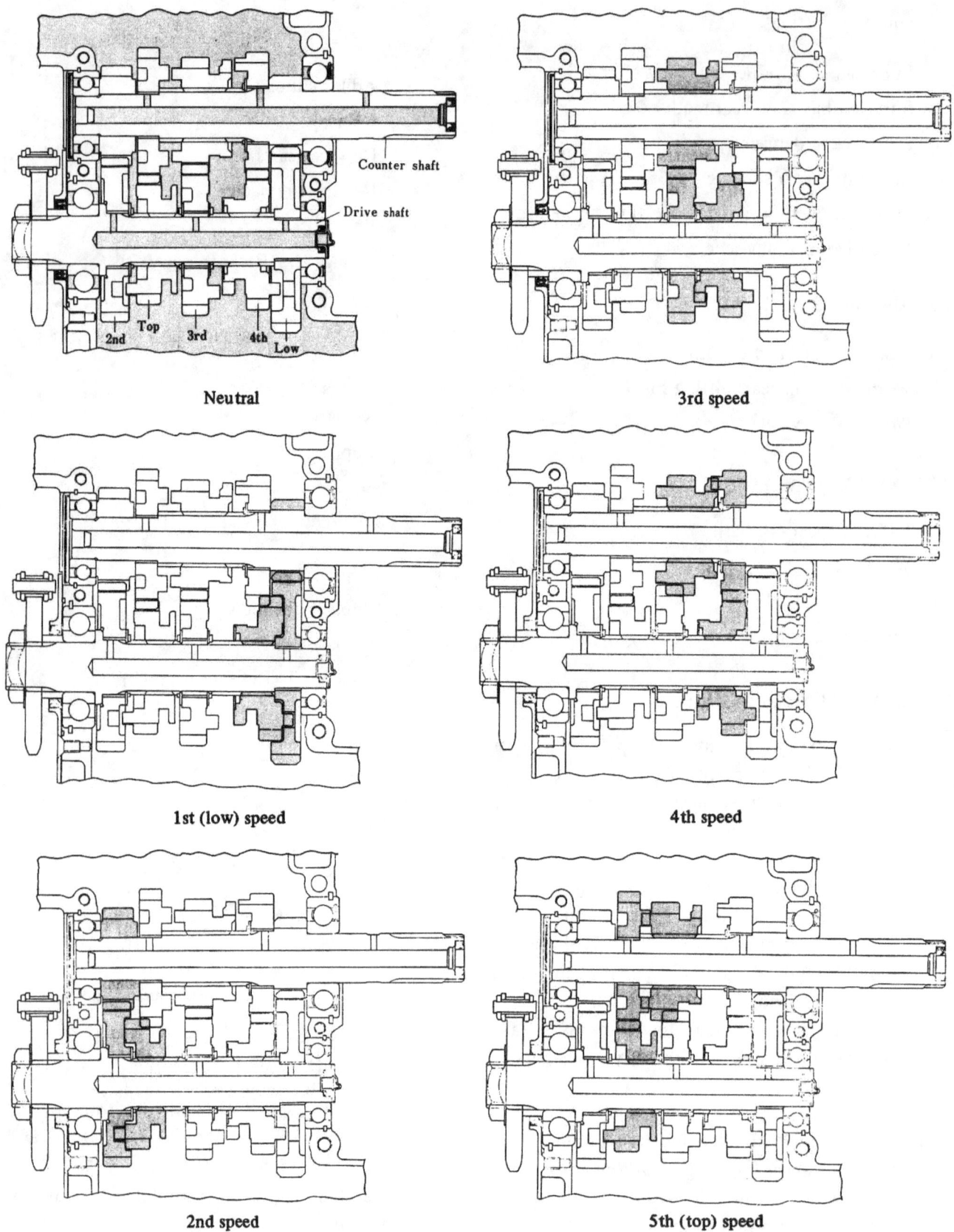

Fig. 5-3 Gear positions

2. As the gear shifting mechanism is shown in Fig. 5–2, Gear shifting pawl and its holder can be actuated by moving the gear shift lever up and down. This turns gear shifting cam, then the shifting fork engaged with it slides laterally. A special device is built-in in this mechanism to ensure the correct gear shifting. When gears are shifted too rapidly, the shifting cam drum tends to rotate beyond the specified limit. A positive stop shifting device is provided for preventing the cam drum from turning too far for this purpose.

Inspection

All parts are to be thoroughly cleaned before inspection.

1. Check for any defect or abnormal wear on gear flanks. Wear of a gear can be obtained by measuring the backlash using a small dial gauge as in Fig. 5–4. First lock the driven gear, then measure play in the direction of the rotation by a dial gauge. If this play exceeds the below specified values, replace the gear.

   Standard backlash:
   for low, 2nd, 3rd and kick gears
   0~0.05 mm (0~0.002")
   for other gears
   0.05~0.1 mm (0.002"~0.004")

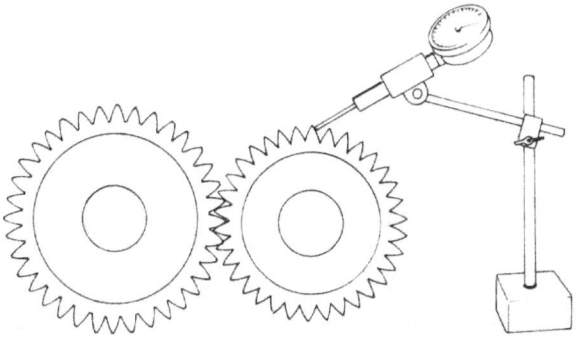

Fig. 5–4 Measuring gear backlash

2. Examine gear dog and dog hole for any defects or excessive wear. Replace it in the case of excessive wear or defects.

3. Check clearance between gear and shaft; if the excessibly worn, burnt or scored parts are found on the gear bore and the shaft, replace them with new ones.

4. Check counter, drive and kick shaft for bend, replace them with new ones if it is found to be bent.

5. Check the clearance between gear shifting fork and shift fork shaft. Check the bend of the shaft at the same time.

   Shifting fork to shaft clearance (standard):
   0.05~0.1 mm (0.002"~0.004")

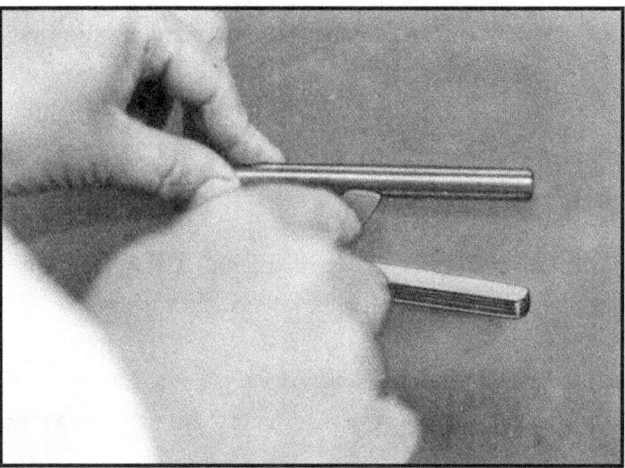

Fig. 5–5 Checking shifting fork shaft for wear and bend

6. Measure the thickness of gear shifting fork at its fingers. If it is less than 4.9 mm (0.19"), replace it.

   Finger thickness (standard):
   4.95~5.05 mm (0.195~0.198")

7. Check wear in gear shifting cam drum. Measure the outer diameter of drum with micrometer. Replace it when the diameter measured exceeds the limit of 44.70 mm (1.7598").

   Drum diameter (standard):
   44.900~44.975 mm (1.7677~1.7706")

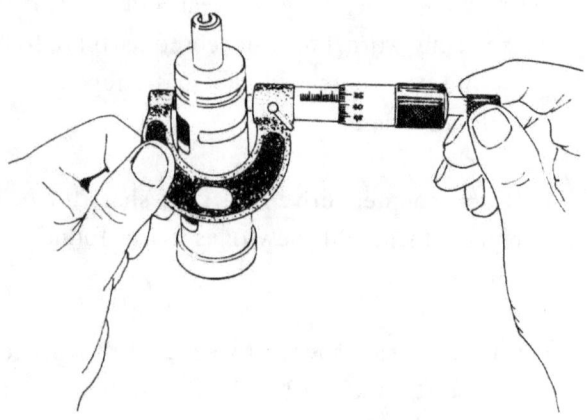

Fig. 5-6 Measuring shifting cam diameter

8. Check wear of bearings. Turn the outer race, as you hold the inner race. If some noise is generated or a smooth turning is not obtained, replace the bearing.

Assembly

Wash all the parts and components and clean them up using compressed air, before assembling.

1. Install 2nd gear to counter shaft by press fit using arbour press machine in the following manner:

    a) Apply Suzuki Super Lock 103Q (99000-32030) onto the bore surface of 2nd driven gear.
    Note: Care must be taken not to apply it on the counter shaft surface.

    b) Press fit the 2nd driven gear, so that the distance between the end of the gear and the end of 1st driven gear is within 109.4 and 109.5 mm (4.307~4.311").

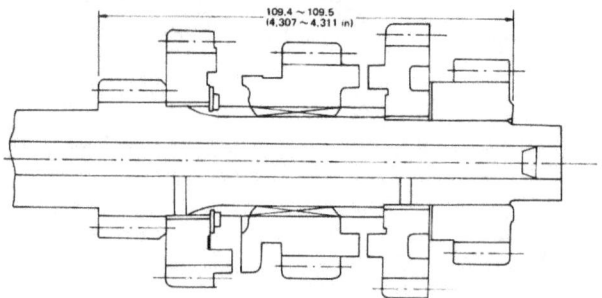

Fig. 5-7 Distance between both end gears

2. Install countershaft assembly, drive shaft assembly and gear shifting mechanism into the lower crankcase. Turn the shaft and check if a smooth turning of the shaft can be attained.

3. Please apply Thread Lock Cement (99000-32010) on all of the screws used for tightening gear shifting pawl, lifter fitting screws, cam guide fitting screws, oil reservoir plate fitting screw.

4. Gear shifting pawl is to be installed by taking due care in the direction of fitting.

5. Assemble kick starter mechanism, keeping it in mind that kick stater ① is installed into kick starter shaft ② with punch marks both on the flank of the kick starter shaft and the spline on the shaft aligned, and also oil guide hole ③ on the kick stater shaft is to face upward when the kick starter comes in contact with kick starter guide ④.

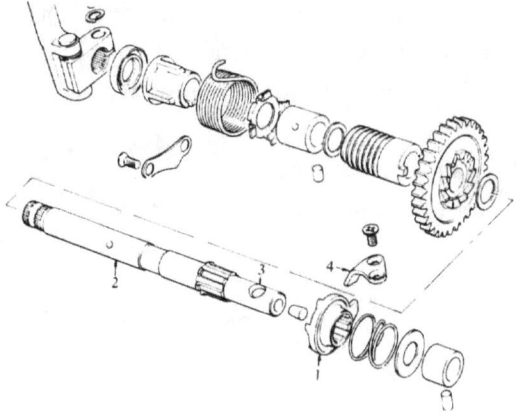

Fig. 5-8 Kick starter mechanism

6. Install the kick starter assembly into lower crankcase.

7. Install the kick starter guide into the lower crankcase with two set screws, appling the Thread Lock Cement on them.

8. Install the kick starter lever into the kick starter shaft so as to align the punch marks ① as shown in Fig. 5-9.

Fig. 5-9 Aligning punch marks

9. Supply transmission oil of 2,500 cc into the transmission case after assembling all parts.

Note: "2200 cc" is indicated on the clutch cover. This merely indicates the oil level needed in re-filling without overhauling engine. When oil is changed without disassembling, a certain amount (about 300 cc) of oil may possibly remain within the casing. That is why the filling capacity of 2200 cc is indicated.

6. LUBRICATING SYSTEM

	Page
DESCRIPTION	43
SPECIFICATION	44
CONSTRUCTION & OPERATION	44
Oil Pump	44
Construction	45
Operation	45
SRIS (SUZUKI Recycle Injection System)	48
Construction	48
Operation	48
TROUBLE SHOOTING	49
OIL PUMP & OIL PIPE	49
Removal	49
Disassembly	50
Inspection & Repair	50
Assembly & Adjustment	51
SRIS	51
Removal	51
Inspection Repair	51
Assembly	52

DESCRIPTION

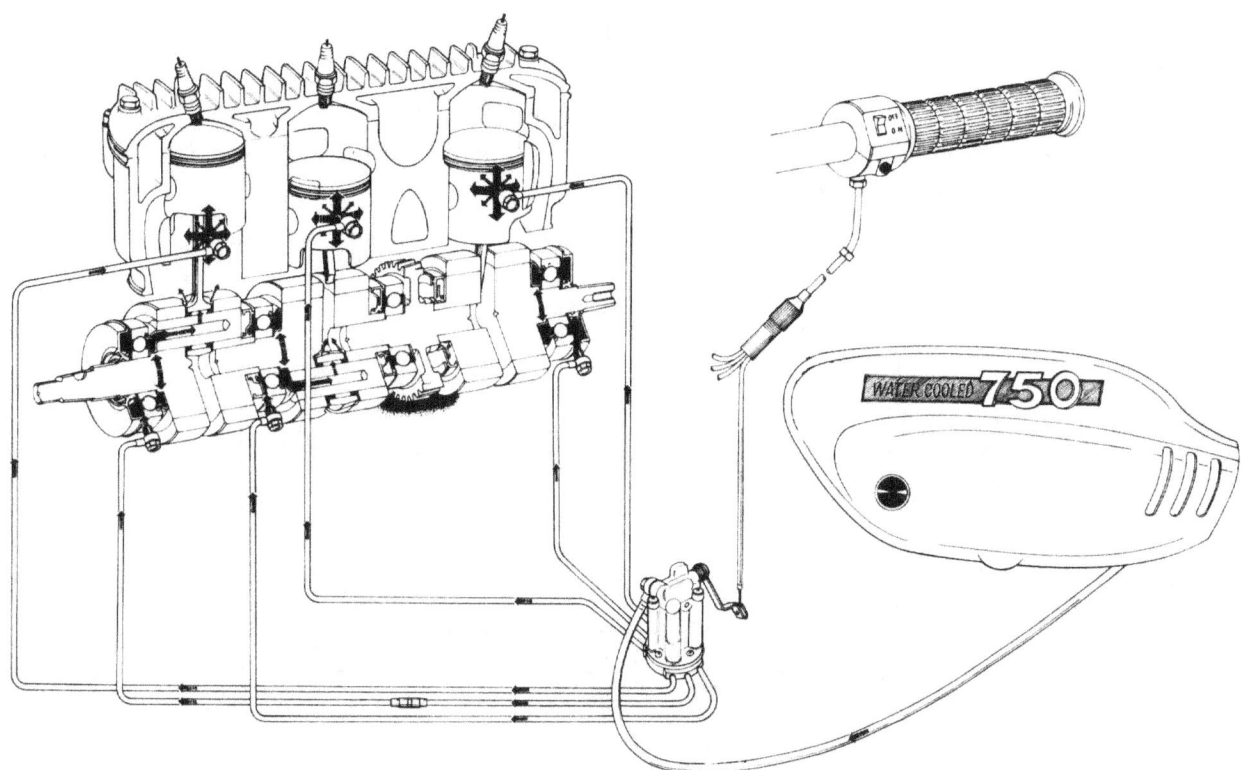

Fig. 6-1   GT750 engine lubricating system

The lubricating system of this engine uses "SUZUKI C.C.I (Cylinder & Crankshaft Injection) System", whereby a required amount of oil is pumped into both the seating or moving portions of each inner part and the stressed points by an oil pump direct from the reservoir of fresh oil with the regulation of this oil flow rate.

The oil pump is of a 6-outlet plunger type which is the original design of SUZUKI. Oil from the pump is distributed to cylinders and crankshaft, and all the inner parts such as a cylinder wall, a crank bearing and connecting rod bearings are equally lubricated.

Fresh oil is always supplied to each inner part without being diluted with gasoline. We see then that wearing of each part can be minimized and its durability is improved.

After lubricating the inside of the engine inside oil is drained into the crankcase. There a new system SRIS (Suzuki Recycle Injection System) is adopted for the recirculation of that oil. This new system has resolved a problem of smoky exhaust gases emission into atmosphere. This is usually due to incomplete combustion of oil in the crank chamber which leak suddenly into the combustion chamber during quick engine acceleration. We have now completed a two-cycle engine free from smoky exhaust gases.

SPECIFICATION

Oil Pump: Plunger type

Delivery quantity (at full throttle opening):
    For cylinder side: 48.3 cc (0.13/0.11 pt. US/Imp) per Hr. at 2,166 rpm
    For crank bearing side: 7.21 cc (0.09/0.07 pt. US/Imp) per Hr. at 2,166 rpm
    Oil pump reduction ratio with crankshaft: 63.72 : 1

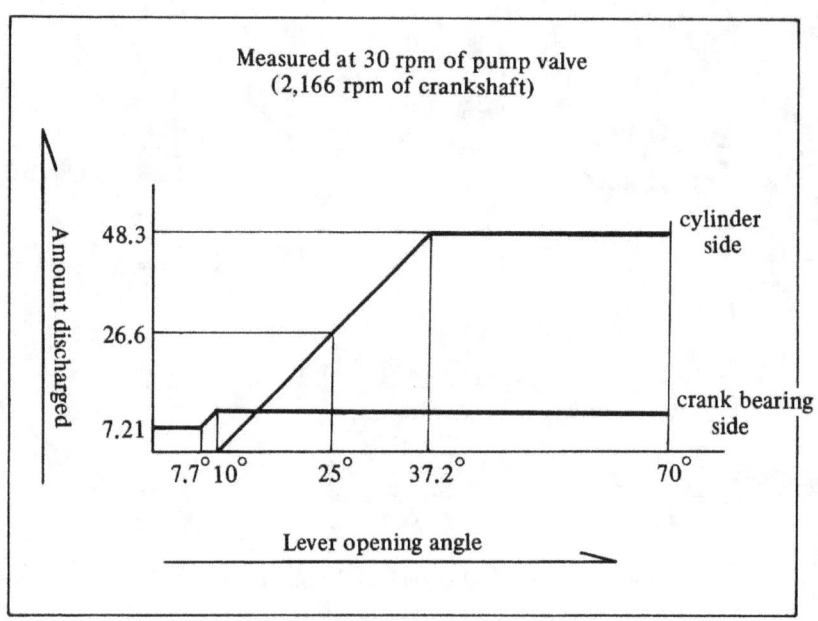

Fig. 6-2   Oil delivering curve

CONSTRUCTION & OPERATION

Oil Pump

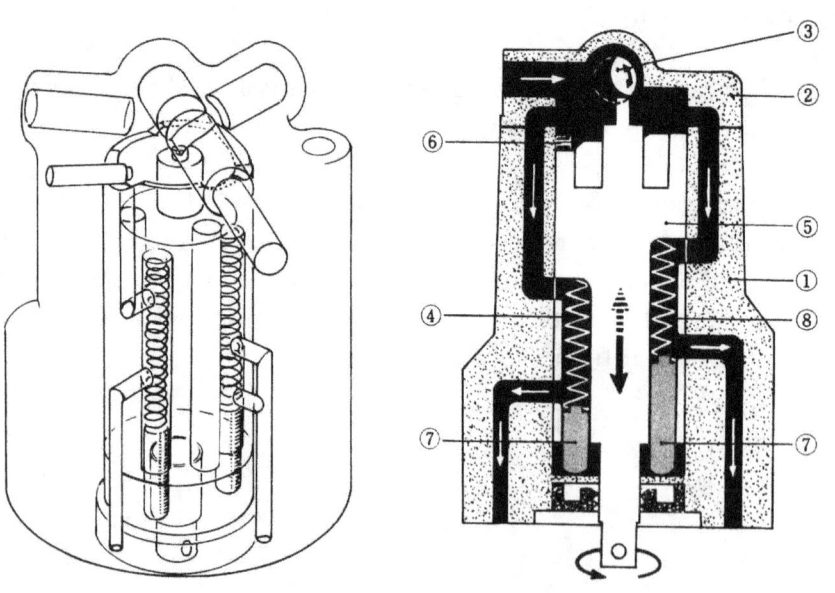

① Oil pump body
② Pump control body
③ Control cam
④ Plunger hole
⑤ Pump valve
⑥ Cam guide
⑦ Plunger
⑧ Spring

Fig. 6-3   Oil pump construction

Construction

As shown in Fig. 6-3, the oil pump consists of the following components:

1) Oil pump body:
   Oil inlet and delivery ports are provided on both upper and lower sides, and on the inner bore parts.

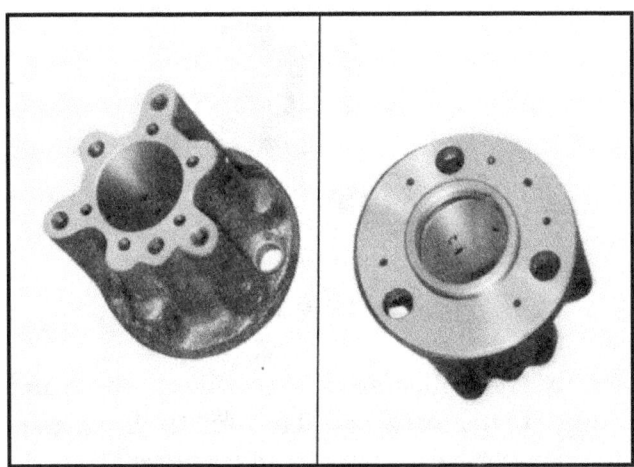

Fig. 6-4 Oil pump body

2) Oil pump valve:
   Three(3) kinds of cam ① are provided on upper stems of valves symmetrical to the valve center, for the total of six(6) different elevations.

   These cams are provided for three(3) different functions; first for oil suction, second for delivering oil to the cylinder and third for delivering oil to the crankshaft.

   On the outer side of the valve, four ports ②, two each on the two row, are provided. The upper two ports are used for oil suction and the lower ones for oil delivery.

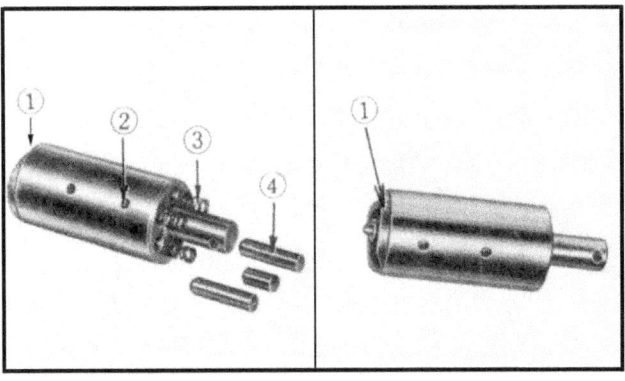

Fig. 6-5 Oil pump valve & plunger

3) Oil pump plunger:
   Six(6) openings are arranged vertically inside of the valve. Three(3) of them are through-hole while a spring ③ and plunger ④ are inserted in the remaining three as shown in Fig. 6-5.

   This plunger, in fact moves in the opposite direction to the vertical motion of the valve and sucks in and delivers oil.
   Two types of plunger are available.

4) Control cam and shaft:
   The vertical motion of the valve, which is subjected to rotating motion is effectively controlled by the cams right above it and by a cam guide ① on the pump body. In this case, the delivery amount of oil can only be controlled by the rotating valve, namely by the engine speed.

   The control cam ② is capable of limiting the vertical valve motion and consequently changes the amount of oil delivery depending upon engine loads. This control cam is driven by a camshaft lever ③ connected to the carburetor throttle cable.

Fig. 6-6 Control cam & shaft

Operation

When the oil pump valve functions and moves upwards being regulated by the valve guide and the control cam, the plunger moves downwards relative to the valve. Oil is, therefore drawn into the valve, when a port on the valve side and the port on the pump body are matched.

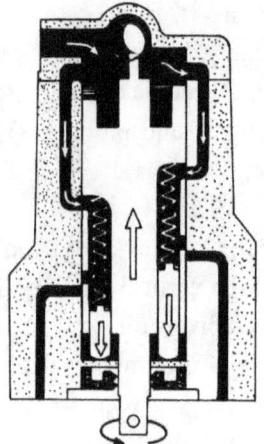

Fig. 6-7 Sucking oil

Then, during the downward strokes of the valve, the plunger moves upwards relative to the valve and oil already sucked into the plunger is discharged. It is to be noted, however, that the oil pump body has separate ports for oiling the cylinder and the crankshaft respectively to deliver the oil.

Oil quantity can be regulated by timing the overlapping period of the outlet ports of the valve and the pump body.

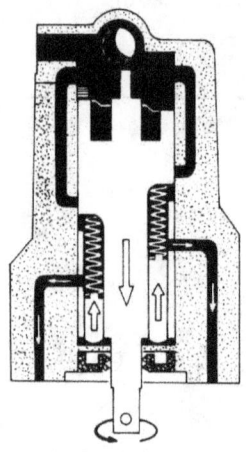

Fig. 6-8 Discharging oil

As mentioned above, four(4) ports two each for each of the two rows are provided on the valve. Correspondingly ports are provided on the pump body for delivering oil to the cylinder and the crankshaft. Because it completes a return stroke twice during one rotation, eights discharges of oil will be obtained for with one(1) rotation of the valve. Actually, however, the total of six(6) oil discharges are required for the cylinder and the crankshaft lubrication because the engine has only three(3) cylinders. In order to meet this requirement, oil for each one delivery to the crankshaft and the cylinder is returned to the original place within one(1) rotation, and the total delivery time is kept at six(6). See Fig. 6-9.

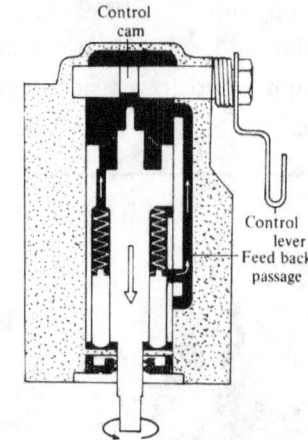

Fig. 6-9 Feed-back passage

For the vertical motion of the valve, the volume formed by the plunger and body (under the plunger) is always changing. In order to facilitate oiling into that portion, an oil circulating passage is provided on the valve body, as shown in Fig. 6-10.

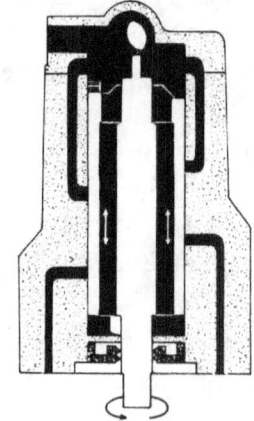

Fig. 6-10 Oil circulating passage

An overall construction and the arrangement under operating conditions are illustrated in the following diagram.

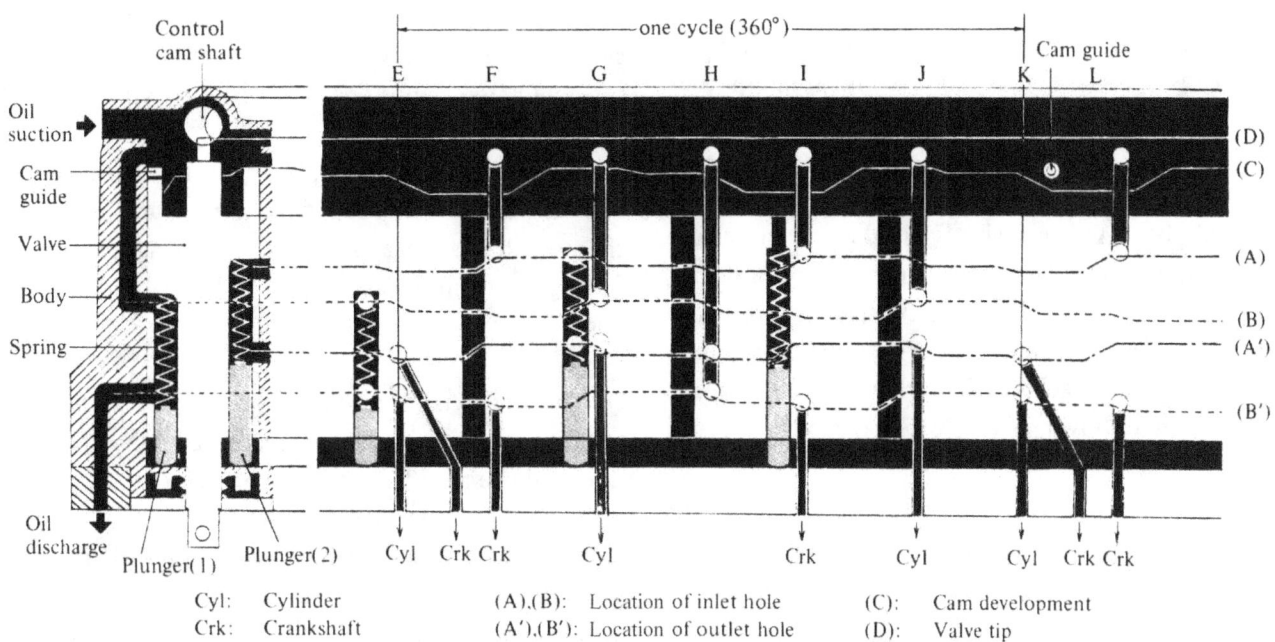

Fig. 6–11 Overall construction and arrangement under operating conditions

(A), (A'), (B) and (B') show the loci of each oil inlet and outlet on the outside of the valve traced when the valve moves up and down as rotating, with its cam traveled along the cam guide on the inside of the pump body.

These loci will be varied in accordance with the movement of the control cam shaft which is shown as a line(D) in the figure, because the reciprocating movement of the valve is regulated by both the control cam and the cam guide.

To take the plunger ② for example, oil is drawn into the valve at the position "F" and discharge it once to cylinder side to a certain extent at "G" and feed back the remaining oil to the control chamber at "H", then suck oil again from the control chamber at "I" and discharge it into cylinder and crankshaft (at "J" and "L") respectively.

Thus each plunger discharges the specified amount of oil into the cylinder and crankshaft totally 6 times within one cycle.

SRIS

Construction

The construction of SRIS (Suzuki Recycle Injection System) is so made that oil accumulating in the crankcase bottom is forced into the scavenging ports of adjacent cylinders through the rubber pipes with the help of positive and negative pressures induced by each cylinder. A check valve is fitted to the outlet of the crankcase lower part in order to prevent the reversion of oil flow. There are two piping forms for this SRIS, the one shown in Fig. 6-12 has been equipped on the machines from the first production, and the other shown in Fig. 6-13 is modified type for later model.

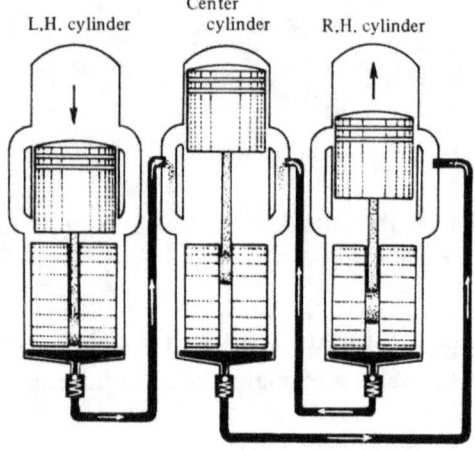

Fig. 6-12   SRIS type 1

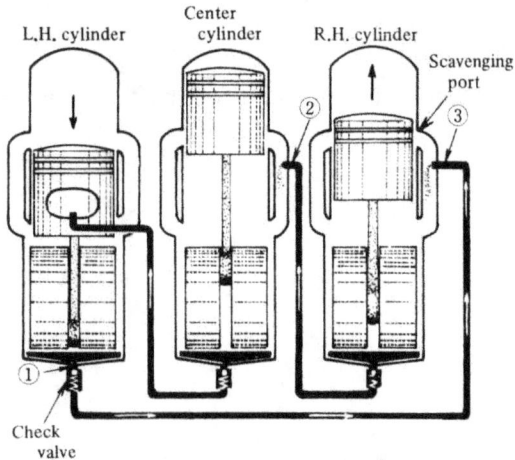

Fig. 6-13   SRIS type 2

Operation

To take the later type (Fig. 6-13) for example, it is understood that when the piston on the left hand cylinder moves downwards, its crank chamber is subjected to a positive pressure, moving the oil outside of its outlet port ①.

Simultaneously with that, the piston on the center cylinder is near the top dead center and its crank chamber has a negative pressure, taking suction of fresh gases from the carburetor and oil from the SRIS hose ②.

On the other hand, a negative pressure is induced in the crank chamber of the center cylinder as mentioned above and the piston of the right hand cylinder is in the upward stroke from the bottom dead center, reducing the positive pressure in the crank chamber. Therefore, a pressure at the scavenging port of the center cylinder cannot attain a sufficiently high value of pressure needed for drawing oil from SRIS hose and oil as stopped at the check valve does not enter into the SRIS hose.

In the cylinder on the left hand side, the crank chamber has a positive pressure, while fresh gases are still flowing into the crankcase of the cylinders on the right hand. Therefore, oil is drawn into the crank chamber from the SRIS hose ③ and though oil is being delivered as a whole, it will no longer be delivered if the pressure is changed from positive to negative as the piston moves upward.

TROUBLE SHOOTING

Symptoms & Probable Causes	Remedies

Piston seizure

  a. Maladjusting of oil pump lever   Adjust (Refer to Fig. 6-19)
  b. Air inside oil pipe/s   Expel air (Refer to Fig. 6-16)
  c. Oil leakage of oil pipe/s & pipe joint/s   Replace or repair
  d. Malfunctioning of check valve   Replace or repair (Refer to Fig. 6-20)
  e. Clogged oil pipe/s   Clean or replace
  f. Low quality motor oil   Change oil (Refer to page 51)
  g. Malfunctioning of oil pump   Check and replace

Smokey exhaust gas

  a. Maladjusting of oil pump lever   Adjust (Refer to Fig. 6-19)
  b. Clogged or pinched SRIS pipe   Clean or replace
  c. Malfunctioning SRIS check valve   Repair or replace (Refer to Fig. 6-20)
  d. Low quality motor oil   Replenish (Refer to page 9, 13)

Excessive oil consumption

  a. Maladjusted oil pump lever   Adjust (Refer to page 10)
  b. Oil leakage   Trace leakage and repair

OIL PUMP & OIL PIPE

Removal

(1) Remove oil inlet pipe from oil tank.
(2) Remove oil pump cover.
(3) Remove oil pump.
(4) Remove starter motor cover fitting bolts and lift up the cover along the by-pass hose.
(5) Remove oil outlet pipe union bolts.

Fig. 6-14   Removing oil pump

Fig. 6-15   Loosening oil pipe union bolts

Disassembly

The oil pump is manufactured with precision and its efficiency may be reduced once disassembled and is restored to the original, possibly leading to an engine trouble. It is constructed, therefore, as nondisassembly type, similar to the previous model. In this respect, it is difficult to accept any claim about an oil pump being reassembled. Also, it would be unacceptable to treat each oil pump inner part as a supply part for replacement. It is recommended that the whole of the oil pump assembly should be renewed, since any inner part is out of order.

Inspection & Repair

1. The oil pipe is checked to see if there is any trapped air inside. If there is any air found within the oil inlet pipe between the oil tank and the oil pump, the air expelling screw at the upper part of the pump is loosened to expell the air completely.

   If air is found being trapped in the oil outlet pipe which carries oil from pump to engine, the following steps are recommended:

   a) For a small amount of air; With the engine idling, the oil pump lever is set to "full open" position and this condition is maintained until all of the air is believed to be expelled completely.

   b) For a large amount of air; The oil pump is dismounted and as shown in Fig. 6-16, oil is filled up from an inlet to exhaust air. It is to be noted that a check valve is fitted to each pipe end to prevent the reversion of oil flow as indicated in the figure.

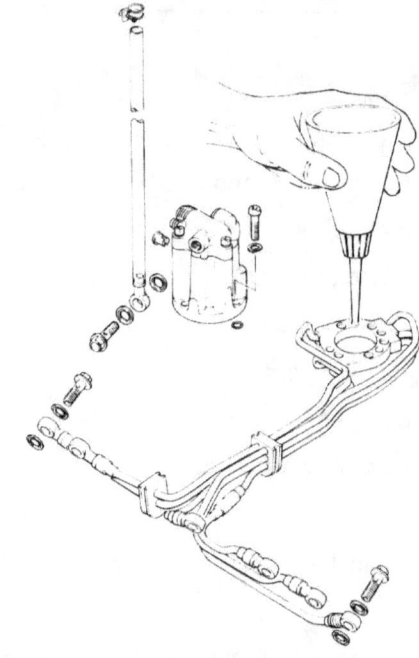

Fig. 6-16   Expelling air in oil pipes

2. Check the oil pump for any air trapped inside. As shown in Fig. 6-17, the expelling air screw is loosened and tightened after confirming the oil discharge.

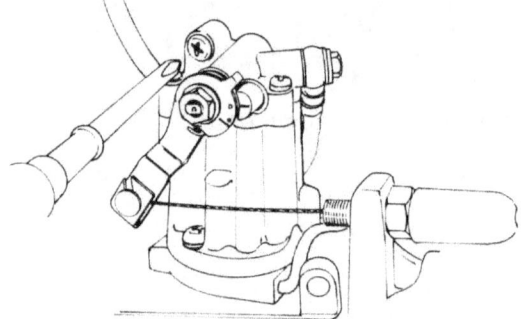

Fig. 6-17   Expelling air in oil pump

3. When an abnormal oil consumption is noted, it is first recommended to replace the oil pump. If the oil consumption does not improve with this, it is most probable that the pump unit has a leakage or the check valve is out of order. These points should therefore be checked.

4. When an engine trouble is caused apparently due to the improper function of the lubricating system and yet a cause of troubles cannot be traced exactly, please check the oil tank cap to see if it is well mounted. It is often seen that a breather hole on the tank cap is closed down due to the improper maintenance.

Assembly & Adjustment

1. Before mounting the oil pump and the oil pipe, oil should be supplied by forced lubrication to the CCI oil passage of the crankcase up to the full level, so as to expel air completely.

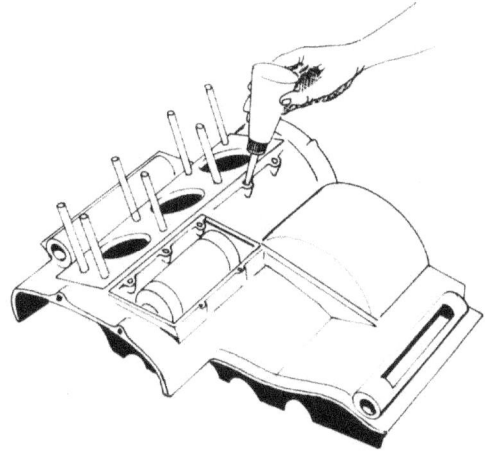

Fig. 6-18 Expelling air in oil passage

2. The oil pipe should also be filled with oil to expel air, as shown in Fig. 6-17.

3. In fitting the oil pump cover after mounting the oil pump, care should be taken not to pinch oil inlet hose between the case and the cover.

4. For the adjustment of oil pump, the throttle is opened gradually as shown in Fig. 6-19 and adjustment is made to align the aligning mark of the oil control lever with that of the stator, when the aligning mark of the throttle valve is on the top of an aligning hole on the side of the carburetor mixing chamber body.

Fig. 6-19 Adjusting oil pump

5. It is recommended to use SUZUKI CCI oil or non-diluent (non-self mixing type) of high quality equivalent to SAE #30 wt.

SRIS (SUZUKI Recycle Injection System)

Removal

1. Remove the oil pipe guide plate from lower crankcase.

2. Disconnect the SRIS pipes at the crankcase lower side by removing the clips with a screw driver.

3. The check valve and union are press-fitted to each of the crankcase and the cylinder on the machine equipping the former SRIS type, while on the later type the check valve is screwed into the crankcase, so that it can be removed easily.

4. Piping from left hand cylinder to right hand cylinder on the later type is made between the left hand crankcase and the right carburetor inlet through the under crankcase fins and the starting motor case. Therefore, when overhauling the engine, be sure to disconnect the pipe ends both at the crankcase and at the carburetor inlet beforehand.

Inspection & Repair

1. Check the oil pipes for crack, bend or pinched part.

2. Check to see if the check valves operate properly by using an injector. If the check valve is found to be clogged with foreign materials, remove the check valve from the lower crankcase and wash it in a solvent.

Note: On the later type, the nylon mesh strainer is provided on the check valve end.

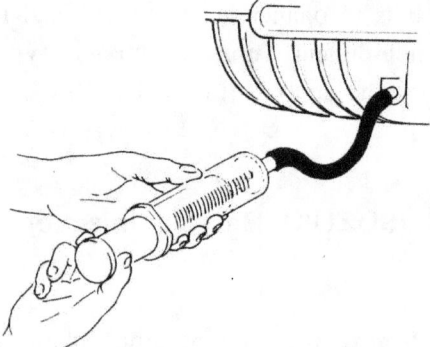

Fig. 6-20 Checking SRIS check valve

Assembly

1. The arrangement of oil pipes from the crankcase to the cylinder is as shown in the figures. Connect each end of the pipes to each union on the front side of the cylinder, where "R", "C" and "L" marks are relieved, so as to match the marks with the cylinder location.

   On the later type, the pipe from the right crankcase to the left cylinder is arranged as shown in Fig.

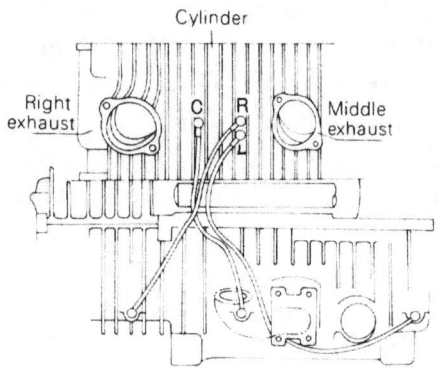

Fig. 6-21 SRIS piping

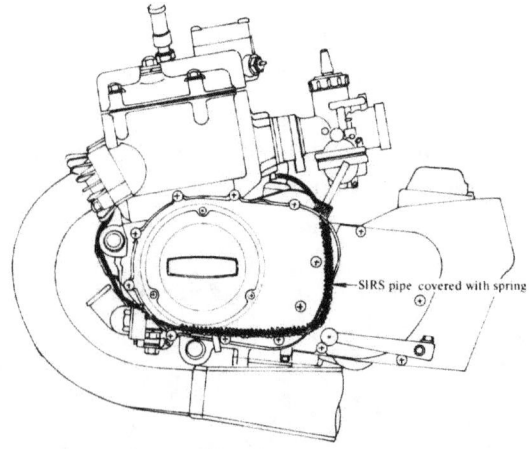

Fig. 6-22 SRIS piping for later model

7. COOLING SYSTEM

	Page
DESCRIPTION	53
SPECIFICATION	54
TROUBLE SHOOTING	54
RADIATOR	55
Removal	55
Inspection & Repair	55
Installation	57
THERMOSTAT	57
Removal	58
Inspection & Repair	58
Installation	58
WATER PUMP	58
Removal	59
Disassembly	59
Inspection	60
Assembly	60
COOLING WATER, ANTI-FREEZE & SUMMER COOLANT and ANTI-LEAKAGE MATERIAL	60
Cooling Water	60
Anti-freeze & Summer Coolant	61
Anti-leakage Material	62
Cooling System Flushing	62

DESCRIPTION

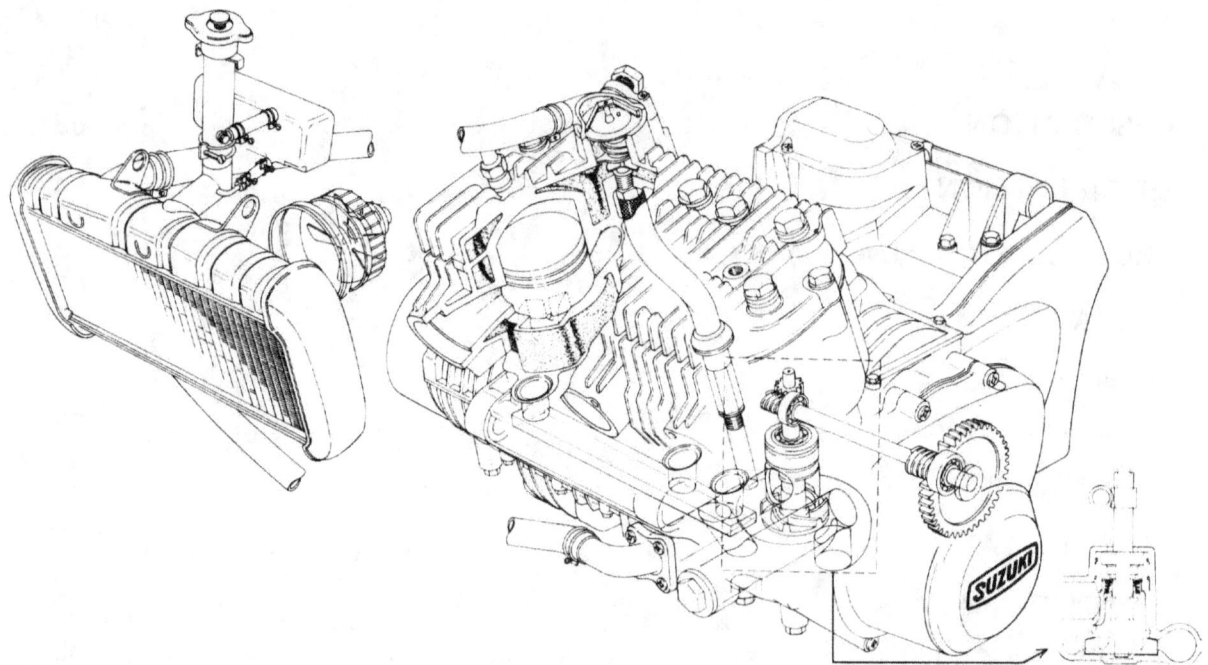

Fig. 7-1 GT750 engine cooling system

The cooling system of this engine uses a pressure forced circulation type and is designed to provide an excellent cooling effect under every imaginable running conditions.

The radiator has a corrugated fin and tube type construction of aluminum material. Therefore, it is characteristic in respect of light weight and heat radiator. Outside of the radiator is provided a reservoir tank as an escape space of the cooling solution due to the expansion from the heating. Expanded cooling solution due to a temperature rise enters into the reservoir tank thus preventing its escape into the atmosphere. The water pump, with forced circulation of cooling solution among the radiator, the engine and the cylinder block, has centrifugal type construction and is fitted to the lower side of the engine. The pump is direct driven by the crankshaft through the starter clutch gear.

The pump takes in the cooling solution from the lower side of the radiator, by circulating it throughout the water jacket of the cylinder block, the cylinder head and the thermostat, and is finally returned to the ratiator. Cooling solution is circulated within a closed circuit as mentioned above. When the engine is still cold, however, cooling water circualtes through a bypass hose from the thermostat and is returned to the water pump directly.

The radiator cap is designed to maintain a pressure of about 1.9 kg/cm^2 (27.0 lb/in^2) in the cooling system and its reverse valve opens to release an excess portion of the pressure out, when applied to a pressure above the said valve.

The thermostat is wax pellet element type and is designed to maintain an optimal level of temperatures in the cooling water.

SPECIFICATION

Water pump specification
    Type   Six(6) - blade impeller centrifugal type
    Delivery capacity   60 liters (15.8/13.2 gal US/Imp) per minute at 6,000 rpm at 20°C (68°F)
    Revolution ratio with crankshaft   1.57 : 1
    Water seal   Mechanical seal

Radiator specification
    Type   Pressure sealed cooling corrugated fin and tube type
    Radiation capacity   200 Kcal/min
    Opening pressure radiator cap valve 0.9 kg/cm² (12.78 lb/in²) ± 10%
    Coolant capacity   about 1.4 liters (1.47/1.23 Qt. US/lmp)
    Radiation area   664 cm² (102.92 in²)
    Core dimension   Height   240 mm (9.45")
                                                  Width   430 mm (17.0")
                                                    Thickness 59 mm (2.32")

Thermostat specification
    Type   Wax pellet element type
    Opening at   82°C (179.6°F)
    Full opening at   95°C (197.6°F)
    Stroke   8 mm (0.3")

Thermo switch and temperature gauge
    Refer "Body Electrical System".

TROUBLE SHOOTING

Symptoms & Probable Causes	Remedy
1. Overheating	
a. Insufficient coolant	Replenish, and check for leak/s
b. Thermostat remain closed by sticking	Replace thermostat
c. Water pump inoperative	Repair or replace
d. Cooling system passage blocked	Clean radiator and water passage
e. Incorrect ignition timing	Adjust ignition timing (Refer to page 11)
f. Brake dragging	Adjust brakes
g. Malfunctioning of cooling fan	Repair
2. Overcooling	
a. Thermostat remain opened by sticking	Check or replace thermostat
b. Extremely cold weather	Cover radiator

Symptoms & Probable Causes	Remedy
3. Loss of coolant	
a. Leaking radiator	Repair radiator
b. Loose or damaged hose connection	Tighten connection or replace hose
c. Leaking water pump cover	Repair or replace
d. Defective cylinder head gasket	Replace gasket
e. Improper tightening of cylinder head bolts	Tighten
f. Cracked cylinder head or block	Replace cylinder head or block
g. Defective radiator cap	Replace radiator cap
4. Noisy cooling system	
a. Defective water pump bearing	Replace water pump ass'y
b. Loose or bent water pump impeller	Replace impeller

RADIATOR

Removal

1. Cooling solution is drained out.
   Refer "Engine Disassembly" on page 22.

2. Remove the fuel tank.

3. Replace the radiator inlet and outlet hoses, the coolant inlet pipe, the radiator reservoir tank and its hose, etc. after loosening hose clamps.

4. The cooling fan and its shroud are removed.

Fig. 7-2 Cooling fan

5. The radiator is dismounted after removing its bumper.

Inspection Repair

1. Check the radiator for any water leakage at its upper tank, lower tank and core. The radiator should be replaced if any water leakage is found.
   Water leakage in the cooling system including the radiator is sometimes caused often by deteriorated materials and fitting conditions with the elapse of time including the shrinking of gasket, bolt loosening and hose deterioration, in addition to a usual apparent cause such as an accident which may involve rolling over of vehicles. In colder areas, the cooling system may sometimes become out of order, due to freezing coolant.
   It is necessary, therefore, to mix cooling water with an antifreeze and summer coolant and an anti-leakage material. New models GT750 coming out of the line have such agents added in the cooling system.
   As to the cooling water, an anti-freeze and summer coolant and an anti-leakage material, please see page 60.

2. Check the core fin of the radiator for mud or other foreign substances which may block smooth air flow. Also, bent or damaged fins, if any, should be remedied immediately.

Note: When more than 20% of the total radiator core area is clogged, the cooling effect of the radiator will be completely lost and it is necessary to replace the radiator in this instance.

3. Check the reverse valve of the radiator cap for its condition. This should be checked using a pressure gauge as shown in Fig. 7-3. When no pressure gauge is available, add a weight of about 7 kg (15.4 lb) onto the cap valve. It should then open when kept in good condition.

Gauge pressure (standard)
0.9 ± 0.1 kg/cm^2 (12.78 ± 1.4 lb/in^2)

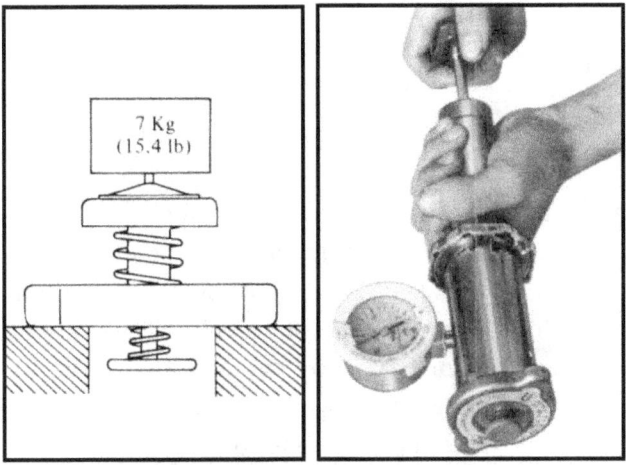

Fig. 7-3   Checking radiator cap

Note: In addition to the reverse valve, the radiator cap is fitted with two(2) other valve mechanisms. The knob(A) is installed for releasing the steam for some abnormal causes.

In this instance, the valve(B) opens, when the knob is pushed down before removing the radiator cap, and the steam within the radiator escapes into the bypass. Therefore, you do not have to worry about burning hands in removing the cap.

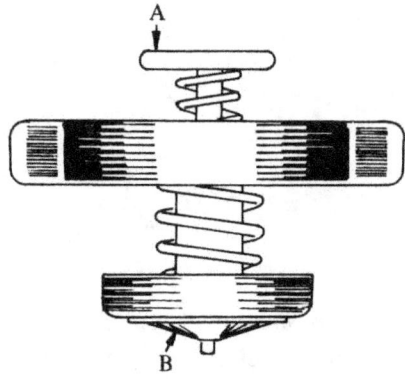

Fig. 7-4   Radiator cap

The valve(B) opens automatically, independent of the knob(A), when the pressure inside the radiator has dropped due to the temperature drop of the coolant and its subsequent contraction. Consequently possible damage on the radiator core due to a negative pressure can be avoided accordingly.

✱ Reason for adopting pressure-sealed cooling system. ✱

Pure water freezes at 0°C (32°F) and boils at 100°C (212°F). The use of this pure water as a coolant, however, would bring up many undesirable points. Usually, you may lower the freezing point and raise the boiling point using additives or by pressurizing the cooling system.

When pressurized pure water is heated, its boiling point rises in proportion to the pressure. Based on this principle, the tank cap is completely sealed. This is a pressure-sealed cooling system.

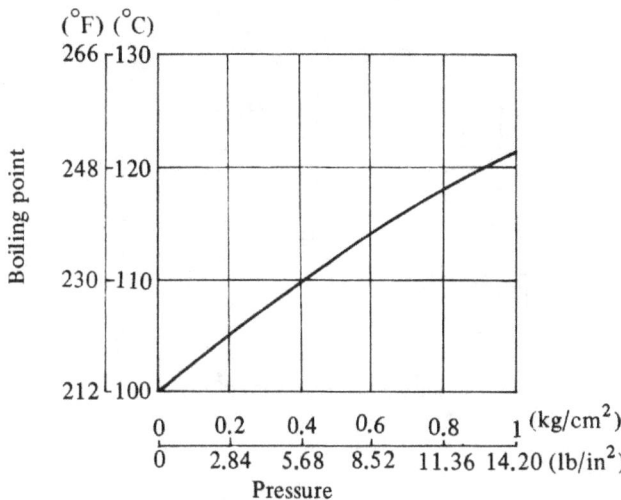

Fig. 7-5   Pressure-boiling point curve

As a coolant rises in temperature and expands, the pressure rises. When it reaches 1.9 kg/cm^2 (27.0 lbs/in^2), a gauge pressure of 0.9 kg/cm^2 (12.78 lbs/in^2), the valve of the radiator cap opens releasing the pressure and to prevent possible damage on the cooling system. As is seen from the above curve, a temperature in that instance is about 120°C (248°F). Actually, however, additives are added in the coolant. Then its boiling point rises further.

Note: A gauge pressure is difined as the difference between the inside pressure and the atmospheric pressure (about 1 kg/cm^2).
In the case of the radiator cap of GT750, the gauge pressure of 0.9 kg/cm^2 (12.8 lbs/in^2) is obtained as a balance between 1.9 kg/cm^2 (27.0 lbs/in^2) and 1 kg/cm^2 (14.2 lbs/in^2).

In replacing the radiator cap, it is required to use a new cap specially designed to a gauge pressure of 0.9 kg/cm^2 (12.8 lbs/in^2). The use of other caps would lead to overheating and a possible damage in radiator.

Installation

Installation is carried out in the reverse order of the removal procedure as mentioned hereinbefore and care should be taken on the following points:

There are three(3) kinds of radiator mounting washer of different thickness and these washers are used only for the intended purpose respectively. Be sure to use these washers in a right place in accordance with a white painted round mark on the mounting plate welded to the upper and lower tanks of the radiator. See Fig. 7-6.

Washer (A): 2.0 mm (0.079 in) thick
Washer (B): 1.6 mm (0.063 in) thick
Washer (C): 0.8 mm (0.031 in) thick

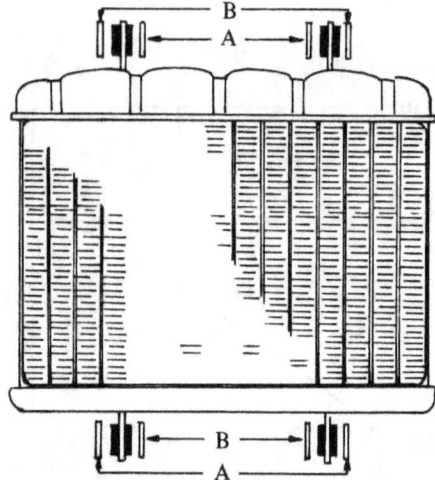

Fig. 7-6 Radiator mounting shims

(1) When marked by a white circle
   a. Upper tank mounting plate:
      The washer(A) is fitted to the plate inside and (B) to the outside.
   b. Lower tank mounting plate:
      The washer(A) is fitted to the plate outside and (B) to the inside.

(2) When unmarked by a white circle
   Fit the washer(B) to both sides of upper and lower tank plates.

(3) When a white circle mark is painted on the surface of the upper tank only, the washers(A) and (B) are fitted only to the upper tank mounting plate in a similar manner to the above (1). The lower tank mounting plate is fitted with the washer(B) only. In case only the lower tank is marked by painting, the procedures should be followed by the reversed order.

(4) In case that a slight gap is still there even though the proper washer has been selected, use the washer(C) to fill it up.

The radiator of GT750 is made of aluminum and attention should be paid to the fact that its improper installation would cause a stress concentration in the mounting plate, probably leading to a danger of cracks during the course of time.

Note: The radiator body and three(3) washers are available as spare parts in the form of a set and a suitable washer should be selected according to the above explanations.

THERMOSTAT

A thermostat is used for controlling the flow of cooling solution. When the temperature of the cooling solution is 82°C (179.6°F) and less, the thermostat valve closes thus preventing the coolant from flowing into the radiator. This runs through the bypass and circulates through the engine. At a temperature of 82°C, the value starts opening to release the cooling solution into the radiator as well. At 95°C (203°F), the valve is wide open and the bypass is closed to release all the coolant into the radiator for cooling.

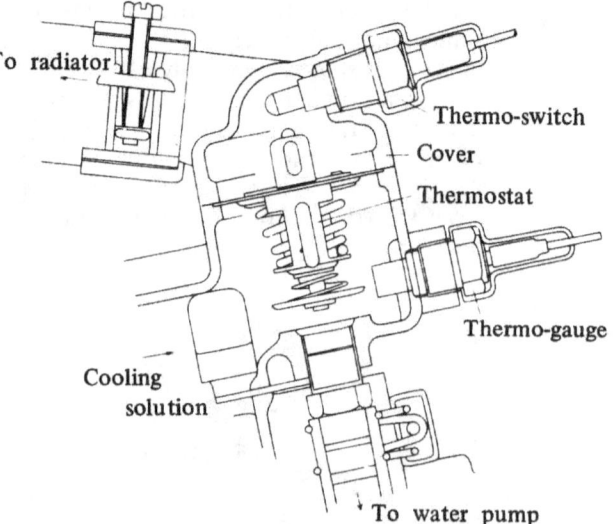

Fig. 7-7 Thermostat location

The thermostat is wax pellet type and its system is so made as to open and close the valve with the help of the expansion and contraction of wax in the pellet.

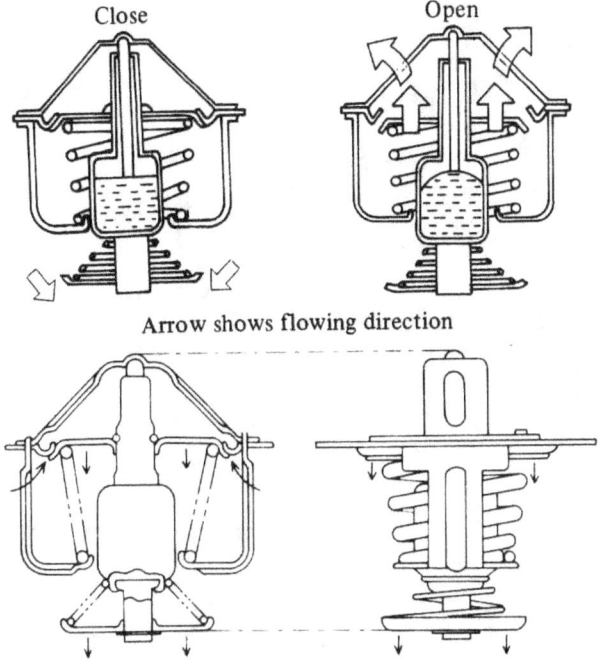

Fig. 7-8 Thermostat operation

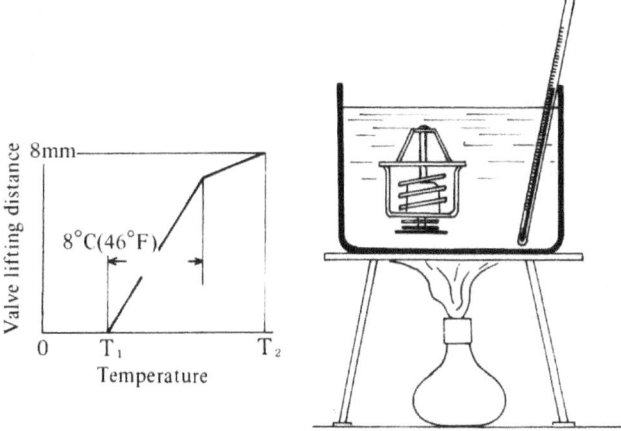

Fig. 7-9 Testing thermostat

Removal

1. Drain off the coolant.

2. Remove the thermostat cover and the thermostat.

Inspection & Repair

1. Check the pellet for any crack.

2. The function of the valve is tested. As shown in Fig. 7-9, both the thermostat and the thermometer are dipped into water within the vessel and water is heated by stirring to obtain a uniform temperature. Then, check the thermostat if it is normally operating at a prescribed temperature.

   * Valve opening temperature T_2:
     82±1.5°C (179.6±34°F)
   * Temperature when the valve is wide open T_2:
     95°C (203.0°F)
   * Stroke at the full opening:
     8 mm (0.3 in)

Note: An improper thermostat may lead to the overheating and the overcooling of the engine, and it is recommended that the thermostat should be replaced if it does not show the above-mentioned performances. Defective thermostat is often caused by the followings:

a) Unsatisfactory performance due to water scale and rust
b) Wax leakage at wax pellet
c) Deteriorated spring

Installation

To be carried out in the reverse order of the removal procedures.

WATER PUMP

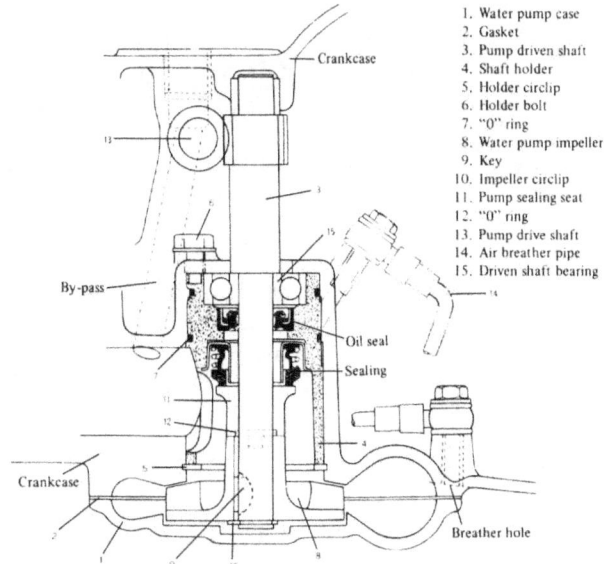

1. Water pump case
2. Gasket
3. Pump driven shaft
4. Shaft holder
5. Holder circlip
6. Holder bolt
7. "O" ring
8. Water pump impeller
9. Key
10. Impeller circlip
11. Pump sealing seat
12. "O" ring
13. Pump drive shaft
14. Air breather pipe
15. Driven shaft bearing

Fig. 7-10 Water pump

The water pump has a six(6)-blade impeller centrifugal type and is mounted in the transmission chamber at the bottom of the crankcase. Care, therefore, should be taken about the sealing against water and oil, and this point should always be borne in mind, in handling the engine and the water pump.

Removal

1. Drain off the coolant.

2. Remove the central muffler.

3. Remove the water pump cover with care so that its fitting surface may not be damaged.

4. Remove the impeller circlip and the impeller.

5. Remove the pump holder circlip and using a snap ring mover (09900–06103). Then, the water pump driven shaft is wrapped in cloth and drawn out downwards using the pliers.

Fig. 7–12 Removing pump holder circlip

Fig. 7–13 Extracting pump holder

6. In overhauling the water pump driving mechanism, please see the item on the "starter clutch."

Fig. 7–11 Removing impeller circlip

Caution: When removing the pump holder, be careful not to hurt the driven shaft surface, or else the impeller may not be reinstalled on assembly.

Disassembly

The water pump driven shaft and its bearing can be removed if drawn out in the reverse direction to the impeller after the pump holder is heated up to 75–85°C (167–185°C).
A water pump seal and an oil seal in the pump holder should not be removed, which otherwise would be damaged.

Note: Both the water pump seal and the oil seal in spare parts are treated as a complete set with the pump holder and these components may not be supplied separately.

Inspection

1. Check the bearing for rough surface or excessive end play.
   Scales or rust, if any, on the pump dirven shaft should be removed with emery cloth.

2. Check impeller blade for any deflection, bend or damage etc. The impeller should be replaced whenever such a defect is found.

3. Check to see if the sealing seat is worn out excessively and an effective sealing cannot be expected, the sealing seat and the pump holder should be replaced.

4. Check the "0" ring around the pump holder for any damage and proper sealing effect should be expected.

   Note: The cooling solution and transmission oil are sealed in two(2) steps, as follows:
   The solution is first sealed with a pump seal, a sealing seat and an "O" ring installed inside of the sealing seat.
   Transmission oil is first sealed with an oil seal. Then, both solution and transmission oil are sealed with two(2) "O" rings outside of the pump holder. The system is so made that the solution or transmission oil, if leaking at the said sealing part, will be drained from the crankcase through a breather pipe.

5. Check water pump drive gears and their bearings for any abnormality.

6. Check the impeller if it is contacting the crankcase or the pump case. A contacting impeller with the crankcase indicates an improper coupling of the pump driven shaft with the bearing. The shaft should be removed for checking.

   Standard gap between impeller and crankcase:
   0.5–1.5 mm (0.02–0.59 in)

Assembly

The assembly is carried out in the reverse order of the disassembly procedure and care should be taken on the following points:

1. In inserting the water pump holder in the crankcase, apply oil over the outside of the holder and a port on the holder side is aligned with another port on the crankcase. In this case, rotate the holder slightly to either direction so that a notch on the holder top will come to the setting bolt of the crankcase.

   Caution: Observe the above alignment method correctly. Otherwise, the holder might be broken and a leakage would occur.

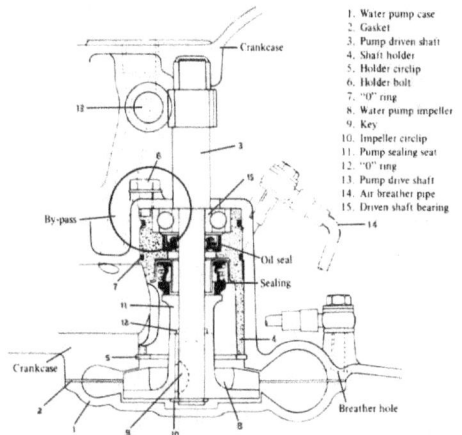

Fig. 7–14   Pump holder notch

2. The impeller is inserted into the pump driven shaft and is secured with a circlip. In this instance, it is necessary to make sure that a gap between the impeller and the crankcase is 1.5 mm (0.59 in). Without this gap, the pump driven shaft should be taken out for a gap adjustment.

3. Apply liquid gasket (99000-33010) on both sides of the waterpump case gasket before mounting the pump case.

COOLING WATER, ANTI-FREEZE & SUMMER COOLANT and ANTI-LEAKAGE MATERIAL

Cooling Water

Generally, drinking water can be used, but for the cooling system of GT750, distilled water must always be used for the following reasons:
Aluminum, which is known for light weight and superior heat radiation efficiency, is used throughout

the cooling system of GT750. This material is liable to rust, as compared with cast iron and bronze which are used generally for the cooling system. In addition to taking some precaution against possible clogging in the water passage, it is necessary to use as pure water as possible. This is to ensure the prevention of the accumulation of foreign substances in the system.

Some drinking water, however, is unsuitable for cooling water and it is usually difficult to judge the hardness of water, upon which the suitability of cooling water depends. In this respect, it is recommended to use distilled water, which contains most likely much less foreign substances and can be obtained with relative ease.

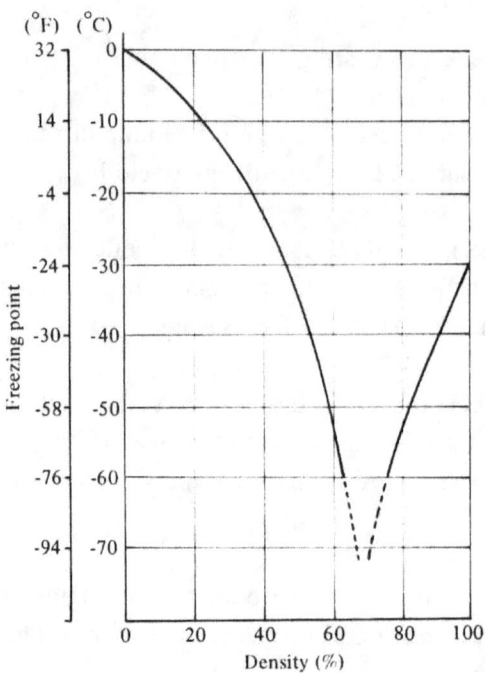

Fig. 7–16 Coolant density-freezing point curve

Anti-freeze & Summer Coolant

As explained in the section of "pressure-sealed cooling system", it is not permitted to use distilled water as it is as cooling water and it is always required to put in additives so that the freezing point of cooling water is lowered or the elevated boiling point. These additives are an anti-freeze & summer coolant, which effectively reduces the freezing point of cooling water or raise its boiling point.

Note: To elevate a boiling point a most effective method use is pressurizing the system and the use of additives is not so important.

All models of GT750 coming from the production line are pre-filled with 50% of GOLDEN CRUISER 1200 anti-freeze and summer coolant in the cooling system. This material can be used for the motorcycle in colder regions where an atmospheric temperature drops to −31°C (−24°F). See Fig. 7–17.

For use in colder regions or storage in the motorcycle, this mixing ration should be increased up to 55% or 60% according to chart (Fig. 7–17).

Caution: Mixing of the anti-freeze & summer coolant is permitted up to 60%. Mixing beyond it would reduce its efficiency as shown in Fig. 7–16.

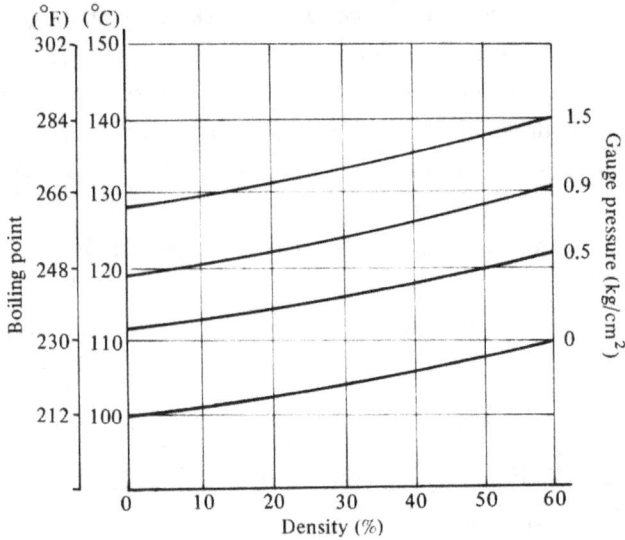

Fig. 7–15 Coolant density-boiling point curve

The above material is also used as rust-proof or corrosion proof material of the cooling system. It can be used. therefore, in summer or in tropical regions as well as in winter seasons and colder regions. We should also note that only those materials prepared for aluminum cylinders and radiators be sued.

As mentioned above, all new models from our line have GOLDEN CRUISER 1200 anti-freeze and summer coolant filled after being tested and guaranteed. In refilling, the same coolant or its equivalent should be used.

Caution: GOLDEN CRUISER is a year-round type coolant and should be able to retain its effectiveness for two(2) years or travelling distance of 35,000 km (20,000 miles). During that period, it is not necessary to exchange nor replenish the coolant except the case of leakage. Also, it is recommended to avoid mixing two(2) kinds of coolant of different brand.

Anti-leakage material

The anti-freeze is characterized by very high values of permeability and the leakage accident of the cooling system is highly likely. The anti-leakage substance is used to prevent such a possible leakage and every new model GT750 is filled with "Suzuki 7 on Bar's Leaks." The same material or its equivalent should be filled in the raidator when cooling water is changed. "Suzuki 7 on Bar's Leaks" is available as one of spare parts in solid form. A suitable amount for use is 1/2 oz (14 gr) per model and in the case of a liquid anti-leakage material available in the market, 70 cc (0.15/0.12 pt US/Imp) should be used.

Caution: Anti-leakage material should not be added except the time of the renewal of cooling water.

Cooling System Flushing

Every two years the cooling system should be serviced by flushing with plain water, then completely refilled with a fresh solution with spceified mixing ratio of distilled water and GOLDEN CRUISER 1200 antifreeze and summer coolant, or a high-quality, inhibited (year-around type) glycol base coolant tested and guaranteed by SUZUKI. In addition, Cooling System Sealer (Suzuki 7 on Bar's Leaks) should be added.

1. Drain the coolant through the crankcase drain valve (refer to page 20).

2. Close the valve and add a sufficient amount of plain water to fill the system.

3. Run the engine until the normal operating temperature is reached.

4. Drain and refill the system, as described in steps 1, 2, and 3, a sufficient number of times until the drained liquid is colorless.

5. Allow the system to drain completely and then close the crankcase drain valve tightly.

6. Add the necessary amount of GOLDEN CRUISER 1200 and distilled water solution to provide the required freezing and corrosion protection.

7. Run the engine until normal operating temperature is reached.

8. Check and adjust level of coolant after the system has cooled sufficiently.

Temperature under which your motorcycle is used	°C	−10	−15	−20	−25	−31	−39
	°F	14	5	−4	−13	−24	−38
Mixing ratio of anti-freeze	%	30	35	40	45	50	55
Amount of anti-freeze /distilled water for 4.5 ltr (4.75/3.95 qt, US/Imp) of cooling solution	ltr	1.35/3.15	1.60/2.90	1.80/2.70	2.00/2.50	2.25/2.25	2.50/2.00
	US.pt	1.40/3.30	1.70/3.10	1.90/2.90	2.10/2.60	2.40/2.40	2.60/2.10
	Imp.pt	1.20/2.75	1.40/2.55	1.55/2.40	1.75/2.20	2.00/2.00	2.20/1.75

Note: This table applies to the use of GOLDEN CRUISER 1200 Coolant only.

Fig. 7−17 Required amount of anti-freeze coolant at each temperature

8. FUEL SYSTEM

	Page
DESCRIPTION	63
SPECIFICATION	63
TROUBLE SHOOTING	63
CARBURETOR	64
Description	64
Carburetor Specification (Setting table)	65
Construction & Operation	65
Starter system	65
Slow system	66
Main system	66
Float system (Fuel supplying system)	67
Removal	68
Disassembly & Reassembly	68
Inspection & Adjustment	68
Starter system	68
Slow system	68
Main system	69
Float system	70
FUEL COCK	71

DESCRIPTION

The fuel system consists of a fuel tank, a fuel cock, a carburetor, a fuel pipe, an accelerator cable and an air cleaner.

Three(3) "AMAL" types of carburetor having bore as large as 32 mm are fitted and a large-sized air cleaner suitable for the carburetor is used.

The fuel tank has a capacity of 17 liters (4.49/3.75 gal US/Imp) and fuel is supplied to the carburetor by way of a diaphragm fuel cock which can be automatically turned "on" and "off".

SPECIFICATION

Fuel tank capacity:
    Total capacity   17 ltr. (4.49/3.75 gal US/Imp)
    Reserve capacity   3.5 ltr. (0.92/0.77 gal US/Imp)
Fuel cock operating pressure   0.35 kg/cm^2 (4.98 lb/in^2)

TROUBLE SHOOTING

Symptoms & Probable Causes	Remedies
1. Overflowing	
a. Improper seating or damaged float needle valve and seat	Clean or replace needle valve, and seat (Refer to Fig. 8–5)
b. Incorrect fuel level	Adjust fuel level (Refer to page 70)
c. Foreign materials in needle valve	Clean (Refer to Fig. 8–11)
d. Defective fuel cock diaphragm	Replace fuel cock (Refer to page 71)
e. Defective float	Replace (Refer to page 70)
2. Hard starting	
a. Clogged starter system	Disassemble and clean (Refer to page 68)
b. Clogged or defective fuel cock	Clean or replace
c. Loose carburetor mounting clamp(s)	Tighten clamps
d. Air cleaner passage blocked	Clean cleaner element
3. Rough idling	
a. Incorrect idle adjustment	Adjust idling (Refer to page 68)
b. Clogged or loose slow system in carburetor	Clean and tighten
c. Incorrect fuel level	Adjust fuel level (Refer to page 70)
d. Improper starter system	Repair starter system
e. Improper air screw adjustment	Adjust opening of air screw (Refer to Fig. 8–8)

Symptoms & Probable Causes	Remedies
4. Excessive fuel consumption	
a. Incorrect fuel level	Adjust fuel level (Refer to page 70)
b. Improper starter system	Repair
c. Air cleaner passage blocked	Clean cleaner element
d. Loose jet and screw/s	Tighten
5. Poor acceleration	
a. Clogged fuel pipe	Clean pipe
b. Defective cock diaphragm	Repair
c. Improper air screw adjustment	Adjust air screw (Refer to Fig. 8–8)
6. Stalling at high speed	
a. Clogged loose main jet	Clean or tighten main jet
b. Incorrect float level	Adjust float level
c. Loose carburetor mounting clamp/s	Tighten
d. Improper fuel cock	Check, clean

CARBURETOR

Description

For model GT750, three(3) "AMAL" type carburetors VM32 SC are fitted with each carburetor having a different specification largely because of the fact that the muffler at the center cylinder is branched to both right and left sides, and hence the distance from the intake of air cleaner to each carburetor differs.

The starter system is operated by a starter cable fitted independently to each carburetor, with the starter lever being fitted to the handle.

To synchronize and balance three(3) carburetors an aligning mark hole is provided on the mixing chamber body of each carburetor to facilitate the adjustment of an unbalance among three(3) carburetors.

Carburetor Specification (Setting table)

Item	R.H. Carburetor	Center Carburetor	L.H. Carburetor
Type	VM 32Sc	''	''
Body mark	31010R	31010M	31010L
Main jet	102.5	100	102.5
Jet needle	5F16-3	''	''
Needle jet	P-4	P-3	P-4
Cutaway	2.5	''	''
Pilot jet	30	''	''
Bypass	1.4	''	''
Pilot outlet	0.6	''	''
Air screw opening	1-½ turns	''	''
Valve seat	2.5	''	''
Starter jet	50	''	''
Float level	26~28 mm (1.02~1.10 in)	''	''

Fig. 8-1 Carburetor setting table

Construction & Operation

The operation of carburetor is considered in the following four(4) stages of the system:
1. Starter system
2. Slow system
3. Main system
4. Float system

Explanations will follow this order, but please see SUZUKI's Service Manual "Carburetor and Carburetion" of 1971 for further details.

1. Starter System

    To start a cold engine a specially rich mixture of air and gasoline is needed. The starter system is used for generating such gases which meet the purpose.

    By operating the starter lever, the starter plunger ② opens with the throttle valve being at a closed position for starting the engine. Then, aspirated air into the engine passes through the air passage ① being branched from the main bore. At that time, a negative pressure is induced within the plunger chamber, which draws fuel from the starter jet ③. When the fuel passes through the emulsion tube ④, air entering through a small hole on the tube emulsifies the fuel. This fuel is further mixed with air within the plunger chamber and atomized, jetting into the main bore from the starter outlet ⑤ before reaching the engine.

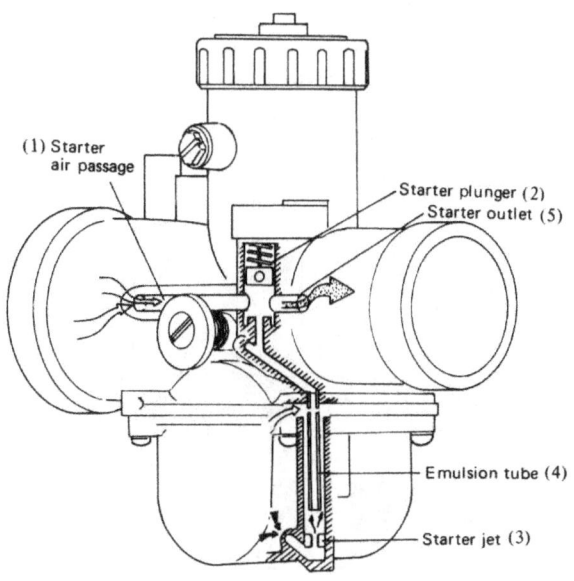

Fig. 8-2 Starter system

The starter cable for operating the plunger is fitted to each carburetor independently to ensure more reliable engine starting.

Note: Care should be taken not to open the throttle grip, when the starter is being used. Otherwise, gases would be diluted and the engine starting would be difficult.

2. Slow System

This system works over a range at a slightly larger opening than the closed position that is, the range is from idling to slow speed condition.

Aspirated air from the air inlet ① due to a negative pressure in the crankchamber can be regulated by the pilot air adjusting screw ② and reaches the pilot jet ③. Fuel is then drawn in and changes into a rich mixture. This mixture is jetted from the pilot outlet ④ and is diluted with air having passed a space between the main bore and the throttle valve. With that dilution, a suitable mixture is formed and supplied to the engine.

With further opening of the throttle valve, the engine speed increases requiring a larger amount of mixed gases, with the same mixed gases being supplied as a jet from the bypass ⑤ to supplying a necessary amount of fuel to the engine.

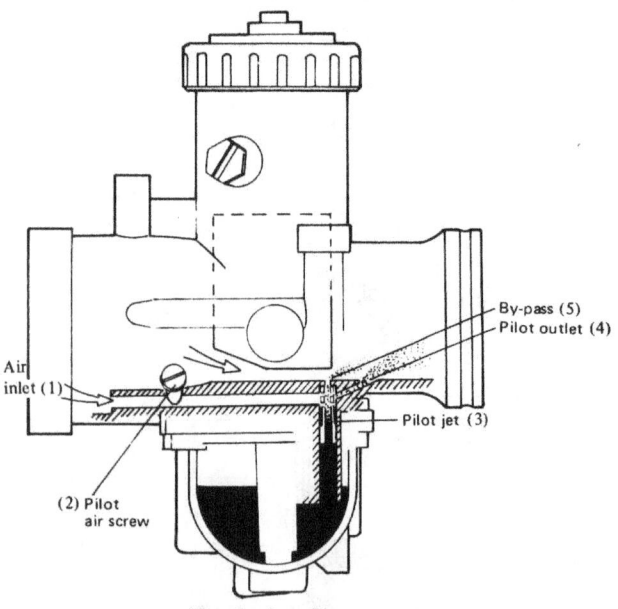

Fig. 8-3 Slow system

∗ This explains why fuel is drawn in from the pilot jet when air flows in the pilot air passageway. ∗

As shown in Fig. 8-4, when air drawn from the part A of a large cross-sectional area reaches the part B having a smaller cross section its velocity is accelerated thus reducing its pressure. (Theoretically, the pressure drop is in inverse proportion to the square of the velocity. A pipe having this effect is called "Venturi".)

This pressure drop induces a lifting force, equivalent to the pressure difference between its pressure and the atmospheric pressure, acting on the fuel. The fuel is carried away at high air speed and is well atomized in a jet from the nozzle.

The above principle applies to the carburetor. In the case of slow system, the part A corresponds to the air cleaner, a tube between the parts A and B correspond to the pilot air passageway and the fuel tube of the part B to the pilot jet for control of a fuel flow, respectively. Also, a pilot air adjusting screw is provided to control the air volume in the air passageway and the delivery of an air-fuel mixture is controlled as a whole. The part C corresponds to the pilot outlet.

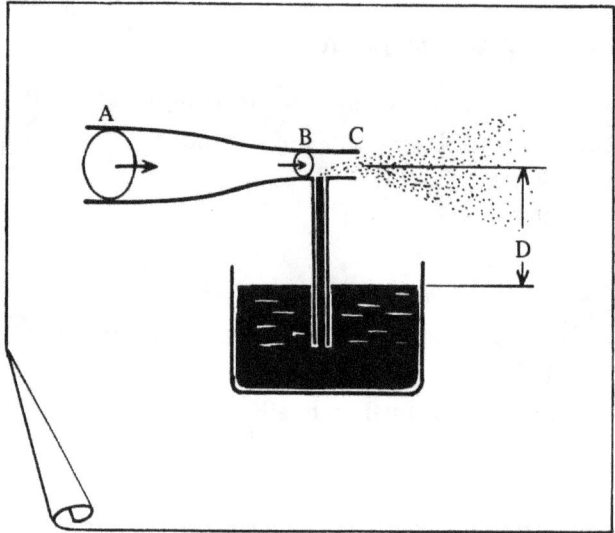

Fig. 8-4 Principle of carburetor

3. Main System

Engine speeds become higher with the throttle valve open, a large amount of air-fuel mixture is needed. Air as drawn does not pass the pilot channel with a large resistance, but flows through the main bore.

It is the main system which is effective in generating the mixture in this instance and the system works over medium and high speed ranges.

As shown in Fig. 8-5, when aspirated air from the air cleaner passes between the main bore and the throttle valve ④, it draws in fuel from the main jet ① and a gap between the needle jet ② and the jet needle ③ by the above-mentioned venturi effect. It further atomizes the fuel before being supplied the engine.

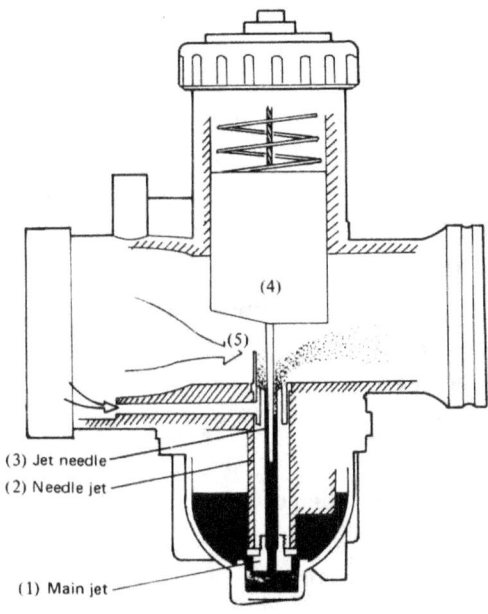

Fig. 8-5 Main system

At the same time, air is introduced from a small air passageway at the lower side of the main bore shown in Fig. 8-5, and passed into the needle jet to facilitate the atomization of the fuel. The screen ⑤ fitted to the top of the needle jet blocks the air flow in the main bore generating a turbulent flow at its back which is needed to facilitate the atomization of the fuel. This is called a "primaty choke".

In the main system, air flow can be regulated at the throttle valve and a matched amount of fuel is regulated at the main jet. Fuel so drawn is further regulated depending upon the extent of the throttle valve opening, finally mixed with air and fed to the engine.

4. Float System (Fuel supplying system)
This system provides one of the most important mechanisms in supplying fuel to the carburetor and, as shown in Fig. 8-6, consists of a float ①, a needle valve ②, a needle valve seat ③ and a valve seat gasket ④. In addition to the function of a valve for adjusting the fuel flow, they play a very important role to keep a constant fuel level in the float chamber.

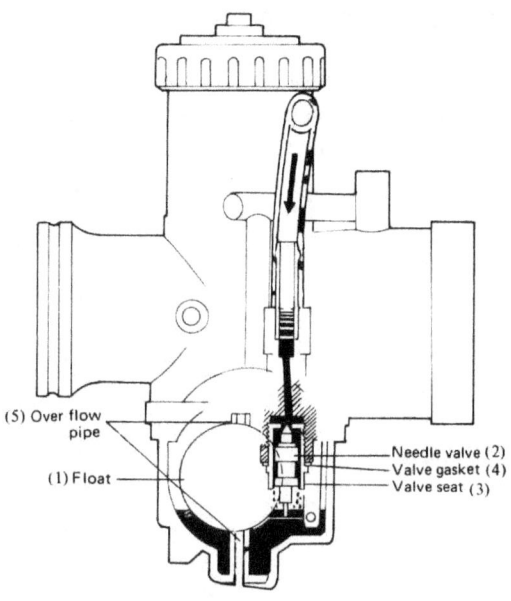

Fig. 8-6 Float system

When fuel in the chamber is below a certain prescribed level, the float ① comes down and the needle valve also sinks correspondingly providing a gap at the valve seat. Then, fuel automatically flows in from the gap up to the preset level, moving the float and the needle valve upward and closing the gap to completely shut off the fuel flow.

The air vent ⑤ is an air breather in the float chamber and facilitates a free fuel flow from the float chamber. Also, it works as an overflow pipe ⑤ to drain the fuel, when the fuel level in the float chamber rises abnormally.

∗ Necessity to keep the fuel level constant. ∗

A mixing ratio of air and fuel is regulated by valve, jet and other related fittings of each system. If the fuel level should not be constant, the ratio would change markedly. It may be understood that the smaller the distance (D) from fuel level to venturi center, the more is drawn. See Fig. 8-4.

Removal

In dismounting the carburetor, clamps on cylinder and air cleaner rides are lossened first and, then, the carburetor is pushed toward the air cleaner. Each cable and tube should be disconnected on the carburetor side.

Disassembly & Reassembly

Each component requires precision manufacturing and utmost care should be taken not to damage the part in disassembly and re-assembly work.

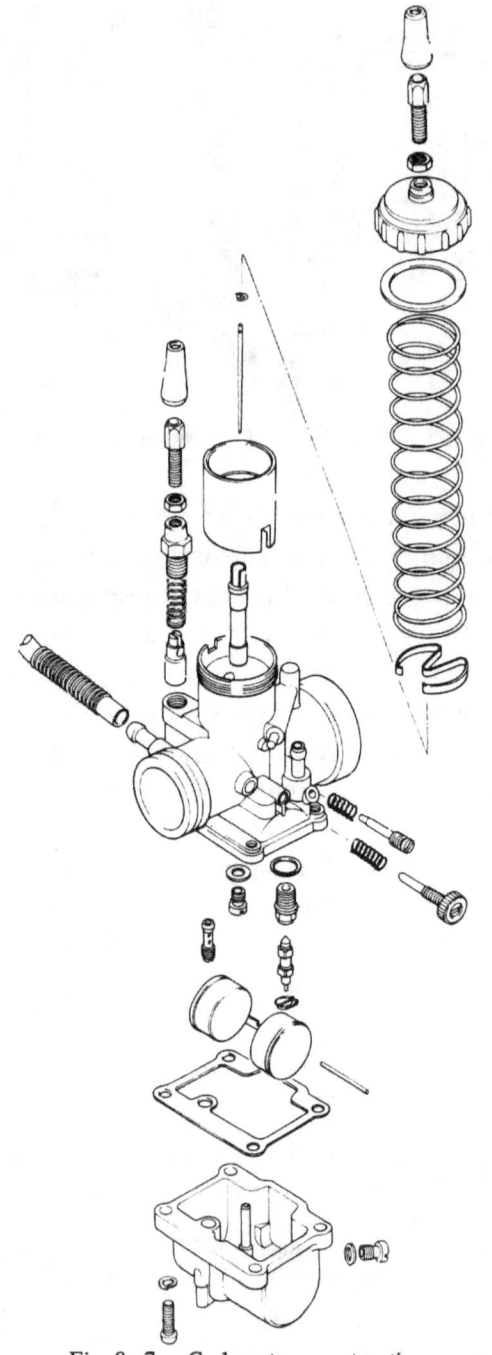

Fig. 8-7 Carburetor construction

Inspection & Adjustment

Before inspection and adjustment the carburetor should be dipped into clean gasoline for the cleaning. After the cleaning, each passageway of the carburetor is blown with the compressed air for removing dusts or other foreign substances.

It is to be noted that a trouble is sometimes caused due to the dusts or other foreign substances in gasoline at the fuel passage and the subsequent clogging of the passage. A wire or any other equivalent tool should not be used in the cleaning work in that instance.

1. Starter system

   If the engine does not start when the starter lever is operated, the following points should be checked:

   a. Clogging of starter jet
   b. Proper working of starter plunger

   Note: If any one of three(3) carburetors is defective in actuating the starter plunger, that is, the plunger not returning to the original position, engine idling will be irregular and it is sometimes seen that the engine stops running immediately after the starting.

2. Slow system

   When the engine is subjected to irregular idling, with the engine speed not increasing smoothly or is subjected to jerking when the engine speed is being increased from the idling with an abnormal condition at low speed, careful inspection would be in order. Check as follows:

   a. Check pilot air adjusting screw ① for its functioning.

   A specified air adjusting screw opening is 1–1/2 for all of the three(3) carburetors. The screw should be tightened once and then lossened by 1–1/2 turns.

Fig. 8-8 Slow system adjusting

b. Check the throttle stop screw ② if it is properly adjusted.
Check also the throttle cable for idle portion. Their adjusting method will be explained in the following section on the main system below.

3. Main system

When jerking and stalling are encountered at medium and high speed ranges proceed the checking, as follows:

a. Check the main jet for its looseness. A loosen jet means an excess fuel being supplied to the engine and the rich gas condition would be given, deteriorating the engine performance.

b. An incorrect fuel level would lead to deterioration in engine performance. As to the fuel level adjustment, please see the section on the float system.

c. An expected engine performance cannot be attained, if the throttle valve cable is maladjusted and three(3) carburetors are not well synchronized. Adjustment can be made as follows:

(1) Adjust throttle cable adjuster of each carburetor and coordinate each throttle cable for an idling portion to allow a play of 2~3 mm (0.08~1.1").

(2) Remove the plug fitted to the mixing chamber body of each carburetor and operate the throttle grip. Then, it is possible to identify an aligning mark on the throttle valve side.
Therefore, the throttle cable adjuster is so adjusted that for each carburetor, the aligning mark will be on top of the aligning hole.

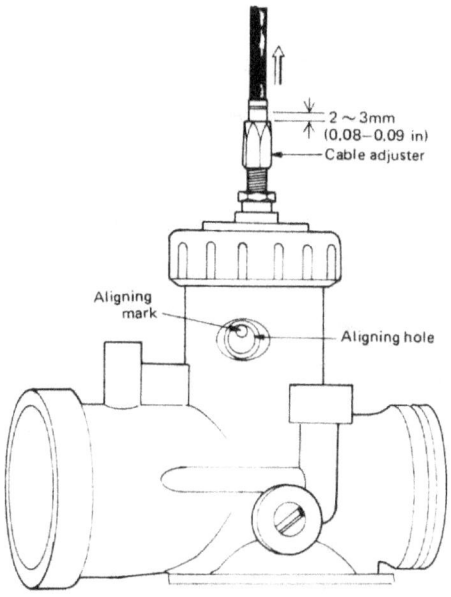

Fig. 8-9 Synchronizing carburetors

(3) The engine is started and warmed up sufficiently. Then adjust idling speed using a throttle stop screw. In adjusting the idling speed, two(2) spark plug caps are removed in turn so that only one(1) cylinder functions and the engine speed should be set to 1,000 rpm for each cylinder.

(4) When each cylinder is adjusted to the speed of 1,000 rpm independently from the adjustment of carburetors, the throttle stop screw of each carburetor is turned back uniformly so that an idling speed of 1,000 rpm can be obtained with the firing of three(3) cylinders.

(5) Finally, the throttle cable adjuster below the throttle grip is adjusted so that the throttle cable will have an idle portion of 0.5~1 mm (0.02~0.04") length.

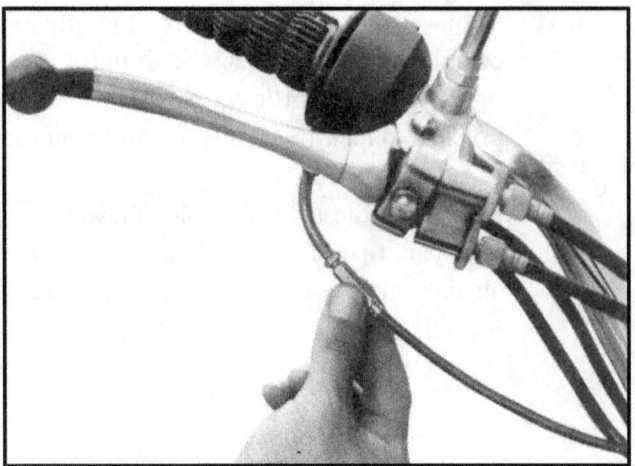

Fig. 8–10 Adjusting throttle cable

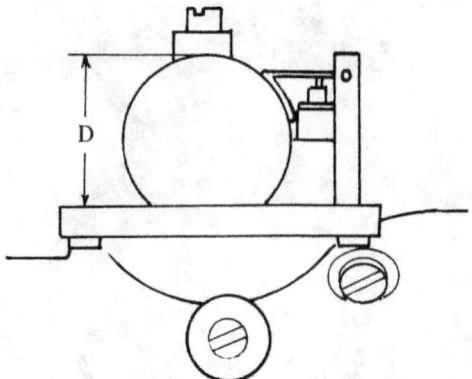

Fig. 8–12 Checking float level

4. Float system

The following three(3) are the check points of the float system:

(a) Checking for any foreign materials between the needle valve and its seat.

An overflowing gasoline, if any, from the carburetor is attributable in most cases to foreign materials caught between the needle valve and its seat, as shwon in Fig. 8–11. Such foreign materials can be removed by tapping the carburetor lightly, but it is usually recommended that the needle valve should be drawn out for cleaning.

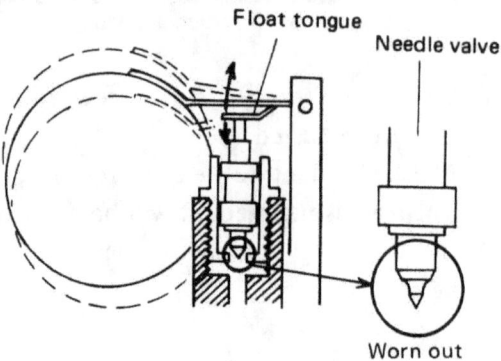

Fig. 8–13 Adjusting float level

For float level adjustment, the tongue of the float arm is bent and as shown in Fig. 8–13, the cap is reversed to give a specified float height.

Standard D = 27±1 mm (1.02~1.10")

(c) Checking if there is any damage on the float or for any water content inside of the float chamber.

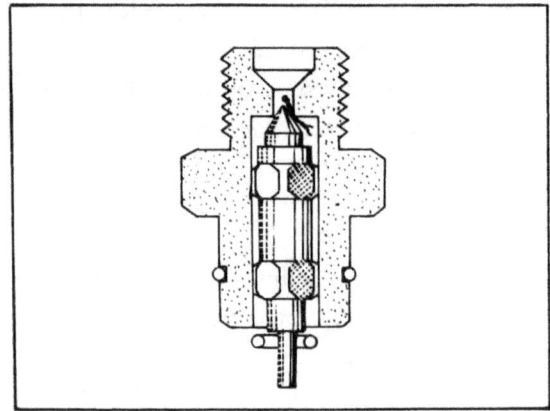

Fig. 8–11 Foreign material on needle valve

(b) The fuel level is adjusted correctly. This is one of the most important steps in the adjustment of the carburetor.

It is recommended that the fuel level should be periodically checked and the needle valve should be replaced if worn out.

FUEL COCK

Description

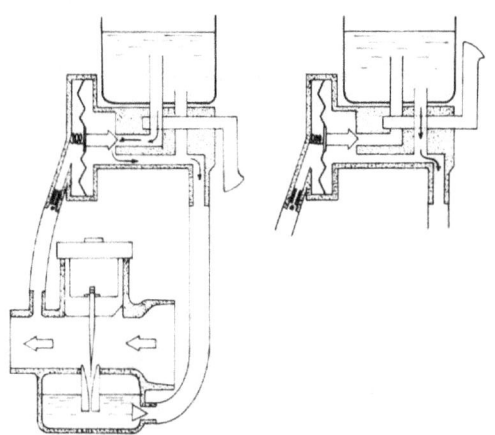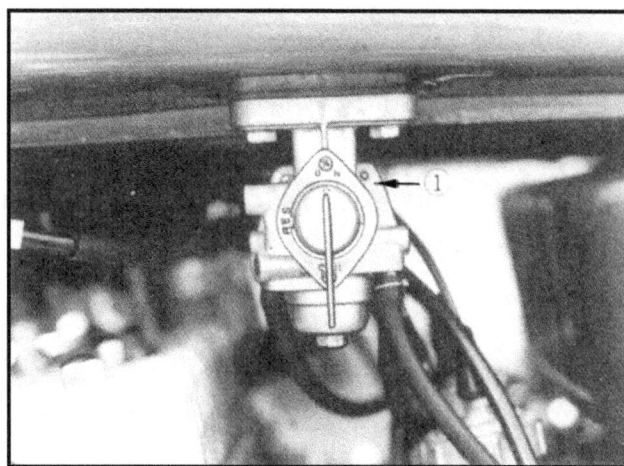

Fig. 8–14 Fuel cock construction

GT750 employs a diaphragm fuel cock which actuates on vacuum from the engine and opens a tap automatically when the engine starts.

The diaphragm chamber includes a diaphragm, valve and spring which presses the valve against the valve seat to close a fuel passage.

From the vacuum chamber to the left hand carburetor runs a strip of tube which transmits the vacuum generated in the carburetor to the cock.

Once the engine runs and vacuum is generated in the carburetor, the diaphragm together with the valve is pulled against the spring by the vacuum, leaving a gap between the valve and seat through which fuel is allowed to flow down to the carburetors.

This fuel cock has three positions, "ON", "RES", and "PRI". Turning the fuel cock lever to "Priming" position allows fuel to flow directly to the carburetor without passing through the diaphragm valve system. When starting the engine of a machine which has been left unused for a long time or the carburetors of which were overhauled, first supply fuel to the carburetor float chamber by turning the cock lever to "Priming" position.

Turn the lever again to "On" position when the engine has started in order to prevent running out of fuel on the way.

Inspection & Repair

1. Check for leakage from cock body or fuel pipe connections.

2. Remove the cock cap and inspect the filter and gasket for defects.

3. Inspect the function of diaphragm cock; take out a fuel and a vacuum pipe from carburetor and suck air from the vacuum pipe with the lever positioned on "ON" or "RES", then check to see if the gasoline flows out or not.

9. EXHAUST SYSTEM

	Page
DESCRIPTION	72
Removal	73
Inspection	73
Assembly	73

DESCRIPTION

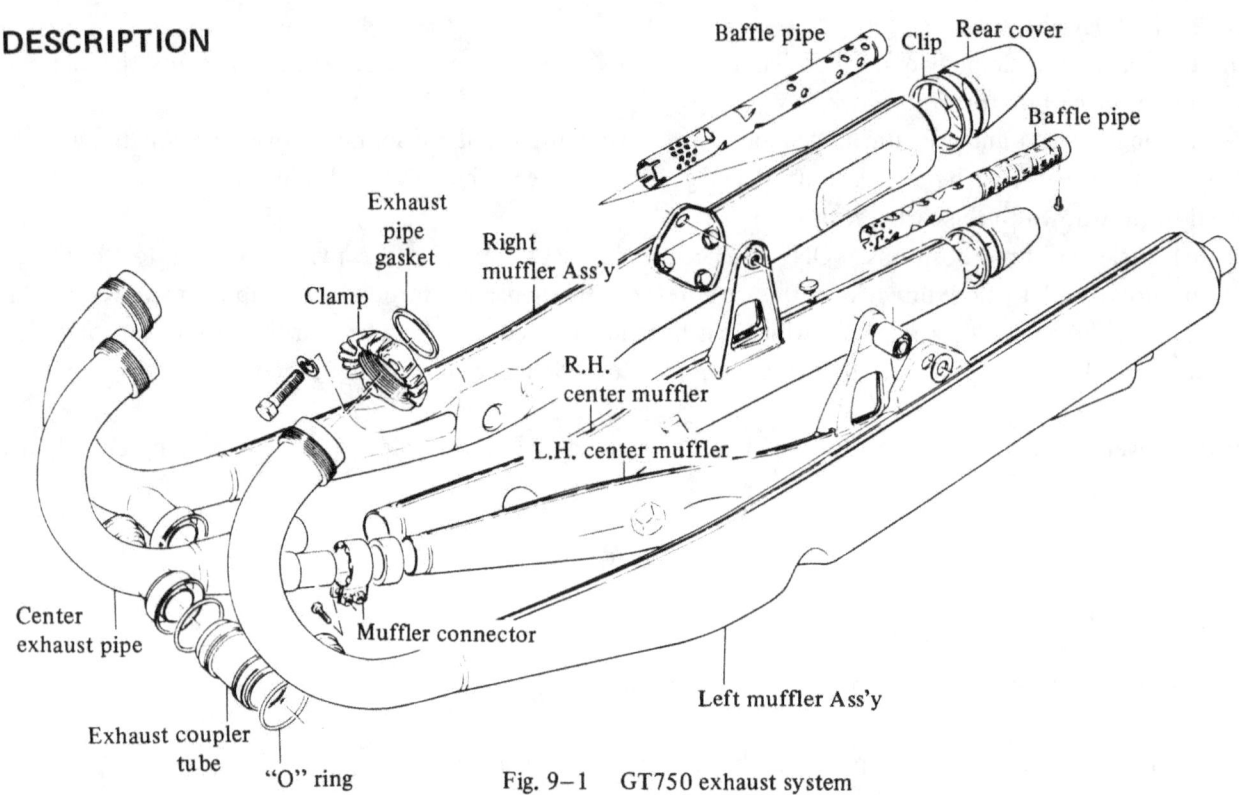

Fig. 9-1   GT750 exhaust system

Exhaust system of this engine consists of the right and left muffler assemblies integrally constructed with muffler and exhaust pipe, and the center exhaust pipe branched at the halfway in two pipes whereto the right and left mufflers are to be fixed.

All mufflers are connected with coupler tubes at the exhaust portion. Inside of each muffler rear body, baffle pipes are installed.

Removal

1. Remove the exhaust clamps of each cylinder by loosening the clamp bolts.

2. Remove the right and left pillion footrest.

3. Disconnect the exhaust coupler tubes, then remove mufflers.

Inspection

1. Check the coupler pipe gasket (Exhaust coupler seal) for leakage.

2. Check for any defect on the exhaust pipe gaskets and "O" rings.

3. Check for any cracks on the muffler body.

* Reason for adopting Exhaust coupler tubes *

The muffler on 2 cycle engine is not used only as a silencer, but as subsidiary equipment for increasing engine out-put. This is because that 2 cycle engine has no valves on the cylinder head controlling the flow of working gas like 4 cycle engine and accordingly have to make its muffler substitute for the valves on 4 cycle engine by utilizing the exhausted gas pulse.

The coupler tubes on GT750 are adopted to heighten further this effect than the ordinary muffler and also to improve the exhaust noise.

Assembly

1. Install the center exhaust pipe into the cylinder exhaust port.

2. Support the right and left muffler at the cylinder exhaust port flanges and the pillion footrests.

3. Install the coupler tubes into each flange on the exhaust pipes with the Exhaust coupler seal (99000-31020) applied on the outside of them.

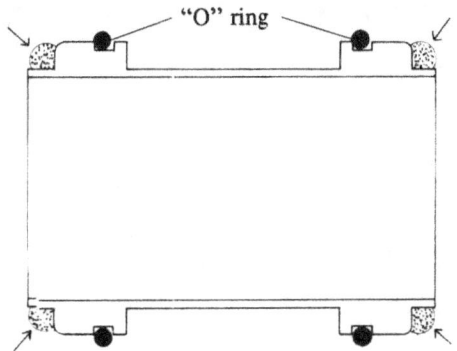

Fig. 9-2   Exhaust coupler tube

4. Tighten the exhaust clamps of right and left muffler firmly and then mount the R.H. and L.H. center muffler.

Caution: (1). The exhaust clamps should be fixed so as to be 1 mm (0.04") of gap between the flank of cramp and the cylinder.

Fig. 9-3   Fixing exhaust pipe clamp

(2). It is recommended to replace Exhaust coupler seal at the time of an overhaul.
It will stop leaking from connecting parts after a while even after replacing.

10. ENGINE ELECTRICAL SYSTEM

	Page
DESCRIPTION	74
TROUBLE SHOOTING	75
STARTING SYSTEM	77
Description	77
Specification	79
Removal	80
Disassembly	80
Inspection & Repair	80
Assembly	83
CHARGING SYSTEM	85
Description	85
Operation	85
Specification	86
Alternator	86
Removal	86
Inspection & Repair	86
IGNITION SYSTEM	90
Description	90
Operation	90
Specification	91
Removal	91
Disassembly	91
Inspection & Repair	91
Timing Adjustment & Test	94

DESCRIPTION

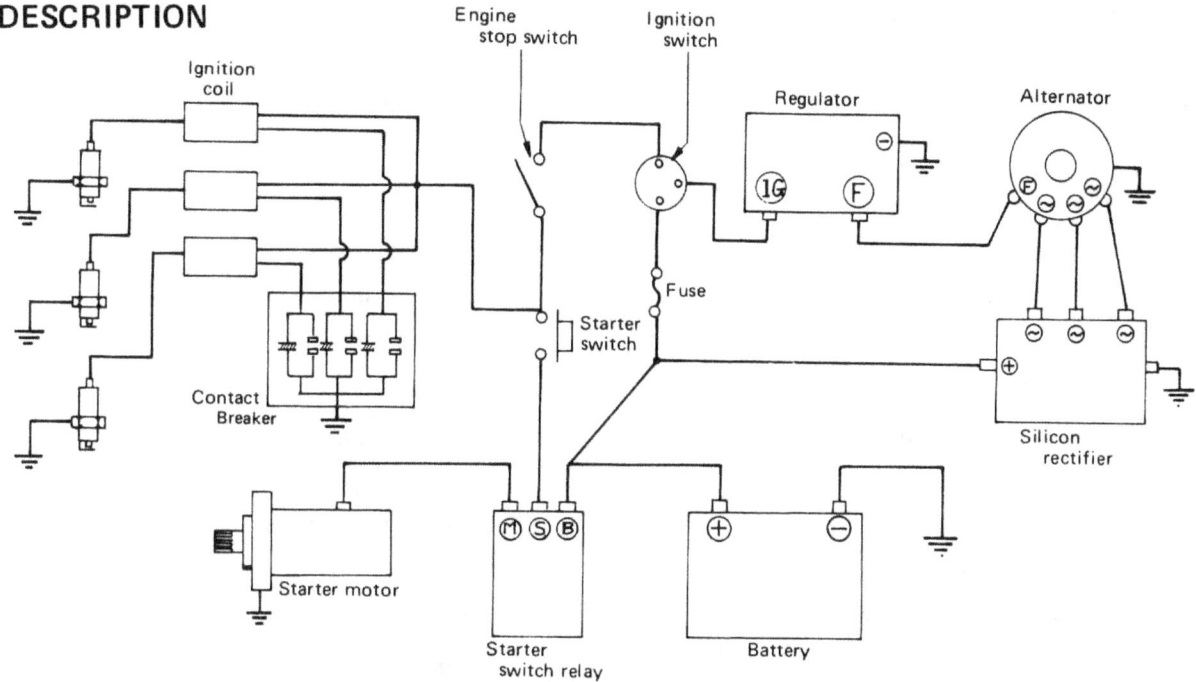

Fig. 10-1 GT750 engine electrical system

GT750 engine is equipped with a 12 volt electrical system, consisting of starting, charging and ignition systems.

Starting system:
The starting motor equipped in this engine is compact and light, and is a sealed type to prevent entry of dirt and dust. It is activated by the magnetic starter relay when the starter button is pushed with both the ignition and the engine stop switches on. The output is transmitted to the engine through the starter clutch which is of over-running type and its driven gear is constant-meshed to the starting motor pinion. The starter relay including the magnetic switch inside is designed to be extremely reduced the possibility of having short circuiting and poor insulation.

Charging system:
The charging system consists of alternator, regulator, silicon rectifier and battery. The alternator generates a high electric output even at low engine speed which enable to eliminate the discharge of the battery in the normal condition.
The function of the alternator regulator is to regulate the generator voltage to a pre-set value by controlling the rotor coil current.

Ignition system:
The ignition system consists of both three ignition coils and contact breaker points. When contact point is closed, the current flow from the battery through the ignition and engine stop switches to the primary windings of the ignition coil, then to ground through the closed breaker point. When the breaker point open, the high voltage current is produced in the secondary coil and led to the spark plug through the high tension cord to make a hot spark between the spark plug gap.

Battery:
The 12V 14AH battery is equipped on the center part of the frame under the seat. The battery is constructed of alternating positive and negative plates with separators between them to prevent a short circuit. The positive plates has fiberglass footed on both sides to prevent them from peeling off. The battery consists of lead peroxide positive plates and spongy lead negative plates and diluted sulfuric acid electrolyte. Six cells are connected in series in the 12 volt battery.

TROUBLE SHOOTING

Symptom & Trouble Cause	Remedy
Starter	
1. Starter does not operate	
a. Poor battery	Charge or replace
b. Poor contact of starter relay terminal	Repair terminal
c. Poor contact of starter switch points	Repair switch
d. Poor connection of battery terminals	Clean and tighten
e. Poor contact of starter brushes	Dress commutator and brushes (Refer to Fig. 10–7)
f. Burned commutator	Lathe cut commutator
g. Shorted starter field coil or armature	Replace
h. Poor tension of brush spring	Replace
i. Worn bushing	Replace
j. Defective starter relay	Replace
2. Starter turns, but crankshaft does not turn	
a. Starter clutch slips	Inspect and replace if inner parts are excessively worn out
b. Defective reduction gears	Replace
Alternator & Regulator & Battery	
1. Battery discharges	
a. Shorted or disconnected alternator stator coil	Repair or replace stator (Refer to page 86)
b. Disconnected alternator rotor coil	Replace rotor
c. Poor contact of brushes and spring/s	Clean or replace (Refer to page 87)
d. Defective rectifier/s	Replace rectifier/s
e. Maladjustment of regulator	Adjust regulator (Refer to page 88)
f. Burned or poor contact of regulator point/s	Dress points or replace regulator
g. Lack or insufficient electrolyte of battery	Replenish electrolyte or replace battery
h. Shorted battery plates	Replace battery
i. Poor connection of battery terminal/s	Clean and tighten
j. Open wiring between ignition switch and regulator "IG" terminal	Repair
k. Open wiring between regulator "F" terminal and alternator "F" terminal	Repair

Symptom & Trouble Cause	Remedy

2. Battery overcharge
   - a. Poor connection of regulator coupler — Repair or replace coupler
   - b. Poor connection of regulator "E" terminal — Clean and tighten
   - c. Burned of melted regulator points — Replace regulator
   - d. Maladjustment of regulator — Adjust regulator (Refer to page 88)

Ignition System

1. Starter turns, but engine will not start
   - a. Excessive moisture on high tension cords and plug gap/s — Remove moisture and dry
   - b. Burned or improperly adjusted breaker points — Adjust or repalce point/s (Refer to page 92)
   - c. Defective ignition coil — Replace
   - d. Defective condenser — Replace
   - e. Open wiring in primary circuit — Repair wiring
   - f. Wet or dirty spark plugs — Replace

2. Hard starting
   - a. Weak battery — Charge or replace battery
   - b. Defective spark plug/s — Replace plug/s
   - c. Defective breaker points — Replace points
   - d. Loose connection in primary circuit — Tighten or repair
   - e. Defective condenser/s — Replace condenser/s
   - f. Defective ignition coil/s — Replace coil/s
   - g. Maladjustment of ignition timing — Adjust timing (Refer to page 94)

2. Engine misses
   - a. Dirty or defective spark plug/s — Clean or replace spark plug/s
   - b. Loose high tension cord/s or defective spark plug cap/s — Tighten, repair or replace cord/s, cop/s
   - c. Improper breaker point/s adjustment — Adjust point/s (Refer to page 92)

STARTING SYSTEM

Description

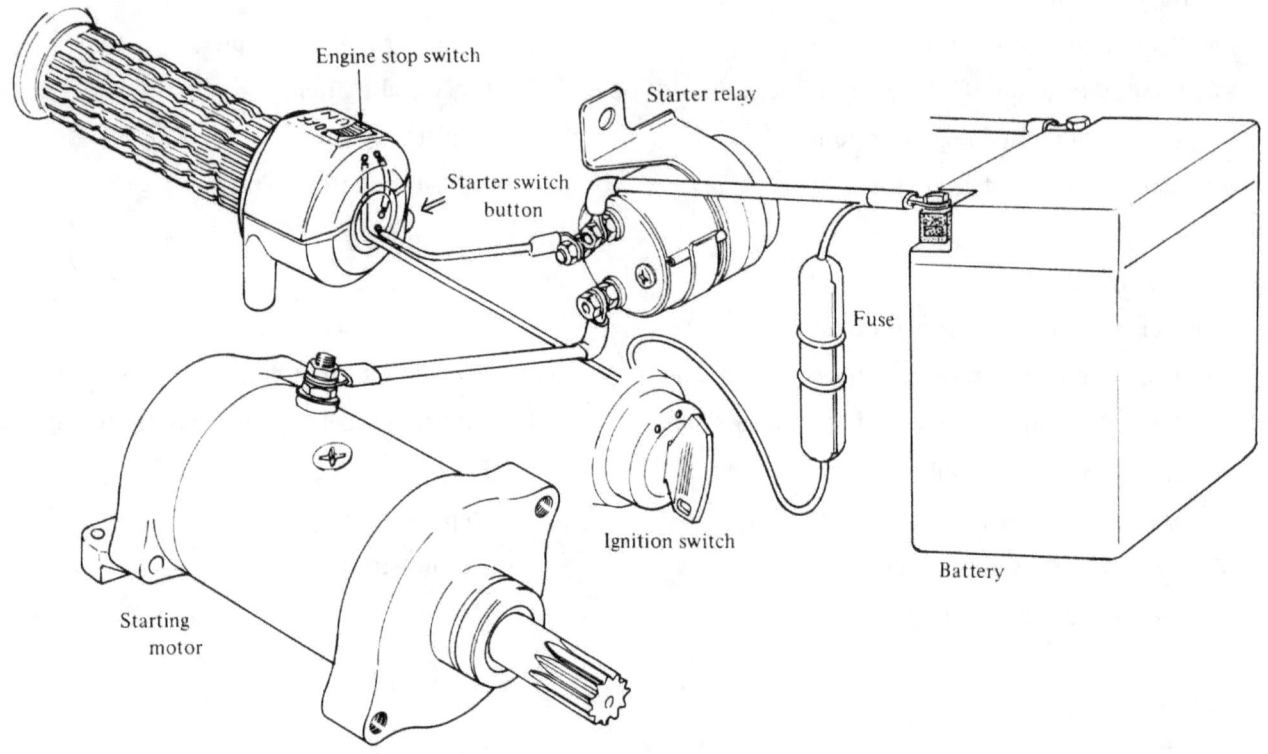

Fig. 10-2 Equipments for starting system

The starting system consists of battery, starter relay, starting motor and two switches as shown in above figure.

The starter relay having magnetic switch inside is provided to flow a large current directly from the battery to the starting motor at starting, since the starter button has no capacity enough to transmit such a large current as to activate the starting motor.

When the starter button is pushed with both the ignition and the engine stop switches on, the solenoid coil of the magnetic switch creates electro magnet with small current from battery and pulls the moving core to close the contacts which closes the circuit between the battery and the starting motor.

The engine stop switch is operated to stop the engine running suddenly in an emergency of the motorcycle being overturned or encountered with some big troubles. Therefore it does not set the starting motor in motion when it is applied even if the starter button is pushed.

The starting motor equipped on the upper crankcase is of cumulative compound type and drive the crankshaft through the starter clutch and its idle gear.

∗ The principal and operation of cumulative compound motor ∗

The cumulative compound motor has the wiring circuit comprising the shunt coil and series coil. In consequence of this wiring, it combines a virtue of series motor which induce a big torque at starting engine with a shunt character of shunt motor to keep the speed constant at any time under normal condition.
The characteristic curve of the cumulative compound motor is shown in Fig. 10-3.

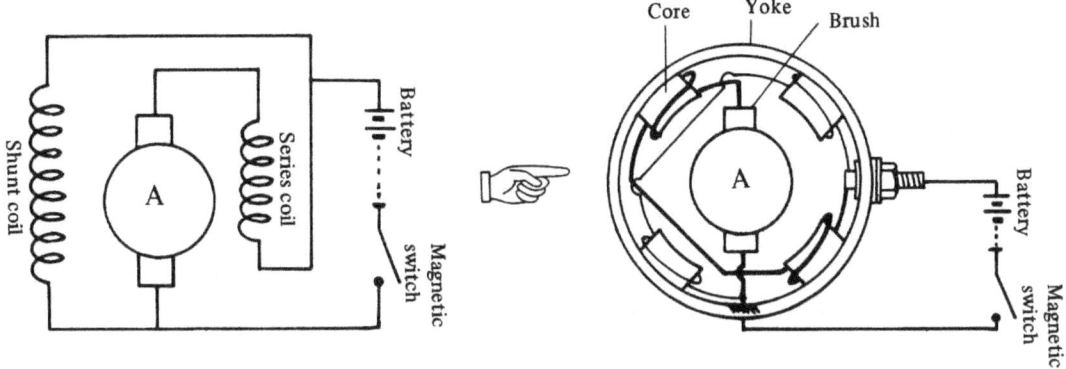

Fig. 10-3 Wiring of cumulative compound motor

The starter clutch equipped on this engine is of over-running type which transmit the starting motor output to the crankshaft and keep the crankshaft free from the starting motor once engine starts.

When the starter clutch gear is driven through idle gear in a direction of arrow as shown in figure, three rollers within the slots are moved to lock the clutch housing and ensuring the starter clutch to rotate.

Since the clutch housing is mounted on the left crankshaft with key, the crankshaft will rotate and ensure the engine to start. Once the engine starts and rotating speed exceeds that of the starter clutch gear, the rollers are moved toward wider section of the slots due to centrifugal force and the engine output is no longer transmitted to the starting motor.

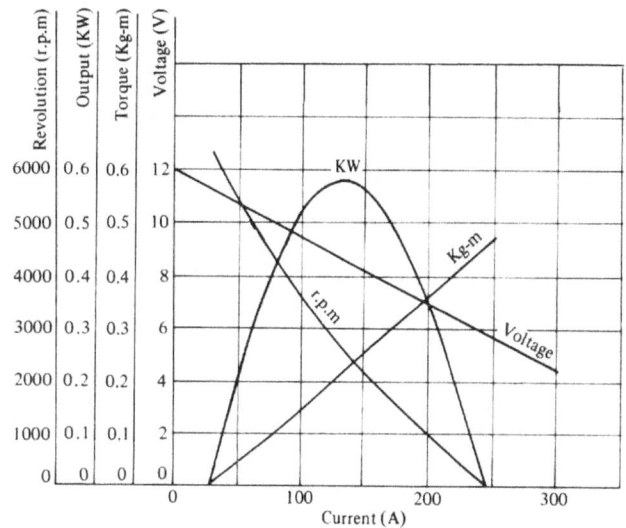

Fig. 10-4 Performance curves of cumulative compound motor

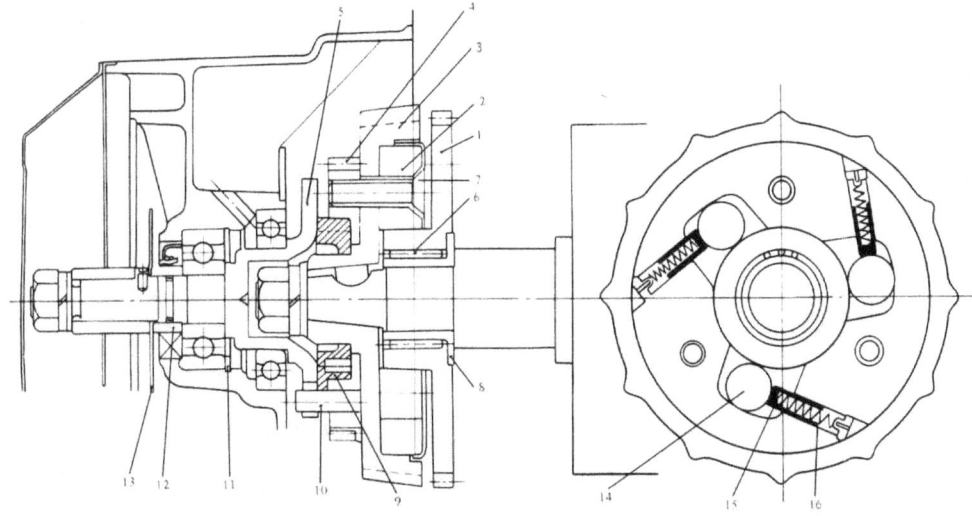

1. Starter clutch gear
2. Starter clutch hub
3. Starter clutch housing
4. Water pump drive gear
5. Breaker cam shaft
6. Needle bearing
7. Screw
8. Crankshaft left bushing
9. Breaker cam shaft dumper rubber
10. Breaker cam shaft drive pin
11. Circlip
12. Spacer
13. Ignition timing plate
14. Starter clutch roller
15. Roller push piece
16. Spring

Fig. 10-5 Starter clutch construction

Specification

Starting motor
- Voltage — 12 Volt
- Output — 0.5 KW
- Actuating time — 30 seconds
- Direction of rotation — Counterclockwise as seen from pinion side
- Number of pinion teeth — 10 teeth
- No-load characteristic:
  - Voltage — At 11 volts
  - Amperage — Less than 50 amperage
  - Revolution — More than 4,500 rpm
- Load characteristic:
  - Voltage — At 8.5 volts
  - Amperage — Less than 150 amperage
  - Torque — More than 0.2 kg-m (1.45 lb-ft)
  - Revolution — More than 1,800 rpm
- Lock characteristic:
  - Voltage — At 5.5 volts
  - Amperage — Less than 280 amperage
  - Torque — More than 0.35 kg-m (2.52 lb-ft)
- Weight — 2.4 kg (5.32 lb)
- Battery — 14 AH
- Reduction ratios:
  - Primary — 4.78 : 1 (starter motor to idle gear 9 : 43)
  - Secondary — 2.50 : 1 (idle gear to crankshaft 22 : 55)
  - Total — 11.95 : 1

Starter Relay
- Rated voltage — 12 volts
- Actuating voltage — More than 8 volts

Removal

1. Drain the cooling system.

2. Remove the fuel tank, then remove three carburetors.

3. Disconnect the starter wire from the starter relay.

4. Remove the starter clutch cover without removing the contact breaker assembly and its related parts which are mounted on it.

5. Loosen the water by-pass hose clamp and then remove the by-pass hose from the thermostat case.

6. Take off the water by-pass hose union ① from the upper crankcase after removing the starting motor cover.

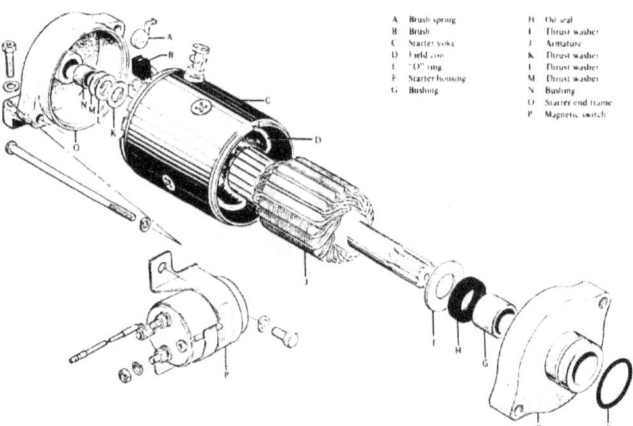

Fig. 10-7 Exploded view of starting motor

Fig. 10-6 Removing starting motor

7. Remove the starting motor fitting bolts, and then dismount the starting motor by sliding it toward the clutch side as shown in above figure.

Disassembly

1. Remove the through bolts, commutator end frame, brushes and washers.

2. Extract the bushes using press machine, if needed.

Inspection & Repair

Armature

1. Inspect the clearance between the armature shaft and the bushings. Replace the bushings if the clearance exceed 0.2 mm (0.008 in).

2. Check the commutator for rough, burned or scored surface, and dress or cut with a lathe to finish proper surface.

3. Check the commutator for out of roundness, it should be less than 0.3 mm (0.012 in).

∗ Necessity of measuring the commutator for out of roundness ∗

Since the commutator rotates at high speed always in contact with brushes, it will be worn out both mechanically by the friction and electrically by the spark, and also its segments are apt to rise against the commutator mica, decreasing the commutation and bringing about the abnormal wear.
Therefore, it is quite necessary to inspect and measure the commutator for the wear or eccentricity periodically. Cut it on a lathe if necessary so as not to exceed 26.5 mm (1.045") in diameter and chamfer the edge of each segment.

4. Check the mica depth, and file off the mica if the depth is less than 0.2 mm (0.008").
   Standard depth ... 0.5~0.8 mm (0.02~0.03")

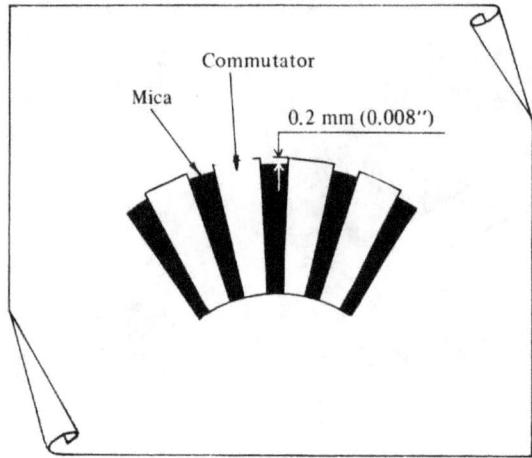

Fig. 10-8　Commutator

5. Check the commutator for ground. Connect one tester prod to commutator, and the other to armature core shaft.

   If the ohmmeter pointer moves or the test lamp on a Growler tester lights, the commutator is grounded.

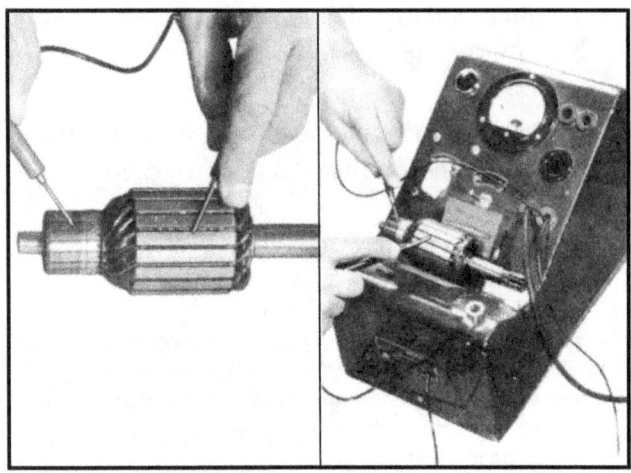

Fig. 10-9　Checking commutator for ground

6. Check the armature for short circuit by placing the armature on a Growler tester and hold a hacksaw blade over the armature core while the armature is rotated. If the hacksaw blade is drawn and vibrates, the armature coil is shorted.

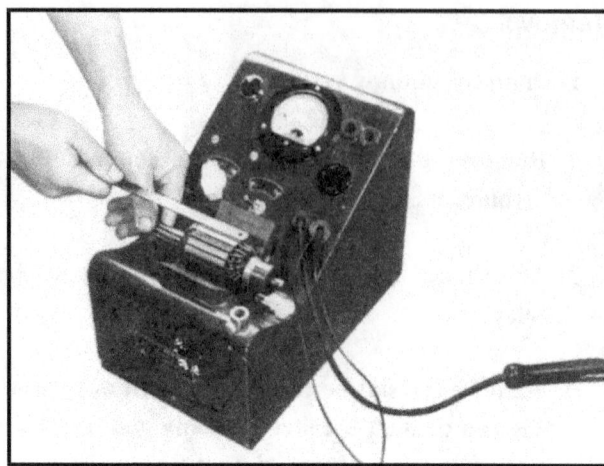

Fig. 10-10　Checking armature for short circuit

7. Check the armature coil for open circuit. Place the armature on a Growler tester and check the reading on the meter with the tester prods connected to each two segments. If the reading is not uniformity, the armature has a open circuit.

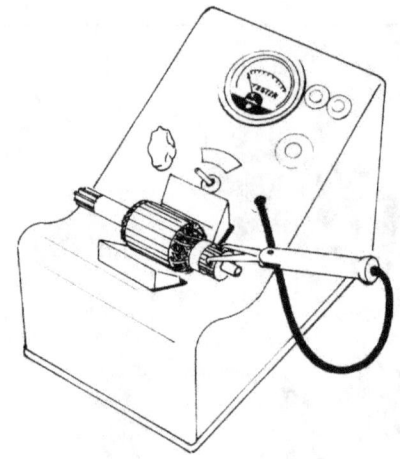

Fig. 10-11　Checking armature for open circuit

Field Coil

1. Check the field coil for open circuit by connecting the test prods to each terminal alternately. If the tester pointer does not move, the field coil has open circuit and should be replaced.

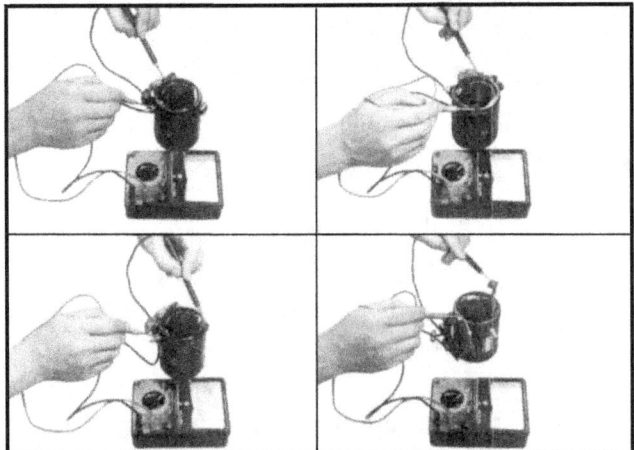

Fig. 10-12 Checking field coil for open circuit

It is also possible to check the field coil for open circuit by exciting the field coils. If the screw driver is not drawn to anywhere when it is inserted into the field yoke, the field coil has a open circuit.

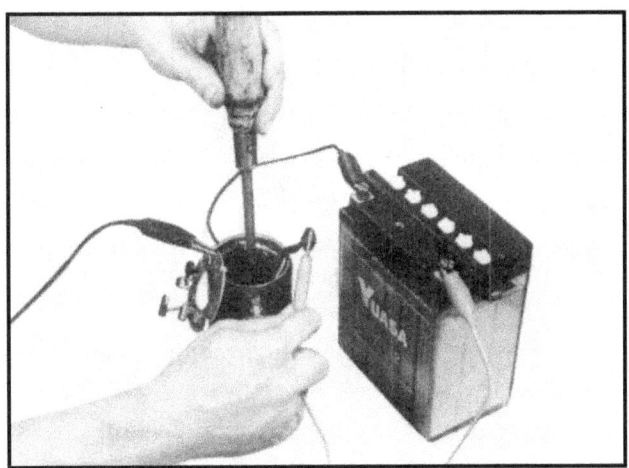

Fig. 10-13 Checking field coil by exiting it

Caution : Be carefull of the following points when testing the fiels coil open circuit by exciting it.
Two kinds of field coils provided on this motor have each different resistance as follows.
  Series coil . . . . 0.02 ohms (Ω)
  Shunt coil . . . . 2.55 ohms (Ω)
When connecting the battery to the field coil as illustrated in Fig. 10-14, a current flow through only shunt coil and the screw driver is drawn toward "A" and "C" cores.

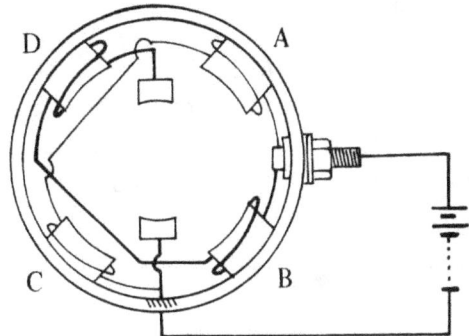

Fig. 10-14 Battery connection for field coil test

On the other hand, when connecting the battery as shown in Fig. 10-15, a current flow through each coil in the order of "D", "B", "A" and "C" in series. In this case, the current is mainly regulated by shunt coil resistance, so that the electromagnetic force is induced on "A" and "C" much more than "B" and "D" coils and accordingly the screw driver will be drawn toward shunt coils.

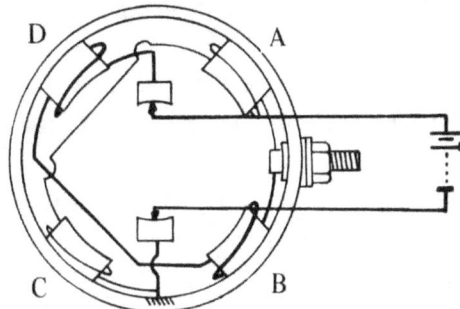

Fig. 10-15 Battery connection for field coil test

2. Check the field coil for ground by connecting one tester prod to the field coil junction on the yoke and the other to the core or yoke. If the ohmmeter pointer moves, the field coil has been grounded and should be replaced.

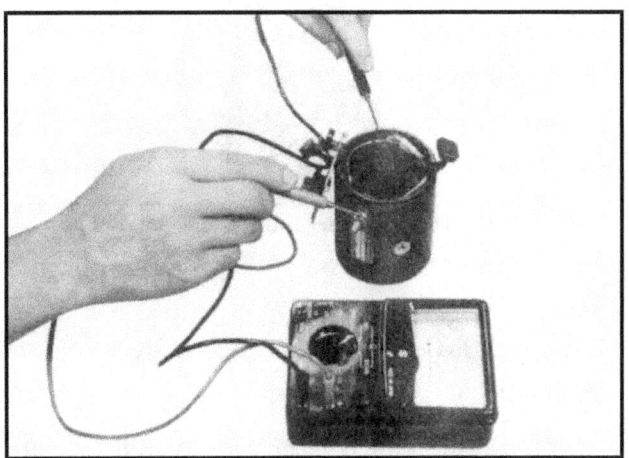

Fig. 10-16 Checking field coil for ground

Brush & Brush Holder

1. Check the brush holder insulation by connecting one tester prod to the brush holder and the other to the base. If the ohmmeter pointer moves, the brush holder should be repaired or replaced.

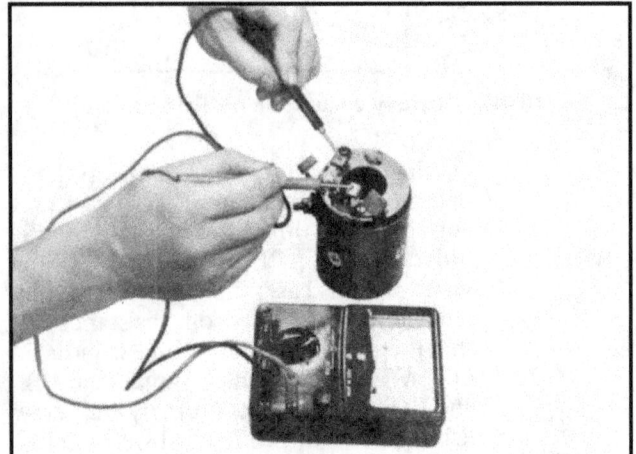

Fig. 10-17   Checking brush holder insulation

2. Check the carbon brush length. If it is less than 10 mm (0.394"), replace the brush.

3. Check the brush spring tension with a spring balance. If it is less than 600 g (0.84 lb), replace the spring.
   Standard spring tension: 1~1.4 kg (2.2~3.1 lb)

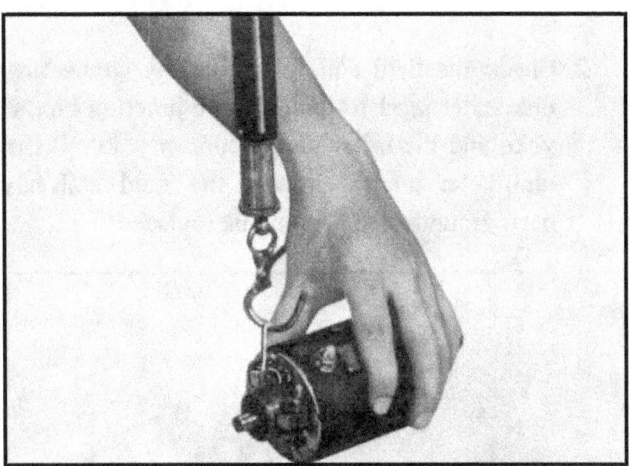

Fig. 10-18   Checking brush spring tension

Starter Clutch

1. Check to see if the clutch rollers operate properly.

2. Check the clutch inner race press-fitted into the clutch gear for wear or deformation. If any deformation is found on the surface of inner race, replace it to avoid the slippage.

Starter Relay

1. Check if the moving core operates properly. When pushing the starter button, if a click is heard from the inside of starter relay, it is judged correct.
   In case the relay has been dismounted from the frame, confirm the click with the battery connected between "S" terminal and mounting plate as illustrated in the figure.

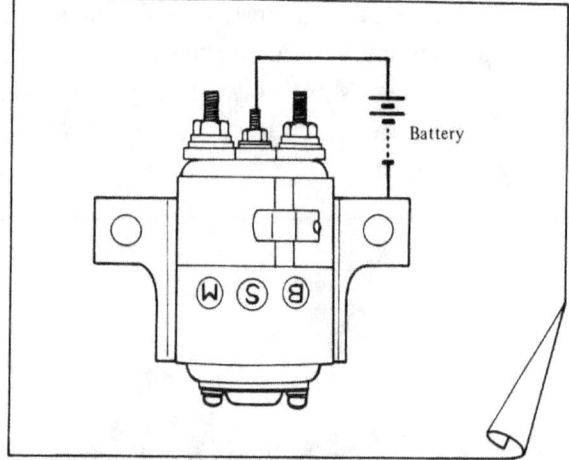

Fig. 10-19   Checking starter relay

2. Check to see if the switch contacts are burnt by opening the cover ①.
   If the contact surfaces have been burnt, dress with a file or emery sand paper.

Assembly

Starting Motor

1. Before assembling the starting motor, apply the multipurpose grease on the armature shaft bushings.

2. Install the carbon brushes into brush holders after the armature is settled in the yoke.

3. Install the armature thrust washers, end frame and housing, then tighten them with the through bolts. Check if the armature shaft turns smoothly with hand.

Starter Clutch

1. When assembling the water pump drive gear onto the clutch housing, apply the thread lock cement on thread of each fitting bolt and then tighten firmly so that the punch mark ① on the housing aligns with the pin ② on the water pump drive gear.

Fig. 10-20 Punch mark and pin

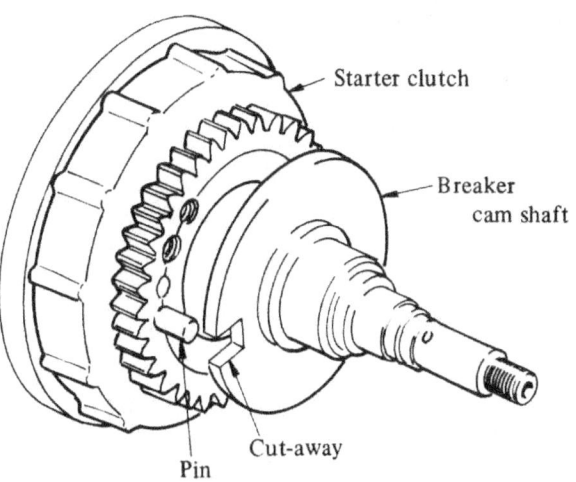

Fig. 10-22 Assembling breaker cam shaft

2. Mount the starter clutch assembly onto the crankshaft and tighten the set nut by 450~550 kg-cm (33~40 lb-ft) with the starter clutch holder (09920-40111).

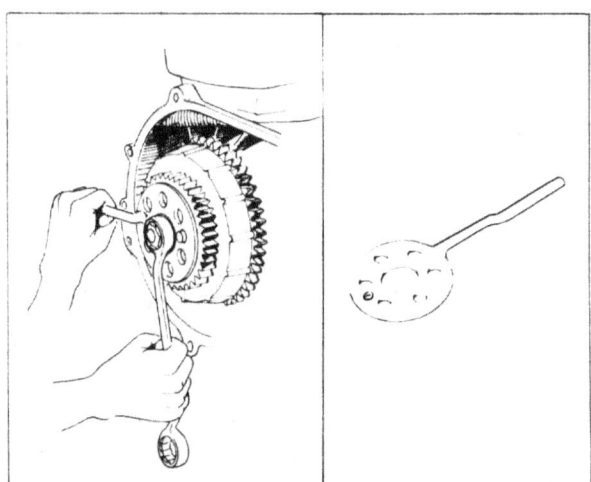

Fig. 10-21 Assembling starter clutch

3. When assembling the starter clutch cover onto the crankcase, turn the breaker cam shaft by hand so as to match the cut-away of breaker cam shaft with the pin on the water pump drive gear.

CHARGING SYSTEM

Description

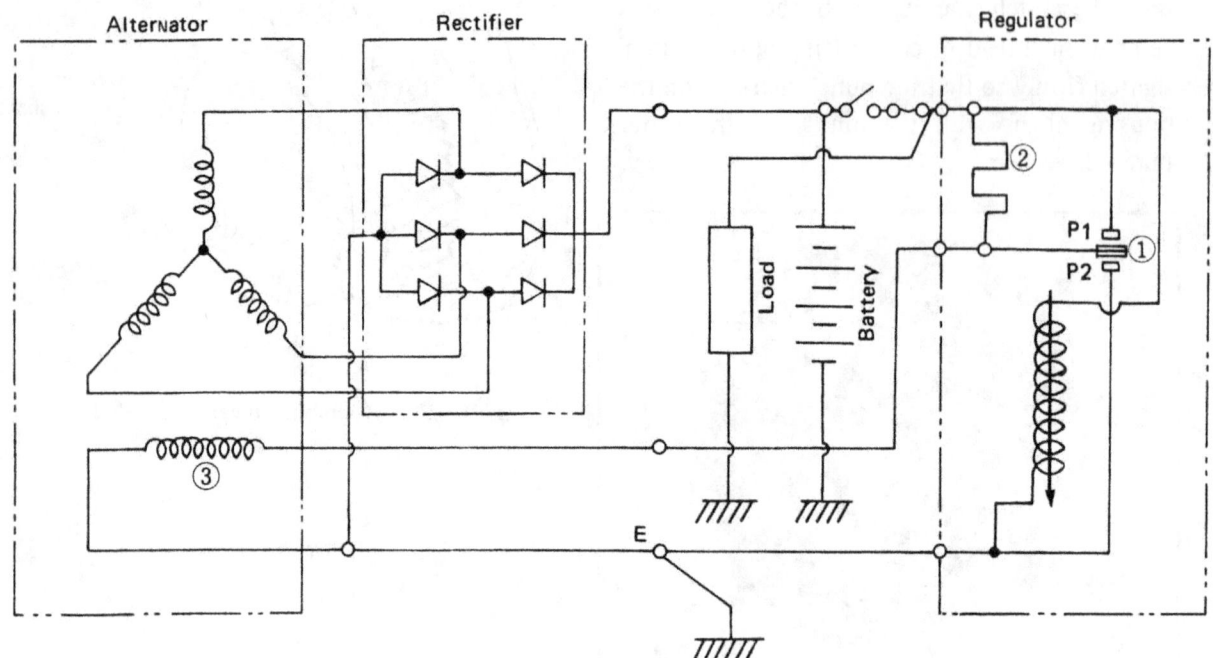

Fig. 10-23 Charging system wiring

The alternator induces a three phase alternating current within the stator coil in proportion to the engine speed, provided that the excitation current supplied from the battery to the rotor coil is constant.

In order to charge the battery, the output current from the alternator should be rectified to a direct current and regulated to a constant voltage (13.5~14.5 volts) in any engine speed.

The silicon rectifier and the voltage regulator are equipped on this system to meet the above demands. The rectifier which consists of six silicon diodes converts a alternating current from the alternator into a direct current.

The voltage regulator which comprises a control resister, contact points and pull-in coil controls the excitation current in the rotor coil.

Operation

When the engine switch is turned on, the current flows through the contact points ① and the control resistance ② in parallel and the rotor coil ③, and the rotor coil is exited. Under this condition, when the engine is started and the rotor is rotated, the three phase alternating current is generated within the stator coil and then rectified to the direct current by the rectifier.

As the charging in the battery is developed, the voltage at the battery terminal naturally becomes higher and also the voltage to the point "IG" increases. Therefore the pull-in force is increased and it pulls the point lever downward so as to open the points from the low speed side (P1). As the point opens, the current flows through the control resistance ② and the excitation current is decreased, resulting in decreasing also alternator output.

Under light load at high revolution, point contacts the high speed side (P2), and the current to the rotor coil is further decreased to control output voltage.

Thus the charging voltage is controled by regulating the excitation current with the control resistance and pull-in coil. On the other hand, stator coil has a self-limiting characteristic in limiting the current flow to the coil to press the value when the revolution increases.

Specification

Alternator:

Voltage	12 volts
Max. output current	20 amperes
Max. output power	280 Watts
No-load revolution	14V, 0 Amp. @ 1050±150 rpm
Output revolution	14V, 20 Amp. @ 3000 rpm
Weight	3.4 kg (7.5 lb)

Voltage regulator:

Regulated voltage	13.5~14.5 volts
Weight	0.22 kg (0.485 lb)

Alternator

Removal

1. Remove the generator cover.

2. Loosen the brush holder fitting screws while firmly pressing the brush holder and then remove, otherwise the brush would spring up and the wire comes off.

Fig. 10-24 Loosening brush holder fitting screw

3. Remove the alternator stator.

4. Pull out the rotor with the Rotor Remover (09930-33110).

Inspection & Repair

1. Check the rotor coil for open or short circuit by placing the tester prods on each slip ring, and then read the resistance. If the reading is less than the standard (around 10 ohms), the rotor coil has a short circuit or grounded.
If the reading is much higher than the standard, the coil has a open circuit. Replace the rotor with new one if differences in the reading are found.

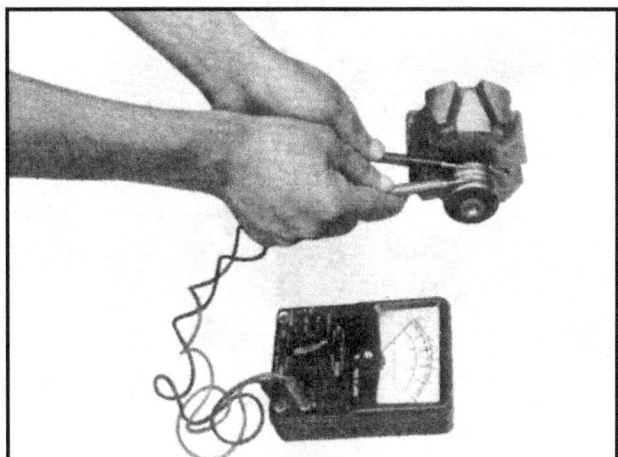

Fig. 10-25 Checking rotor coil for open and short circuit

2. Check the rotor coil for insulation by connecting one tester prod to either slip ring and the other to the rotor core finger. If the ohmmeter pointer moves, the rotor or slip ring is defective and the rotor assembly should be replaced.

3. Check the stator coil for insulation by connecting one tester prod to either stator coil terminal and the other to the stator core. If the ohmmeter pointer moves, the stator assembly should be replaced.

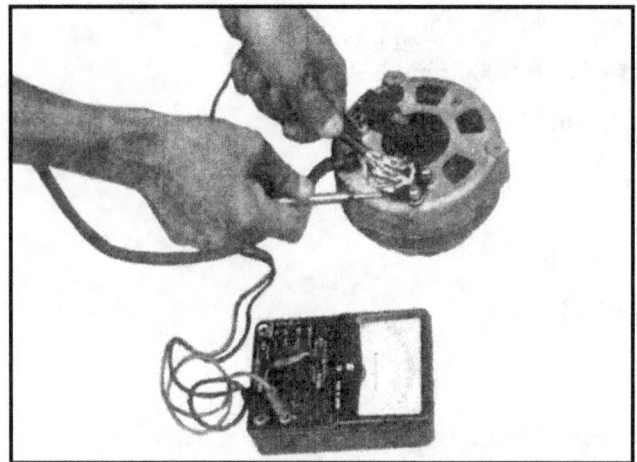

Fig. 10-26 Checking stator coil insulation

4. Check the stator coil for open circuit by placing the tester prods to each stator coil terminal alternately. If the ohmmeter pointer does not move, the stator coil has a open circuit and should be replaced.

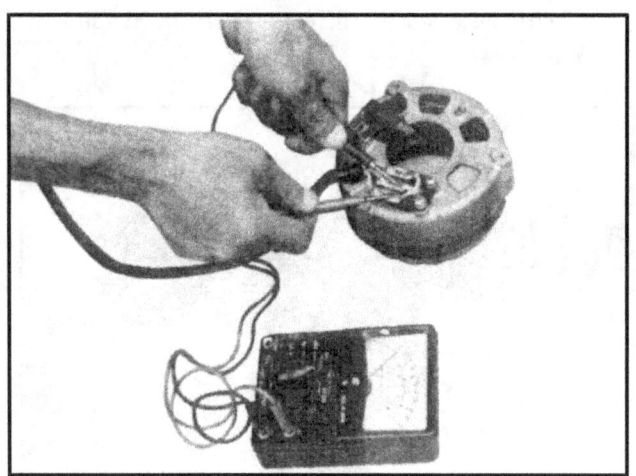

Fig. 10-27 Checking stator coil for open circuit

5. Check the carbon brush for cracks or wear. If it is worn out beyond 5.5 mm (0.217"), replace the brushes. The overall length of brand-new brush is 12.5 mm (4.93").

Note: When replacing the brushes, replace with the brush holder assembly which includes the brush, spring and holder.

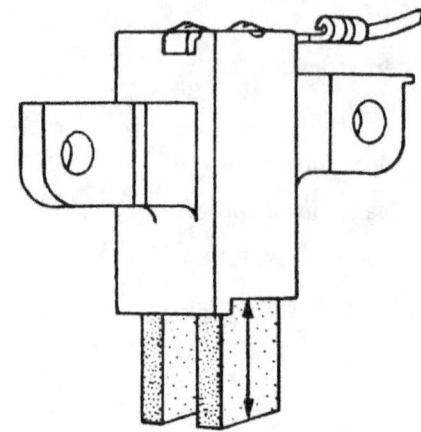

Fig. 10-28 Carbon brush length

6. Check the silicon rectifier for open. Measure the resistance between each terminal. If the silicon rectifier is in good condition, less resistance is measured in the normal direction (for example, Yellow→Red) and no current flows in the inverse direction.

Caution: The standard ohmmeter has an inverse polarity, so that a current flows from (−) lead to (+) lead.

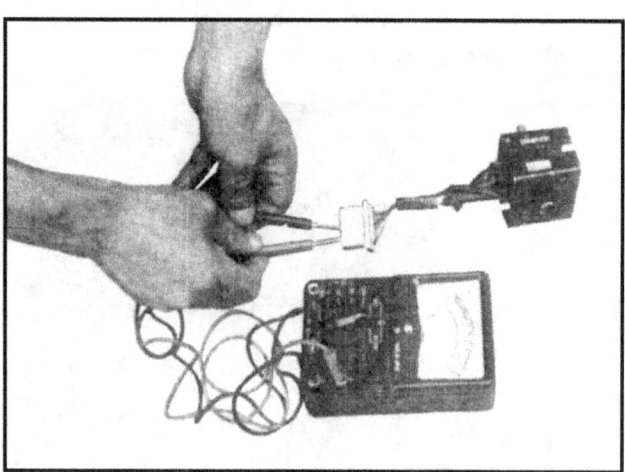

Fig. 10-29 Checking silicon rectifier for open

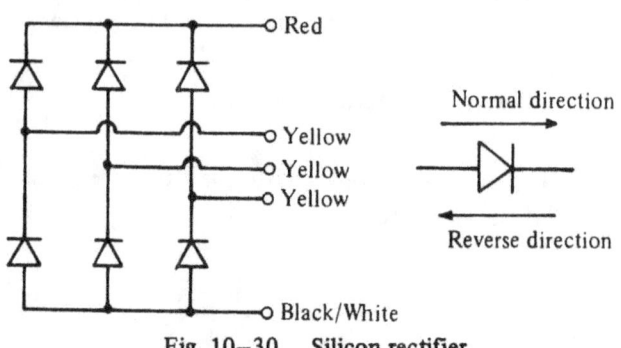

Fig. 10-30 Silicon rectifier

7. Measure the resistance between "IG" (orange lead) and "F" (green lead) terminals. The resistance should be none. If the resistance is there, the voltage regulator low speed point is defective. Open the cover and press the regualtor lever ① to open the points, then measure the resistance again. The specified resistance is 10 ohms.

If the resistance is excessively higher than the specified value, the control resistor is defective.

Caution: The voltage regulator cover is sealed to keep the inside mechanism free from dust and moisture, and further-more the unnecessary adjustment at normal service.
In case it is adjusted from lack of replacement in market, open the cover and inspect it as follows, keeping in mind once it is serviced it will not be guaranteed.

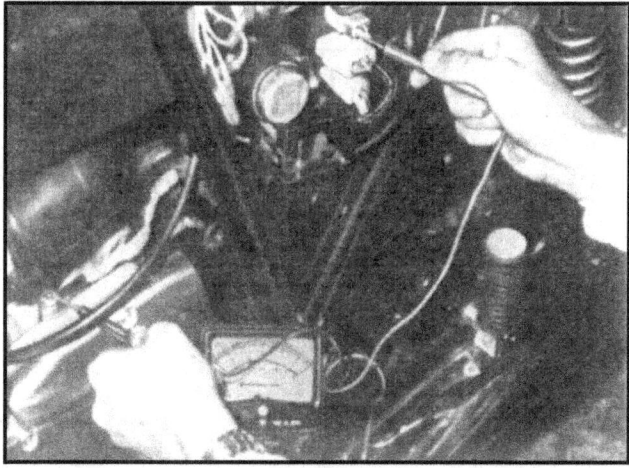

Fig. 10-32   Measuring alternator output

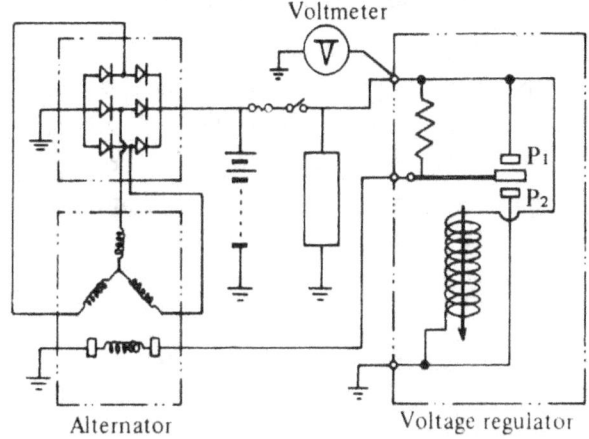

Fig. 10-33   Voltmeter connection

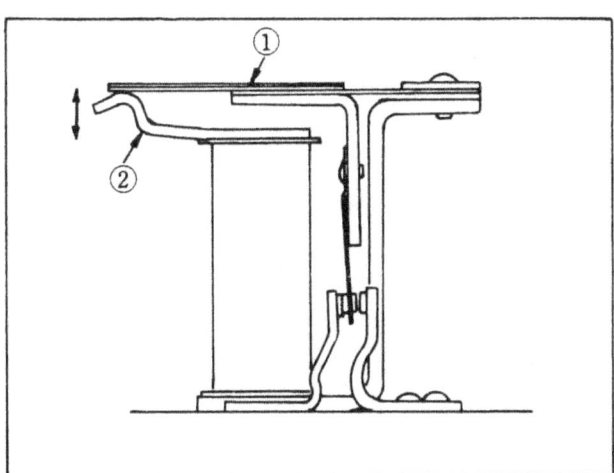

Fig. 10-31   Adjusting regulator

8. Measure the regulated voltage. Insert one tester prod into a cell of the coupler where the orange lead is connected and the other to the engine for grounding. Set the engine to run at 2,000~3,000 rpm and check the voltmeter reading. The specified regulated voltage is 13.5~14.5 volts.

If the reading is excessively different from the above specified voltage, adjust the regulator by so bending the lever ② as to have a meter reading of 13.5~14.5 volts.

9. Check the alternator no-load performance according to the following procedures.

a. Disconnect the starter switch relay lead which is colored red from the connector, and also the fuse lead at the connector side where the white tape is wound. Then connect the fuse lead with the relay lead connector, and the voltmeter between the red lead which was connected to the starter switch relay lead originally and the crankcase.

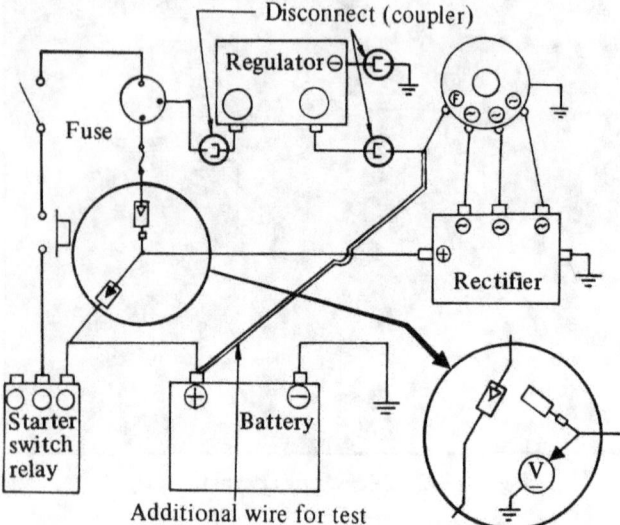

Fig. 10-34 Wiring for measuring output

b. Disconnect the regulator coupler, and then connect the green lead in the coupler and the battery positive terminal with a suitable lead. This is done to supply a constant current from the battery to the rotor coil directly without being regualted by the voltage regulator.

c. Start the engine and set it to run at 1,500 rpm and 2,500 rpm. Check the voltmeter reading.
The specified voltage:
    1,500 rpm   More than 16 volts
    2,500 rpm   More than 27 volts

In case that the no-load voltage is in good condition but the battery is discharged, check the voltage regulator or battery.
If the voltage reading is less than the specified value, the connection of coupler, silicon rectifier or alternator is defective. Repair or replace them.

IGNITION SYSTEM

Description

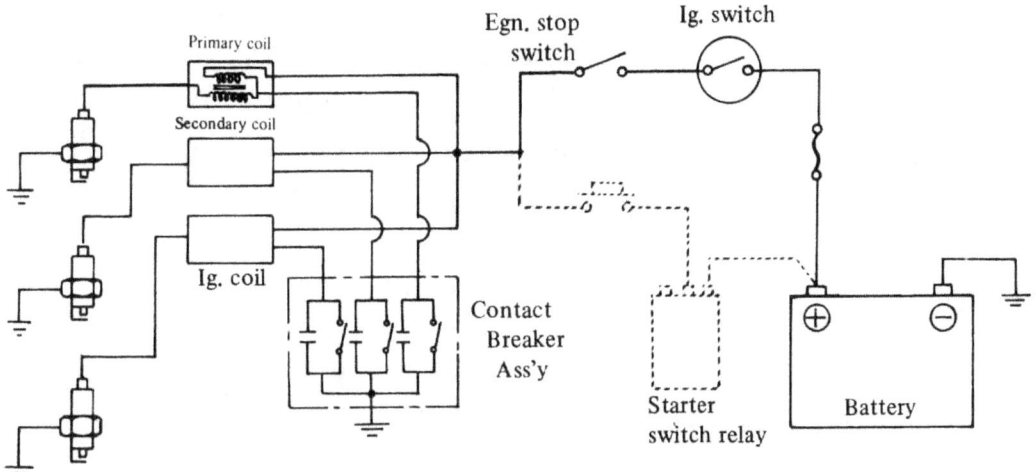

Fig. 10-35 GT750 ignition system wiring diagram

The ignition system consists of the contact breaker assembly, three ignition coils, three spark plugs, an ignition switch and a battery. The contact breaker assembly is located on the engine left side and made up of each three contact points and condensers on the stator base, which are marked with "L", "C" and "R" corresponding to the cylinder location, and the breaker cam shaft on which the cam and timing plate are installed. The breaker cam shaft is not coupled to the crankshaft directly, but through the pin on the water pump drive gear to prevent the vibration.

The ignition coils which are combined with the holder are installed under the fuel tank to obtain the excellent cooling and increased insulation.

Operation

When the ignition switch is turned on and the crankshaft is rotated, a current from the battery flows through the primary coil windings of each ignition coil and contact points if they are closed.

At the time when the point is just opened, a counter electromotive force which is much higher voltage than before is induced within the primary coil by the self induction, and moreover it is stepped up to a high tension current within the secondary coil by the mutual induction so enough as to ignite the spark plug.

A condenser connected in parallel with the contact point is equipped to absorb the electric energy and keep it from sparking between the contact breaker points.

Specification

- Spark plug
  - Standard: NGK B-7ES or DENSO W22ES
  - Optional: NGK B-6ES, B-8ES or DENSO W20ES, W24ES
  - Point gap:
    - NGK: 0.7~0.8 mm (0.028~0.032")
    - DENSO: 0.6~0.7 mm (0.024~0.028")
- Contact point gap: 0.3~0.4 mm (0.012~0.016")
- Condenser capacity: 0.16~0.20 μF
- Ignition timing: 24° ± 2 B.T.D.C.

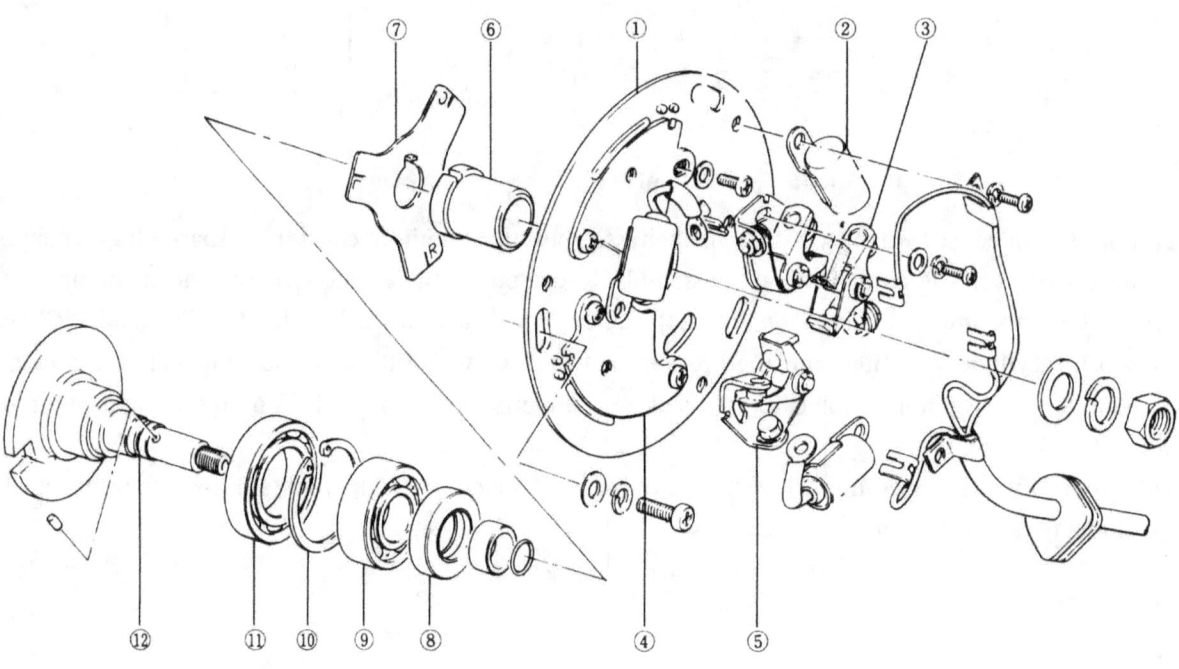

① Contact point base
② Condenser
③ Contact point assembly
④ Contact point set plate
⑤ Contact point shifting plate
⑥ Point breaker cam
⑦ Timing plate
⑧ Oil seal
⑨ Cam shaft inner bearing
⑩ Clamp
⑪ Cam shaft outer bearing
⑫ Cam shaft

Fig. 10-36 Exploded view of contact breaker assembly

Removal

1. Dismount the fuel tank from the frame, and remove the ignition coil assembly.

2. Remove the contact breaker cap, and the contact point base with the points and condensers on it after scribing a mark both on the base and the case near the fitting bolt in order to indicate the position of the base in the case of reassembling.

3. Disconnect the contact breaker lead coupler from the holder plate.

Disassembly

1. Dismount each contact point and condenser from the base by removing fitting screws.

2. Remove the breaker cam shaft nut and washers, then take off the breaker cam and timing plate from the shaft.

3. Extract the breaker cam shaft from the case.

Caution: When removing the breaker cam shaft inner bearing from the case, use the Snap ring opener (09920-70120).

Inspection & Repair

1. Check the contact breaker point for wear, dirt or oil film.

   a. If the point surface is worn out or pitted, the conductivity is decreased and results in misfiring. Dress the surface with either a point file or emery sand paper. If the excessive wear is found, remove the contact points of both the moving and stationary sides and dress them with an oil stone, or replace with new one.

   b. If the dirt or oil is left on the point surfaces, it will bring about the burnt surface. Clean with a waste cloth soaked in trichloretehylne.

   c. Check to see if the points are in perfect contact. Dress or replace the points if necessary.

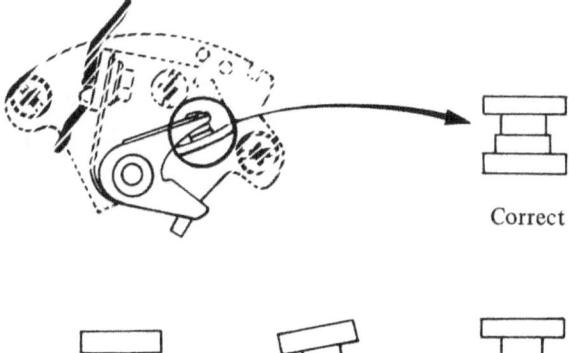

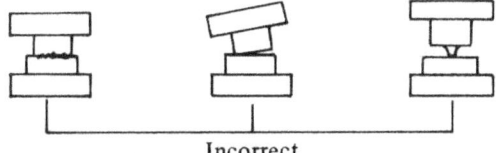

Fig. 10-37 Contact point

   d. Check to see if the point gap is between 0.3~0.4 mm (0.012~0.016") using the filler gauge, when the point gap is at maximum opening.

2. Check the ignition coils for defects using an electro tester.

   a. Connect the ignition coil to be tested with the tester as illustrated in the figure.

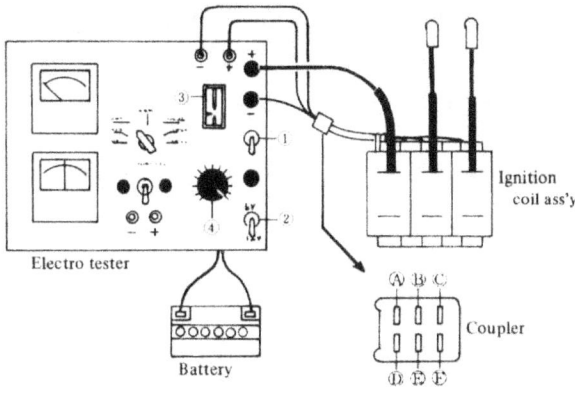

A: Black lead ⊖ . . . . . D: Orange lead ⊖ . . . . for L.H. coil
B: Black/Yellow ⊖ . . . E: Orange lead ⊖ . . . . for M. coil
C: White lead ⊖ . . . . . F: Orange lead ⊕ . . . . for R.H. coil

Fig. 10-38 Testing ignition coil

   b. Turn down the change-over switch ② for electric source to 12 V (use a 12 volt battery), and that ① for coil test to "COIL TEST". Then the spark will jumps between the three prong gap ③ if the coil has no defects.

   c. Adjust the tester three prong gap turning the dial ④ to have 6 mm (0.24") of distance. Check the spark for about 5 minutes.
   The coil is satisfactory if the gap is more than 6 mm and the spark is still strong and blue.

   d. When testing the ignition coil without removing from the frame, remove the spark plug cap and connect the positive tester lead to the high tension cord and the negative lead to the spark plug.

   e. Start the engine and check to see if the spark is maintained over 6 mm of distance.

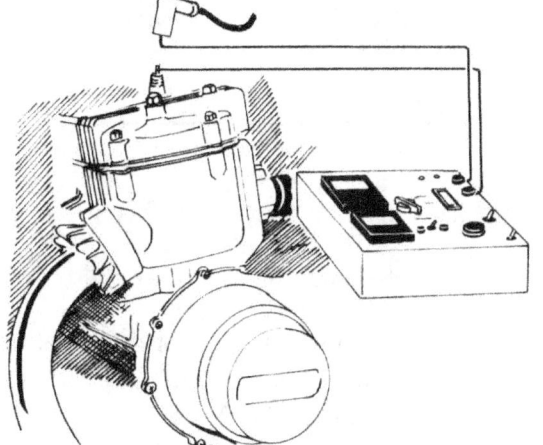

Fig. 10-39 Testing ignition system

3. Check the spark plug cap and high tension cord for crack or deterioration. If it is found to be in improper condition, replace it with new one because the high tension current may leak through the defective parts, resulting in misfiring.

4. Check the spark plug for defects.

   a. Check the plugs for cracks or chips on the porcelain.

   b. Check the electrodes for wear.

   c. Check for excessive carbon deposits. If carbon deposit is excessive, it indicates that the improper heat range spark plug has been used or a too rich fuel-air mixture has been supplied. Replace with a hot type plugs (B-6ES or W20ES) or adjust the carburetors. If the porcelain is excessively white-colored or the electrode is worned out, replace with a cold type plugs (B-8ES or W24ES). When NGK and DENSO plugs are not available, other corresponding plugs may be used in accordance with the conversion chart writen on page

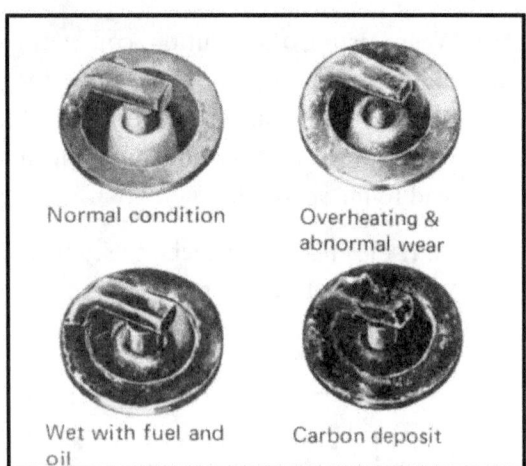

Fig. 10-40 Condition of spark plug

   d. Check the plug gasket for defect.

   e. Check the porcelain for glaze or blister.

   f. Adjust the plug gap to the specified value:
      0.7~0.8 mm (0.028~0.032") for NGK make
      0.6~0.7 mm (0.024~0.028")
      for DENSO make

5. Check the condenser capacity using the electro tester.

   a. Connect a 12 V battery as the electric source for the electro tester.

   b. Position the selector knob ① to "C. Capacity".

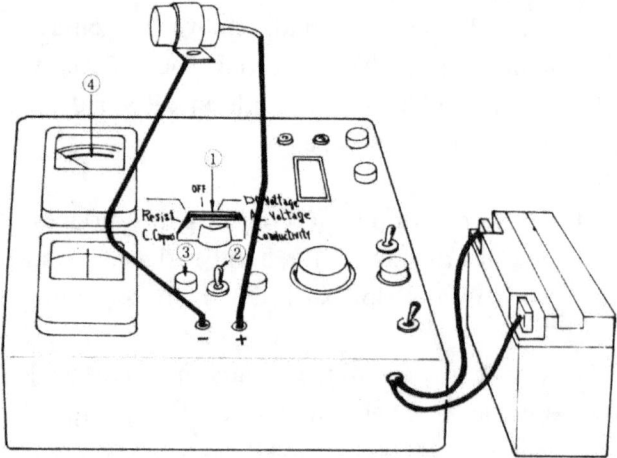

Fig. 10-41 Testing condenser

   c. Turn up the change-over switch ② for calibrating test, and turn the capacity adjusting knob ③ to "CAP. CAL." until the meter pointer ④ comes to show the equivalent value to the capacity (inscribed in the name plate) of the standard condenser built in the electro tester.

   d. Connect the tester leads to the terminal marked "TEST-TERMINAL", and the other ends of the lead to the condenser to be tested as illustrated in the figure.

   e. Turn down the change-over switch ②, then the pointer will show the capacity of the condenser to be tested.
      The specified condenser capacity is 0.16~0.20 μF.

6. Check the condenser insulation resistance using the electro tester.

   a. Position the selector knob to "Insulation" (Megohm).

b. Turn up the change-over switch to "CAL" position, and then turn the zero adjustment knob marked "RES. CAL." untill the meter pointer comes to 0.

c. Connect the tester leads to the terminals marked "TEST-TERMINAL", turn down the change-over switch, and apply the other ends of lead to the condenser to be tested. The pointer will move to the right and then quietly back to the left.
Keeping the connection till the pointer comes to stand still, read the pointer on the scale by Megohm. Bring the condenser wire near the body, so a spark will jump between the wire and the body.
The specified insulation resistance is over 10 Meg-ohm.

Timing Adjustment & Test

When adjusting the ignition timing, both the ignition timing and the breaker point gap should be adjusted. Start the adjustment from the cylinder at left always.

1. Adjust the point gap to 0.35 mm (0.014″) for the points with marking "L" on the base at the position where the point gap is at the maximum opening. Loosen the point set plate fitting screw and move the plate with a screw driver.

Fig. 10-42 Adjusting point gap

2. Remove the spark plug from left cylinder head, and install the timing dial gauge holder into the plug hole and set the gauge stem where the small needle ① of the dial gauge indicates "4" at T.D.C. Turn the outer ring scale ③ so that the large needle indicates "0" on the scale.

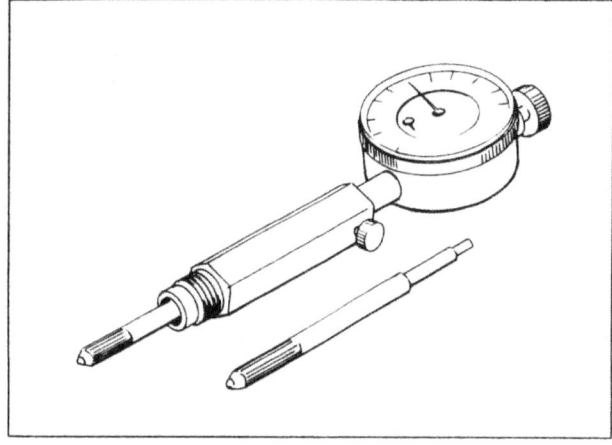

Fig. 10-43 Dial gauge

3. Connect one of the leads of timing tester to the positive terminal where a white and a black leads are connected, and the other to somewhere on the engine to ground it.

Fig. 10-44 Adjusting timing

4. Turn the crankshaft counterclockwise slowly, and tone of the timing tester buzzer changes and the lamp on the tester goes out. These changes tell you the precise position where contact points begin to open that is ignition timing. Read the dial gauge at this moment. The standard ignition timing is 3.64 mm (0.143″) for left cylinder.

Caution: Be carefull that the gauge stroke is not uniform because of the difference in inclination of spark plug hole at each cylinder.

Standard ignition timing : 24° ± 2 (B.T.D.C.)

Crank angle (B.T.D.C.)		22°	23°	24°	25°	26°
Piston distance from B.T.D.C. mm (in)	R & L	3.20 (0.126)	3.35 (0.134)	3.64 (0.143)	3.94 (0.155)	4.25 (0.167)
	C	2.88 (0.113)	3.15 (0.124)	3.42 (0.136)	3.72 (0.146)	3.99 (0.157)

R & L : Right and left cylinder
C : Center cylinder

Fig. 10–45 Ignition timing table

If the reading is different from the standard, turn the contact point base to and fro until the correct timing is obtained.

5. Adjust the points with markings "R" and "C" in a similar manner as "L" after adjusting point gaps to 0.35 mm (0.014") by moving each point set plate ①.

Note: If the dial reading on the center and right cylinders is different from the standard, move the shifting plate ② by loosening two fitting screws.

Fig. 10–47 Ignition timing marks

Fig. 10–46 Adjusting ig. timing for R.H. and L cylinders

6. When adjusting the ignition timing with timing marks ① both on the timing plate and on the casing, rotate the crankshaft counterclockwise to check if the point opens when "L" marking line on the timing plate is in alignments with an aligning mark of the casing in the adjusting window. If it is out of order, turn the contact point base to and fro until the correct timing obtains.

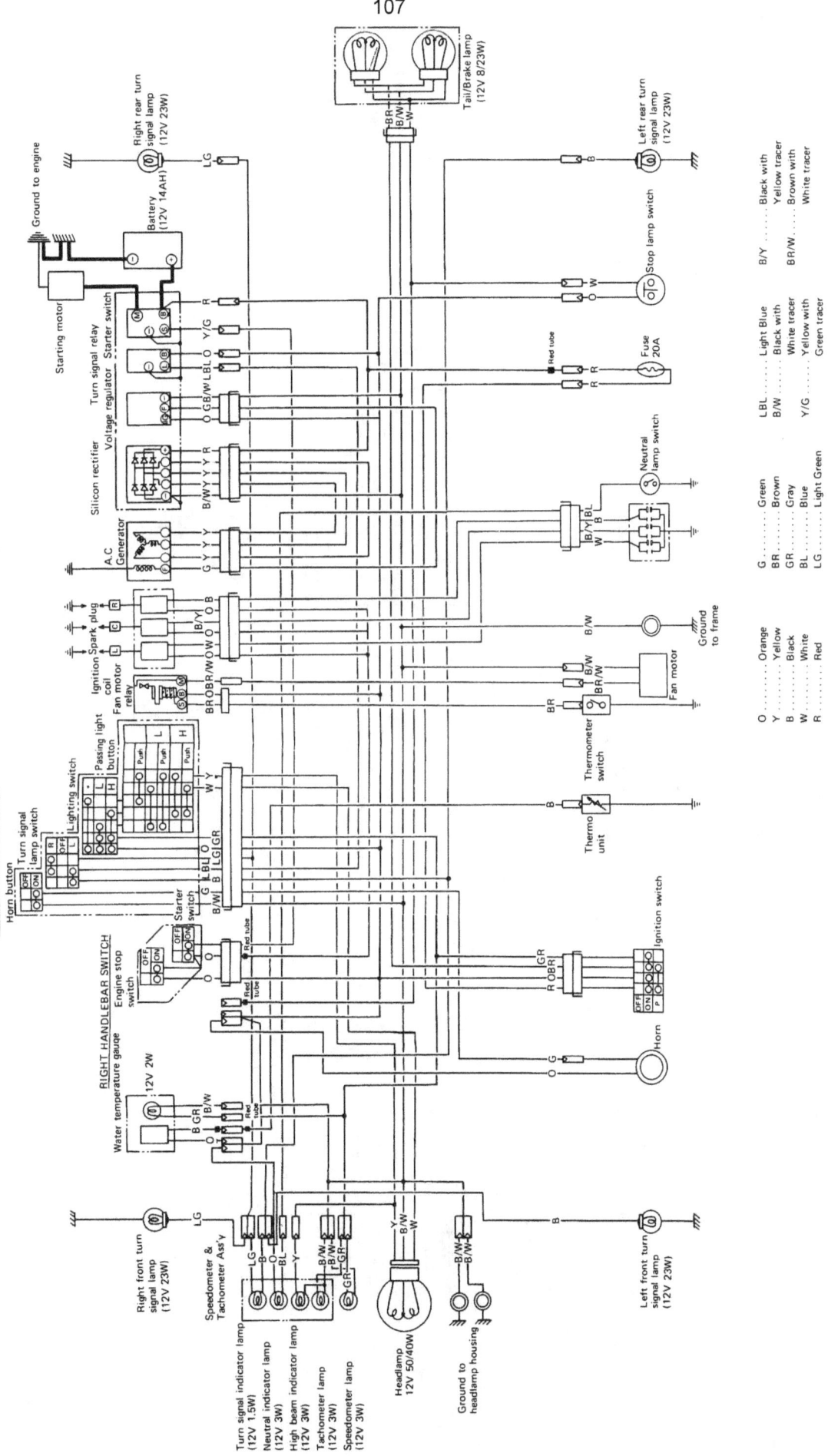

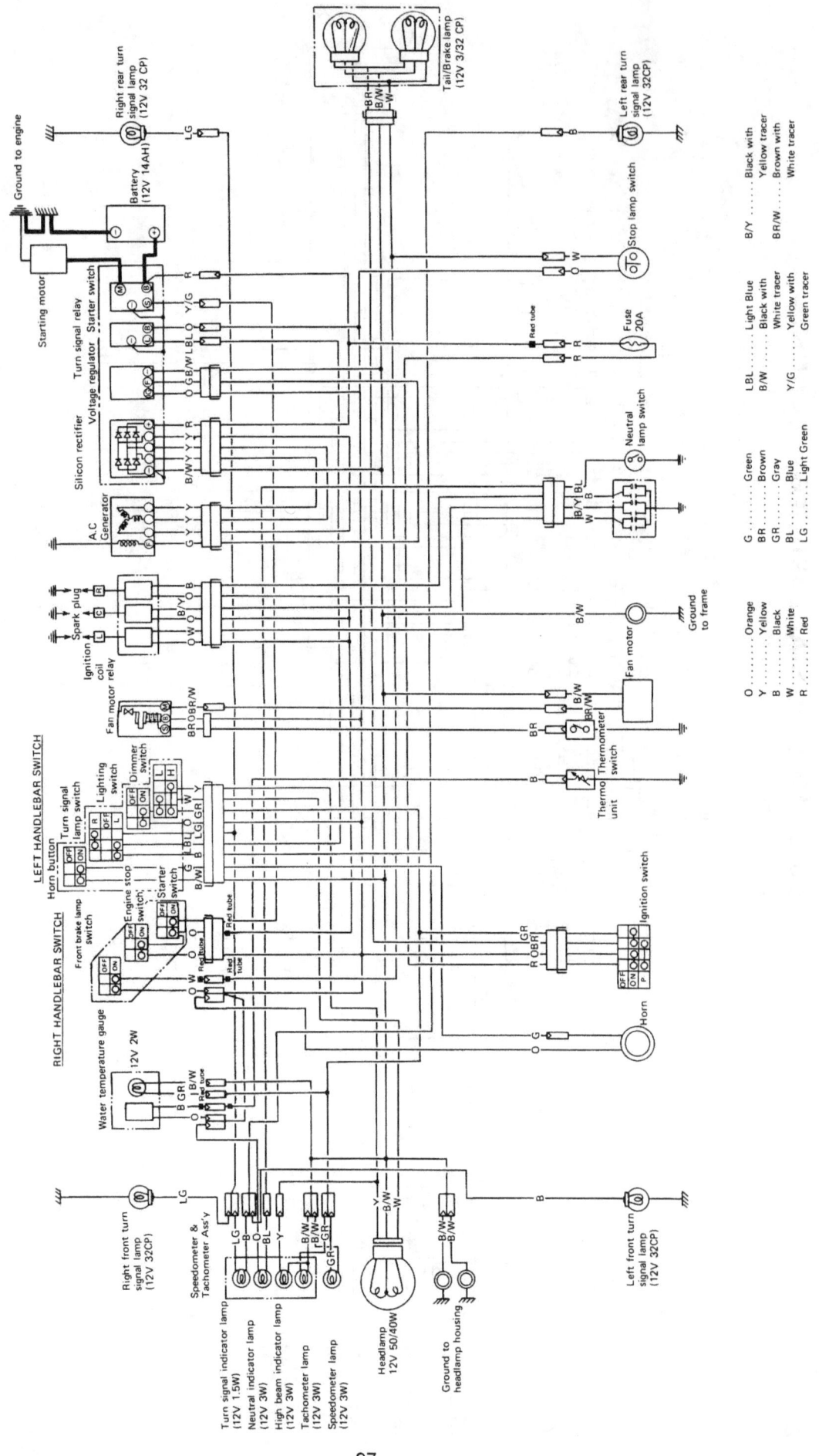

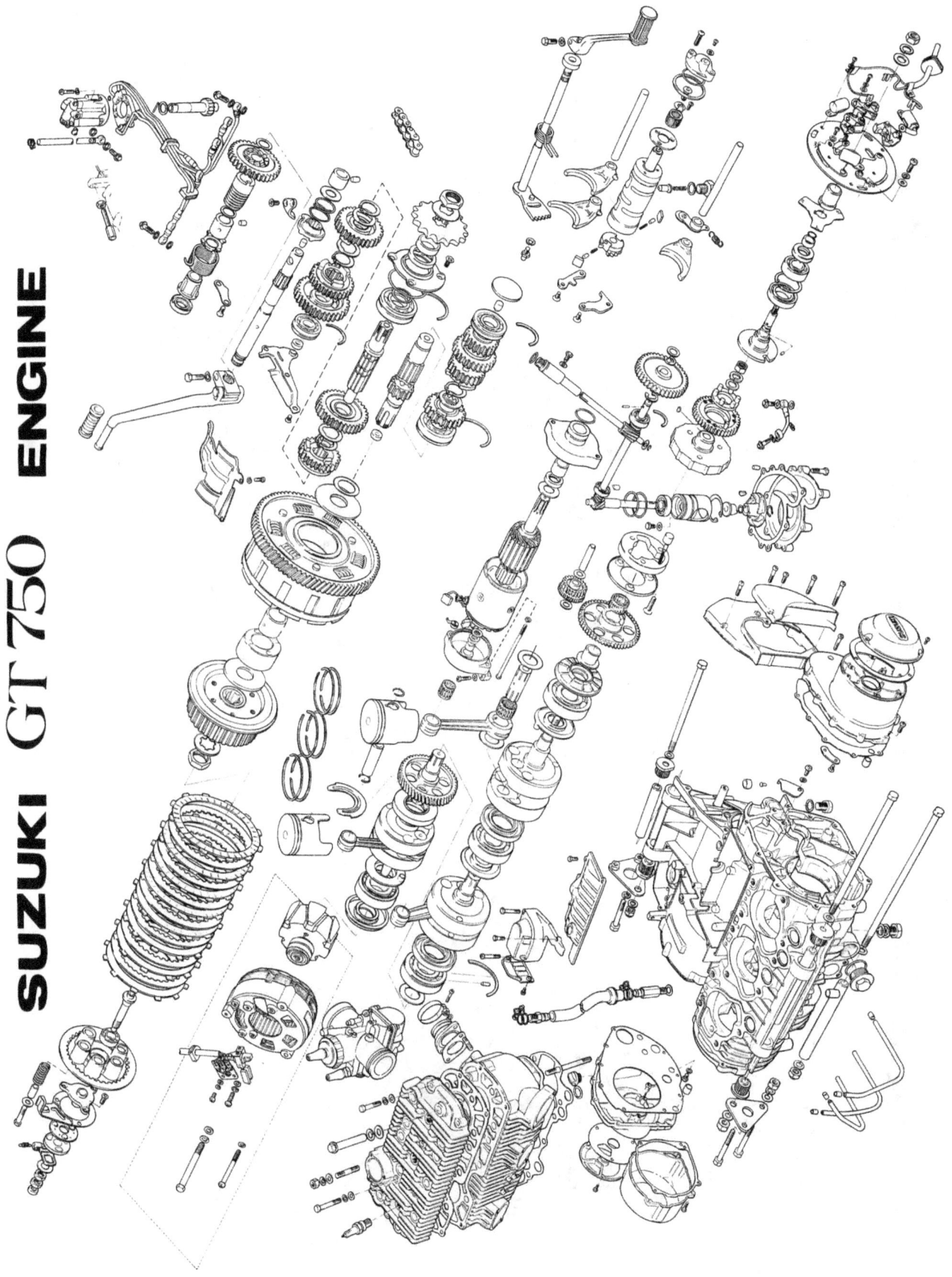

SUZUKI GT 750 COOLING SYSTEM

COOLING WATER CAPACITY 4.5 ℓ
(1.2/1.0gal, US/Imp)

THERMOSTAT
BEGINS TO OPEN AT 82°C
(180°F)
FULLY OPENS AT 95°C
(203°F)

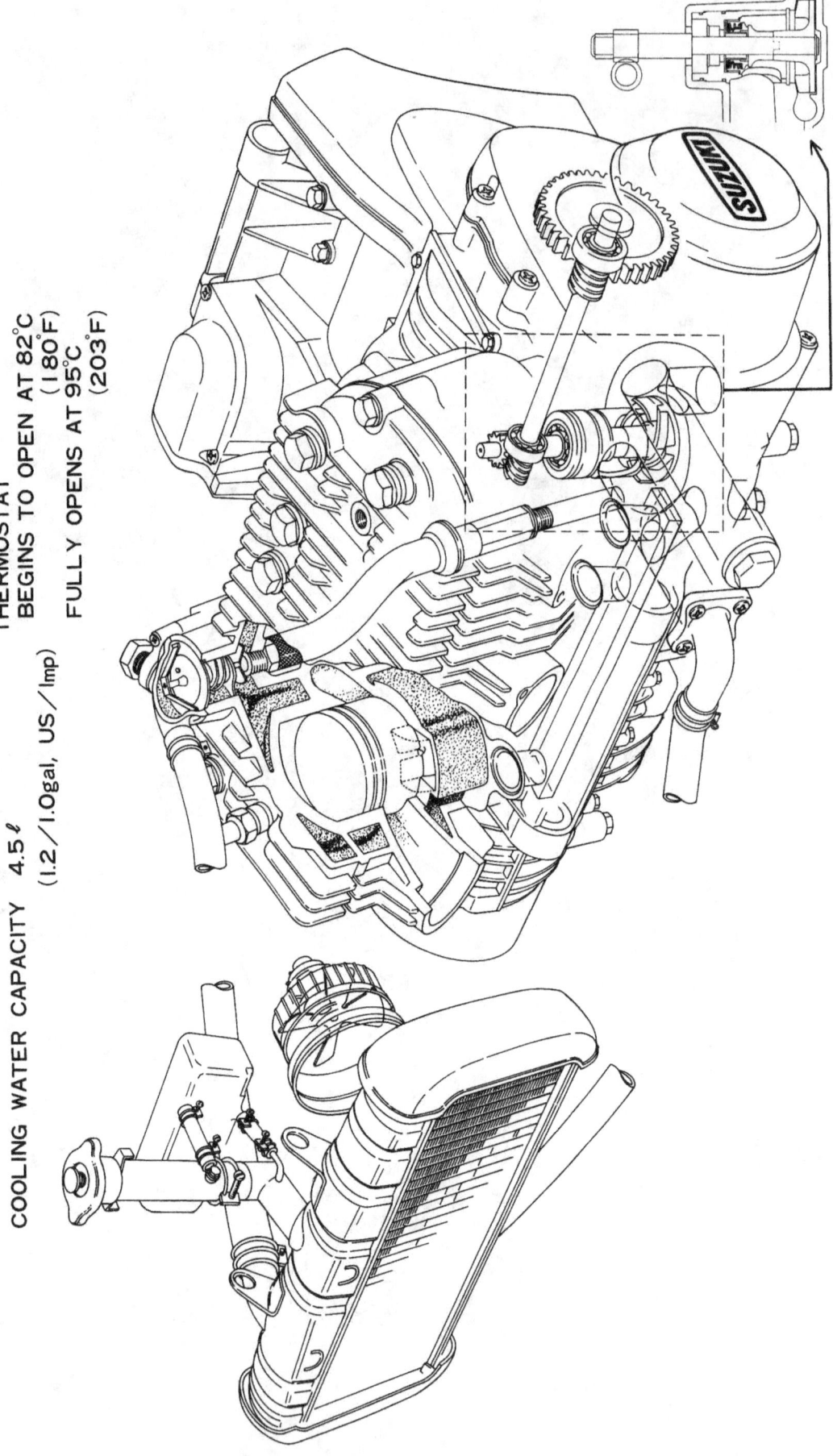

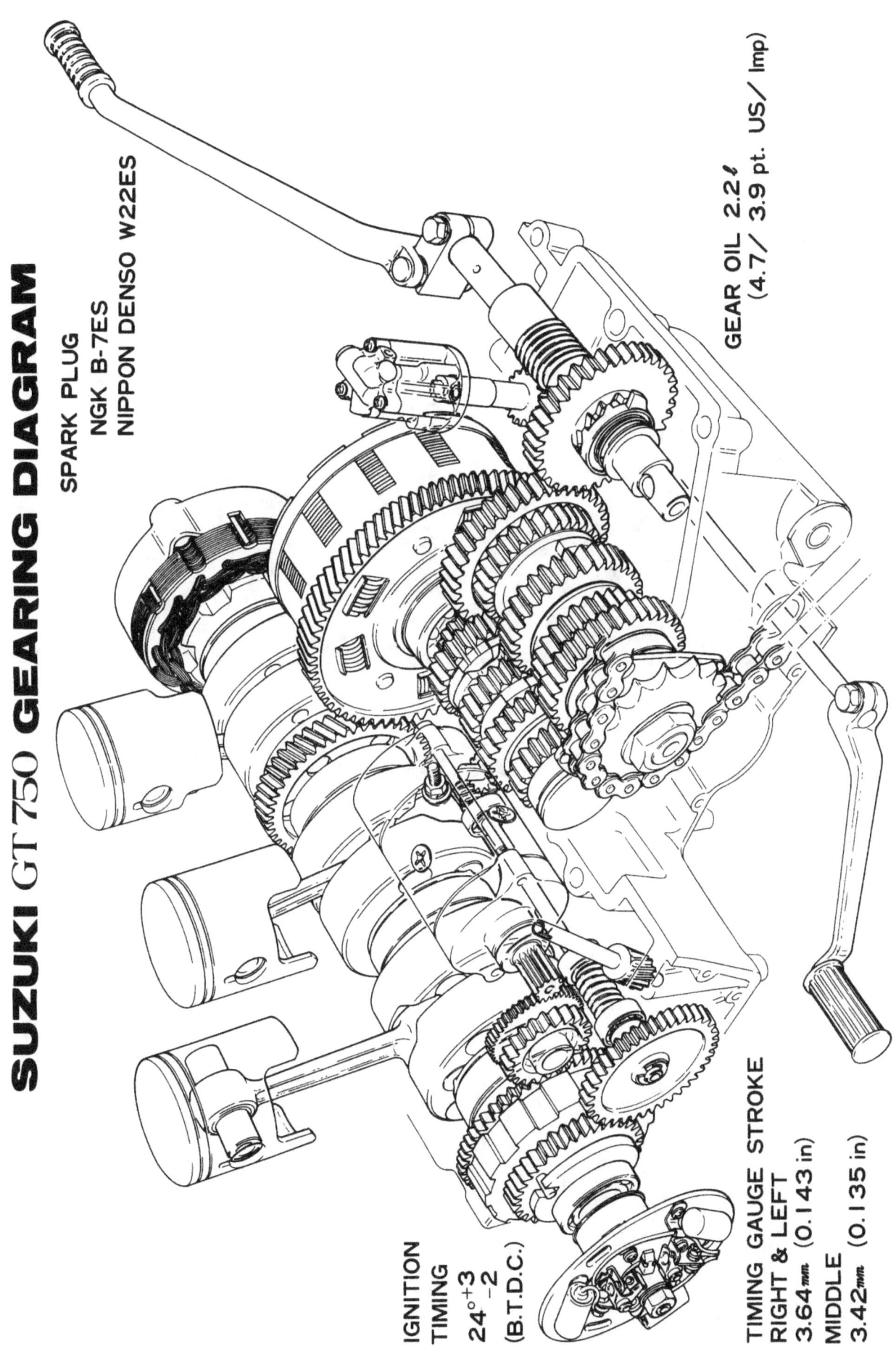

SUZUKI MOTOR CO., LTD.

# SUZUKI
SERVICE MANUAL

MODEL
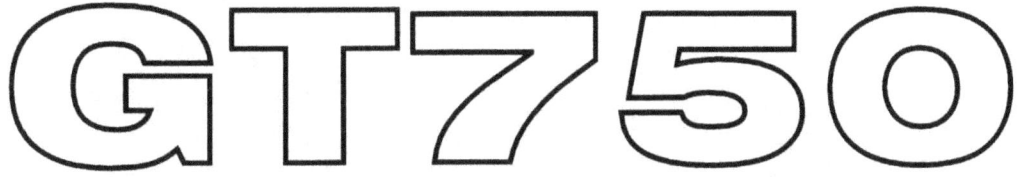
SERVICE GUIDE

FOREWORD

Suzuki GT750 is a unique high power, high performance sport motorcycle having a two stroke cycle, water cooled, three cylinder engine of 750 cc capacity unparalleled in world's sport motorcycle today. It is a luxurious motorcycle incooporating advanced mechanisms not only in engine but in all of the main parts.

In servicing GT750, conventional methods and experiences may not apply and also we have many items which we would like users to observe. Although they are already fully publicized in Owner's Manual, we still depned heavily on the agents like you for giving correct guidance to users of GT750.

This Service Guide is compiled summarizing the instructions for servicing of these new mechanisms and also important items to be observed by users in handling. We believe that the best performance of GT750 can be maintained using your rich experiences and technical knowledge together with the aid of this Service Guide.

In this Service Guide, we emphasize the aspect of Trouble Shooting and the outline of, and the instruction for the maintenance of, the new mechanisms are explained in line with it. In using this Service Guide, please refer to the separate chapters for trouble items and instructions of each block (Engine, Electrical system, Clutch system & Transmission and Body).

A more complete Service Manual giving much detailed and over-all description is now under preparation and will be sent to you whenever it is completed later on.

$ SUZUKI MOTOR CO., LTD.

TABLE OF CONTENTS

FOREWORD   Page

1. GENERAL INFORMATION 2
   1. PERFORMANCE CURVES 2
   2. DIMENSIONS 3
   3. SPECIFICATIONS 4
   4. SPECIAL TOOL 6

2. ITEMS NEEDING SPECIAL ATTENTION IN HANDLING 7
   1. COOLING SOLUTION and COOLANT 7
   2. TIRE SERVICES 9
   3. USING PASSING SWITCH 9
   4. REPLACING MUFFLER COUPLER GASKET 9
   5. REMOVING REAR WHEEL 9
   6. MAJOR PARTS REQUIRING TIGHTENING 10
   7. LIST OF SAFETY RELATED PARTS 10

3. ENGINE 12
   1. LOW POWER or LOSS OF POWER 12
   2. HARD STARTING 19

4. CLUTCH AND TRANSMISSION SYSTEM 21
   1. CLUTCH SYSTEM 21
   2. TRANSMISSION SYSTEM 23

5. LUBRICATION SYSTEM 24

6. ELECTRICAL SYSTEM 26
   1. ENGINE ELECTRICAL SYSTEM 26
   2. BODY ELECTRICAL SYSTEM 29

7. BODY 30
   1. FRONT FORK 30
   2. BRAKE 30
   3. DRIVE CHAIN 31

8. SERVICE DATA 32

9. PERIODICAL INSPECTION 34

1. GENERAL INFORMATION

1. PERFORMANCE CURVES

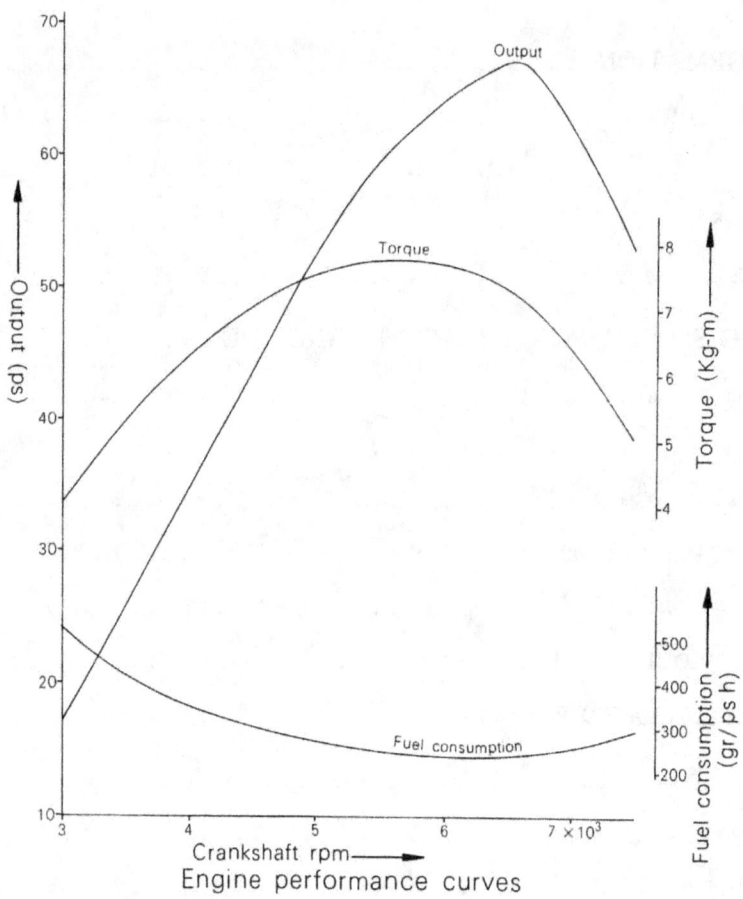

Engine performance curves

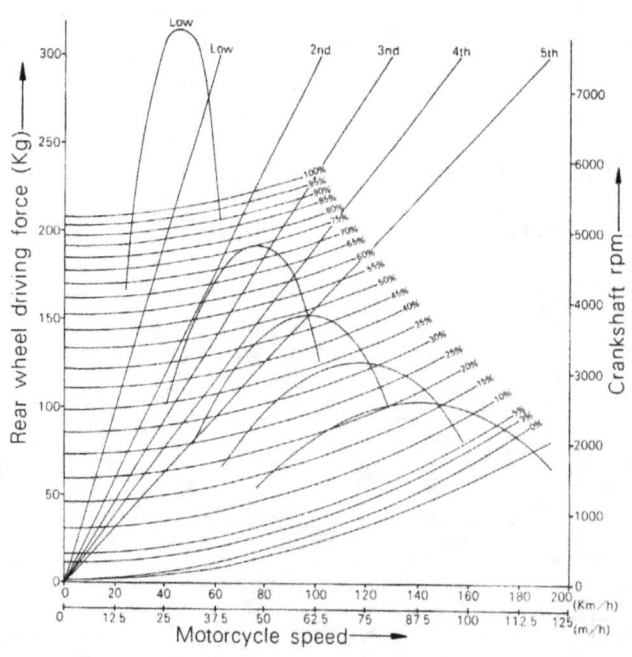

2. SUZUKI GT750 DIMENSIONS

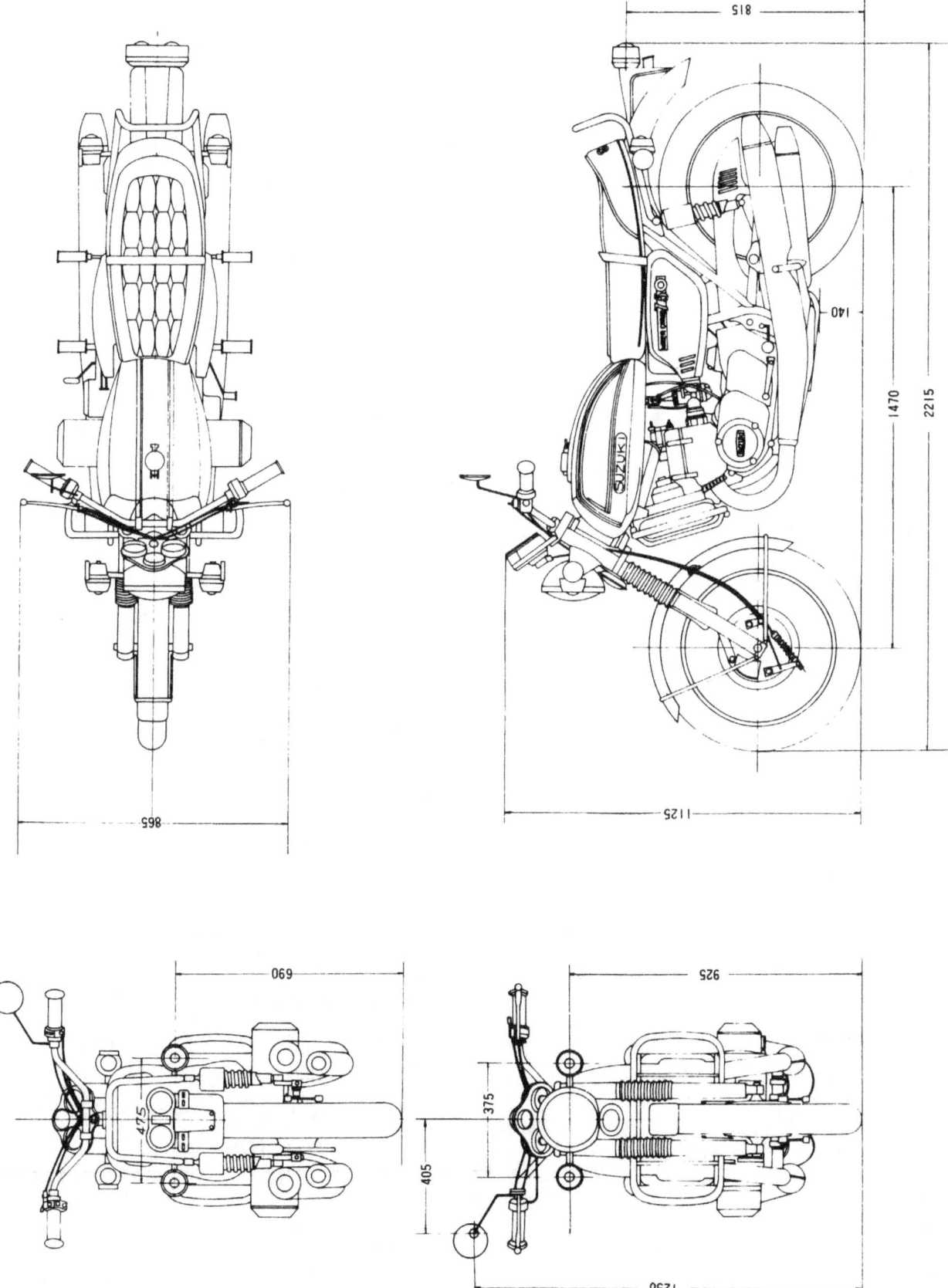

3. SPECIFICATIONS

Dimensions and Weight

Overall length	2215 mm (87.2 in)
Overall width	865 mm (34.0 in)
Overall height	1125 mm (44.3 in)
Wheelbase	1470 mm (57.8 in)
Ground clearance	140 mm (5.5 in)
Tires front	3.25–19 in 4PR
rear	4.00–18 in 4PR
Dry weight	214 kg (482 lb)

Performance

Maximum speed	184–192 kph (115–120 mph)
Acceleration (0–400 m)	12.6 sec.
Braking distance	14 m (46.0 ft) @ 50 kph (30.0 mph)

Engine

Type	2-cycle, water cooled, piston valve engine
Dimensions (L x W x H)	607 x 499 x 445 mm (26.3 x 19.7 x 17.5 in)
Weight	84 kg (38.2 lb)
Cylinder	Sleeved, aluminum, three
Bore x stroke	70 x 64 mm (2.76 x 2.52 in)
Piston displacement	738 cc (45.0 cu-in)
Corrected compression ratio	6.7 : 1
Maximum horse power	67 hp/6,500 rpm
Maximum torque	7.7 kgm/(55.7 lb-ft)/5,500 rpm
Starter	Electric and kick

Cooling System

Type	Water cooled, pressure forced circulation
Radiator	Corrugated fin and tube pressure type
Water pump	6 brade impeller centrifugal type
Thermostat	Wax pellet element type
Cooling solution capacity	4.5 ltr (1.2/1.0 gal, US/Imp)

Fuel System	
Carburetor	VM32SC, three
Air cleaner	Resin-processed, paper filter
Fuel tank capacity	17 ltr (4.5/3.7 gal, US/Imp)

Lubrication System	
Engine	SUZUKI CCI
Gear box	Oil bath 2.2 ltr (4.7/3.9 pt, US/Imp)
Oil tank capacity	1.8 ltr (3.8/3.2 pt, US/Imp)

Ignition System	
Ignition system	Battery
Ignition timing	24° (R.L 3.63, C3.42 mm) B.T.D.C.
Spark plugs	NGK B-8ES or Nippon Denso W24ES

Transmission System		
Clutch		wet multi-disc
Gear box		5-speed constant mesh
Gear shifting		Left foot, lever operated return change
Primary reduction ratio (gear)		1.673 : 1 (82/49)
Final reduction ratio (chain)		3.133 : 1 (47/15)
Gear ratios	low	2.846 : 1 (37/13)
	second	1.736 : 1 (33/19)
	third	1.363 : 1 (30/22)
	fourth	1.125 : 1 (27/24)
	top	0.923 : 1 (24/26)
Overall reduction ratios		
	low	14.92 : 1
	second	9.09 : 1
	third	7.14 : 1
	fourth	5.89 : 1
	top	4.48 : 1

Suspension	
Front suspension	Telescopic fork with hydraulic damper
Rear suspension	Swinging arm with hydraulic damper

Steering	
Steering angle	40° (right & left)
Caster	63°
Trail	95 mm (3.74 in)
Turning radius	2.6 m (8.5 ft)

Brakes	
Front brake	Mechanical, 2 panel 4 leading shoes
Rear brake	Mechanical, leading/trailing shoes

Electrical Equipment	
Generator	Alternator 12V 280W
Starter	12V 500W
Cooling fan	12V 27.6W
Battery	12V 14AH
Head Lamp	12V 50/40W
Tail/brake lamp	12V 8/23W
Neutral indicator lamp	12V 1.5W
Turn signal indicator lamp	12V 1.5W
Speedometer lamp	12V 3W
Tachometer lamp	12V 3W
Turn signal lamp	12V 23W
Fuse	20A
Water temperature gauge	12V 2W

SPECIFICATIONS SUBJECT TO CHANGE WITHOUT NOTICE.

You may find some slight differences between your motorcycle and this service guide. This is because of differences of traffic regulations in different countries.

4. SPECIAL TOOL

Special tool	Part No.	Applied for
Snap Ring Remover	09900−06103	Front fork, water pump
Chain Joint Tool	09900−21801	Drive chain
Starter Clutch Remover	09920−13110	Starter clutch
Clutch Sleeve Hub Holder	09920−53110	Clutch sleeve hub
Rotor Remover	09930−33110	Alternator rotor

2. ITEMS NEEDING SPECIAL ATTENTION IN HANDLING

SUZUKI GT750 is a motorcycle incorporating various new and highly advanced mechanisms. Accordingly, due care must be taken in its operation. Please fully pay attention to and advise customers of the following items for proper operation and maximum performance.

1. COOLING SOLUTION and ANTI-FREEZE & SUMMER COOLANT

    Improper use of cooling solution and anti-freeze will cause corrosion or deposition of foreign substances in the water passage of cylinder and radiator, thereby deteriorating the function of cooling system. Consequently this results in shortening an engine life. The following instructions should be observed.

    (1) Cooling Solution

    As generally known, there are hard and soft water. The use of hard water as cooling solution will result in corrosion or deposition in the water passages of cylinder and radiator due to large contents of calcium and other ingredients.

    Soft water, on the other hand, does no harm to water passages as compared with hard water because of small contents of those ingredients.

    Therefore, soft water should be used as cooling solution. And because it is generally difficult to distinguish soft water from hard water, please advise customers to definitely use distilled water for GT750.

    (2) Anti-freeze & Summer Coolant

    A most serious problem inherent in water cooled engines is the freezing of cooling solution in winter or in cold northern district or the boiling under severe operating conditions. While the boiling is prevented by pressurizing the cooling system, the addition of anti-freeze chemicals to the cooling water is necessary as an anti-freeze and ethylene glycol is commercially available for this purpose. However, even the use of soft water for GT750 will cause corrosion over an extended period of operation due to the existence of extremely small quantity of the ingredients. This is because the cylinder, cylinder head and radiator of GT750 are all made of aluminum alloy for increased heat radiation and substantial weight reduction in the radiator and cylinder. Such being the case, it is necessary to use for GT750 special anti-freeze having an anti-corrosion effect on aluminum alloy and other anti-freeze are not to be used. Suzuki prepares "SUZUKI CCI ANTIFREEZE & SUMMER COOLANT as one of the parts and all the GT750 being shipped are filled with a mixture of this anti-freeze and distilled water in the ratio of distilled water 5: Coolant 5. Please strongly recommend customers to use SUZUKI CCI ANTIFREEZE & SUMMER COOLANT tested and guaranteed by Suzuki or equivalents in the market.

    A standard anti-freeze quantity is 50% under an ordinary operating condition and it should be determined in accordance with a local climate (especially winter-time temperature) under which GT750 is used. Proportionately a larger quantity is required because a freezing temperature must also be covered in distircts with sub-zero temperatures. Determine the amount of coolant according to the following table.

Temperature under which	°C	−10	−15	−20	−25	−31	−39
your motorcycle is used	°F	14	5	−4	−13	−24	−38
Mixing ratio of anti-freeze	%	30	35	40	45	50	55
Amount of anti-freeze	ltr	1.35/3.15	1.60/2.90	1.80/2.70	2.00/2.50	2.25/2.25	2.50/2.00
/distilled water	US.pt	1.40/3.30	1.70/3.10	1.90/2.90	2.10/2.60	2.40/2.40	2.60/2.10
for 4.5 ltr (4.75/3.95 qt, US/Imp) of cooling solution	Imp.pt	1.20/2.75	1.40/2.55	1.55/2.40	1.75/2.20	2.00/2.00	2.20/1.75

Note: This table applies to the use of Suzuki CCI Coolant only.

Suzuki Anti-freeze is of the quality to serve approximately 2 years or 35,000 km (20,000 mile) and is classified as a long life anti-freeze. Don't mix up with any other brands.

(3) Replenishing Cooling Solution:

Every new motorcycle is filled with cooling solution when shipped from the factory. During transportation, however, a loss in quantity sometimes occurs, in that case cooling solution should be added in the following manner.

When loss is small

fill up with distilled water.

When loss is large

fill up with 30 ~ 55% solution of Suzuki Anti-freeze.

The specified cooling system capacity is 4.5L (4.75/3.95 qt, US/Imp) and water level should be 5–15 mm (0.2–0.6 in) from the bottom of radiator reservoir tank.

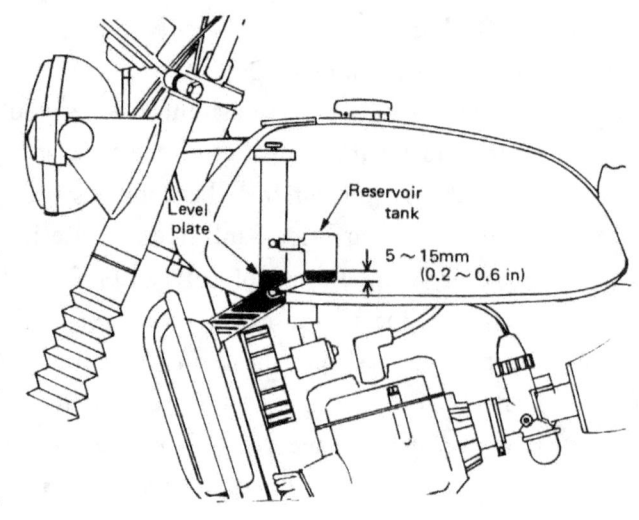

In order to facilitate the daily inspection of cooling solution in the cooling system, the level plate (gage) colored in white is provided inside the water inlet pipe. Please recommend customers to check the solution level before starting the engine, peeping into the water inlet pipe whether the solution level is in the vicinity of this plate.

Solution level can be distinguished from the white plate, for the cooling solution is colored in green.

(4) Loosening Radiator Cap:

In loosening radiator cap, (for inspection of cooling solution) please advise customers to press down fully a pressure release button first for reducing inner pressure, then take the cap off slowly wrapping it with waste cloth.

(5) Changing Cooling solution:

The cooling solution must be changed every two years or 35,000 km (20,000 mile) as a rule. Remove the radiator cap and cooling system drain plug and drain all the used cooling solution. Refit the cooling system drain plug and pour cooling solution mixed with 50% of anti-freeze and put ½ oz (14 gram) of Anti-Leak materials (Bar's Leaks) specified by Suzuki into the radiator.

Run and warm up the engine to open thermostat. After it has been warmed up, wait for a while until it gets cold and then add the cooling solution again if cooling solution level in the radiator is found to be under the level plate provided inside the radiator inlet pipe.

Note: Please reccomend to the customers never to add any anti-leak materials to the cooling solution except the time when changing the cooling solution, since the motorcycles are shipped with the mixture of cooling solution and Bar's Leaks filled.

2. TIRE SERVICES

(1) The tire pressure and its wear have great effect on stability and control of large and high performance type motorcycles such as GT750. The tire pressure should always be kept within the specified value and replacement with new tire is necessary when the remaining depth of tread is less than 1.6 mm (0.063 in) for front and 2.0 mm (0.079 in) for rear tire. Stability at high speed is significantly dependent on tire specifications. Therefore, customers should be advised of the use of Suzuki genuine specified tire (front: 3.25–19" 4PR, rear: 4.00–18" 4PR) or the other well-known brands.

Specified tire pressure	normal riding	continuous high speed riding
Front	1.6 kg/cm² (22.7 lb/in²)	1.8 kg/cm² (25.6 lb/in²)
Rear .... solo riding	1.8 kg/cm² (25.6 lb/in²)	2.0 kg/cm² (28.4 lb/in²)
dual riding	2.0 kg/cm² (28.4 lb/in²)	2.0 kg/cm² (28.4 lb/in²)

(2) When removing a tire from wheels for a flat-tire repair or for other purposes, please provide aligning marks both on tire and wheel rim to facilitate proper assembly without deranging the wheel balance.

3. USING PASSING SWITCH

(This device is not installed on the motorcycles for the U.S. and CANADA market.)

Passing switch is used for flashing head light when an oncoming vehicle is not visible or to warn the other drivers throughout the day and night.

Please advise customers not to use this passing switch too often in ordinary driving conditions since it will give a glaring effect to on-coming drivers.

4. REPLACING MUFFLER COUPLER GASKET

New technique is adopted in the muffler of GT750 to couple the exhaust pipe portion of each muffler by means of a coupler tube.

Increase in power at low speed and improvement of exhaust noises are attained through this technique.

It is recommended to replace at the time of an overhaul coupler tube gaskets which are called Exhaust Coupler Seal (Part No. 99000–31020) and is available as a reel to be used for ten units.

5. REMOVING REAR WHEEL

As is detailed later, since the drive chain of GT750 uses a joint of a flaring type, cutting and jointing of the chain can not be done without chain joint tool (special tool No. 09900–21801) and chain joints (Suzuki genuine parts.) Therefore, when repairing flat tires after loosening the rear axle, a chain is removed from rear sprocket by sliding the rear wheel to its foremost position. Under a normal condition the drive chain is taken off from the rear sprocket in this manner, but if there is a difficulty, chain is easily taken off by removing engine sprocket as well as engine sprocket cover. As to the drive chain and joint tool, refer to the item of "Drive chain" at page 31.

6. MAJOR PARTS REQUIRING TIGHTENING

The following bolts and nuts are so important to ensure the safety that the tightening torque of these parts should be checked periodically.

No.	Item	Tightening Torque	Q'ty
1	Front Axle Nut	360–520kgm (26–38 lb-ft)	1
2	Front Axle Stopper Nut	130–230kgm (9.5–17 lb-ft)	4
3	Front Torque Link Bolt & Nut	130–230kgm (9.5–17 lb-ft)	2
4	Handlebars Clamp Bolt	90–200kgm (6.5–14.5 lb-ft)	4
5	Front Fork Upper Bracket Bolt (R & L)	180–300kgm (13–22 lb-ft)	2
6	Front Fork Upper Bracket Bolt (Center)	90–140kgm (6.5–10 lb-ft)	1
7	Engine Mounting Nut	250–400kgm (18–29 lb-ft)	4
8	Rear Swinging Arm Pivot Shaft Nut	500–750kgm (36–55 lb-ft)	1
9	Front Footrest Bolt	300–450kgm (22–33 lb-ft)	2
10	Rear Torque Link Nut	180–280kgm (13–20 lb-ft)	2
11	Rear Shock Absorber Nut	180–280kgm (13–20 lb-ft)	4
12	Rear Axle Nut	540–800kgm (39–58 lb-ft)	1

7. LIST OF MAJOR SAFETY RELATED PARTS

Suzuki always pursue not only extreme high performance, but also driver's safety in our products. But driver's safety could be realized under such conditions that are provided with both safety design and production for the products in manufacturer side, and good aftersales and service in dealer side. In this connection, it is highly required to check up the important items for motorcycle safety driving in accordance with the following check list taking opportunities of periodical inspection.

Block	Item	Check for
Fuel System	Fuel hose	Fuel leakage
	Fuel tank	Fuel leakage
Suspention System	Front fork ass'y	Crack, Faulty welding of bracket
	Front fork upper bracket comp.	Crack, Faulty welding
	Front axle	Crack
	Rear axle	Crack
	Rear swinging arm comp.	Crack, Faulty welding
Steering System	Handlebar	Crack
	Handlebar upper clamp	Crack
	Handlebar lower clamp	Crack

Block	Item	Check for
Braking System	Front hub drum comp.	Crack
	Rear hub drum comp.	Crack
	Front hub panel comp.	Crack
	Rear hub panel comp.	Crack
	Front torque link	Crack
	Rear torque link	Crack
	Front brake shoe	Crack, Peeling off of lining
	Rear brake shoe	Crack, Peeling off of lining
	Front brake cam shaft	Crack, Deformation of serration
	Rear brake cam shaft	Crack, Deformation of serration
	Rear brake rod ass'y	Crack
	Brake pedal	Crack, Faulty welding
	Brake lever	Crack
	Front brake cable ass'y	Detachment of cable end
	Rear brake cable ass'y	Detachment of cable end
Frame	Frame	Crack, Faulty welding

3. ENGINE

1. LOW POWER or LOSS OF POWER

    The following are considered to be primary causes of low power.
    Servicing must be made according to the procedures described below.

    A. Low compression
    B. Incorrect ignition system
    C. Malfunction of fuel system
    D. Insufficient air intake
    E. Overheating

    All the servicing and maintenance work herein described can be made without demounting the engine from body. Cooling water should be drained prior to the service.

A. **In the case of low compression**

(1) Remove the cylinder head and check for any leakage through head gasket.
(2) Remove cylinder and check for sticking and wear of piston rings.
    – Inspection of wear of piston ring –
    Insert the piston ring at the skirt of cylinder then measure piston ring end gap. Replace the piston ring if the gap exceeds 0.7 mm

    Standard piston ring end gap.......... 0.15–0.35 mm (0.006–0.014 in)

    Both the 1st and 2nd rings are of Keystone type.
(3) A defective crankshaft oil seal is also conceivable. An engine overhaul is necessary to check this. However, it is better to measure the compression of each cylinder first to know the possibility of defect under the same condition (run by starting motor with throttle fully open) and check if 3 cylinders show approximately a same compression. If any differency can be seen, it will result from defective oil seal.

B. **In the case of incorrect ignition system**

(1) Adjust ignition timing if needed
    – Adjusting ignition timing –
    Adjust ignition timing from the cylinder at left. By moving the contact point base and set plate, adjust point gap to 0.35 mm (0.014 in) of the point with marking "L" on the base, then rotate a crankshaft counterclockwise to check if the point opens when "L" marking line on timing plate is in alignments with an aligning mark of the casing in the adjusting window. If it is out of order, adjust the set plate untill the correct timing is obtained. Subsequently adjust the points with markings "R" and "C" in a similar manner as "L" after adjusting point gaps to 0.35 mm (0.014 in) by moving each point set plate attached on the shifting plate.

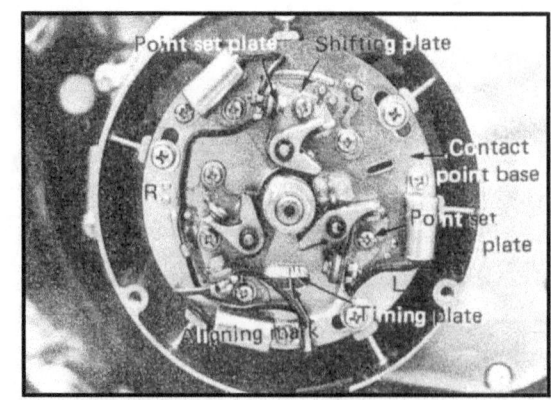

When using a timing gauge for adjustment, adjust according to the following table keeping in mind that the gauge stroke is not uniform because of the difference in inclination of spark plug hole at each cylinder.

Standard Ignition Timing $24°\,^{+2}_{-2}$ (B.T.D.C.)

Crank angle (B.T.D.C.)		22°	23°	24°	25°	26°
Piston Distance mm (in)	R & L	3.20 (0.126)	3.35 (0.134)	3.64 (0.143)	3.94 (0.155)	4.25 (0.167)
	C	2.88 (0.113)	3.15 (0.124)	3.42 (0.136)	3.72 (0.146)	3.99 (0.157)

R & L : Right and Left cylinder
C : Center cylinder

(2) Check for defective spark plug. A standard spark plug is NGK B-7ES and DENSO W22ES. If too wet with this plug, use B-6ES and if too hot, use B-8HS. When NGK and DENSO plugs are not available, other corresponding plugs may be used in accordance with the following conversion chart.

Spark Plug Conversion Chart

NGK	DENSO	Champion	AC	Autolite	Bosch	KLG	Lodge
B - 6ES	W20ES	N88, N84 N6 N5	45XL, 45N	AG5 AG4	W160T2 W175T2	FE70 FE50	HBLN
B - 7ES	W22ES	N4	44XL, 44N 43XL, 43N	AG3	W225T2	FE75	HL14, HLNP
B - 8ES	W24ES	N3	42XL		W240T2 W260T2		HF2HL, 2HL HLN

(3) Check for defective contact points or condensers.
Examine contact points whether the surface is even and whether whole area contacts. Examine the condenser by electro tester whether insulation and capacity are normal. Standard condenser capacity is 0.22 μF.

C. In the case of malfunction of fuel system

(1) Check for clogged jet or fuel passages in the carburettor. Also check whether proper adjustment is made. Three VM32SC carburettors are used. Since the setting is different with right/left cylinders and with middle cylinder, use the following table for carburettor setting.

Carburettor Position	Identification stamp	MJ	JN	NJ	CA	PJ	BP	PO	AS	VS	GS
Right & Left	310 10R 310 10L	102.5	5F16 - 3	P - 4	2.5	30	1.4	0.6	1½	2.5	50
Middle	310 10M	100	–do–	P - 3	–do–	–do–	–do–	–do–	–do–	–do–	–do–

— Inspection and adjustment of carburetor —

* Regulating fuel level

Remove a float chamber cap from carburettor and measure the height of the float while holding the carburettor upside down.

Standard D = 27.0 mm (1.06 in)

If D is out of order, adjust the float height with the tongue bended up and down as illustrated to the right.

Caution: Before adjusting float tongue, check needle valve for wearing. If it is excessively worn, replace it with new one.

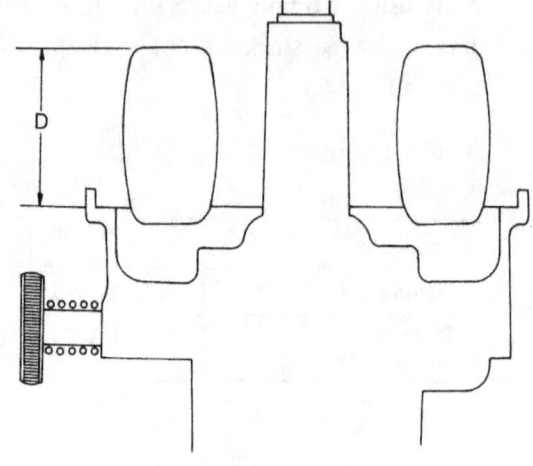

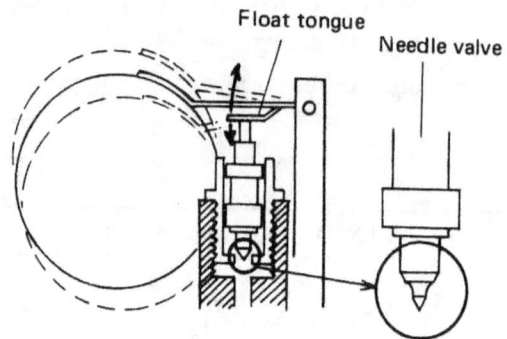

* Adjusting idling speed and synchronizing technique.
○ Turn the cable adjuster on the top of carburettor to have a play of 2–3 mm (0.08–0.09 in) between the cable and cable adjuster.
○ Remove aligning hole plug from a mixing chamber body of each carburetor, then adjust three carburettors by turning cable adjuster so that an aligning mark on the side of throttle valve comes on upper surface of the hole with the throttle grip gradually wound up.

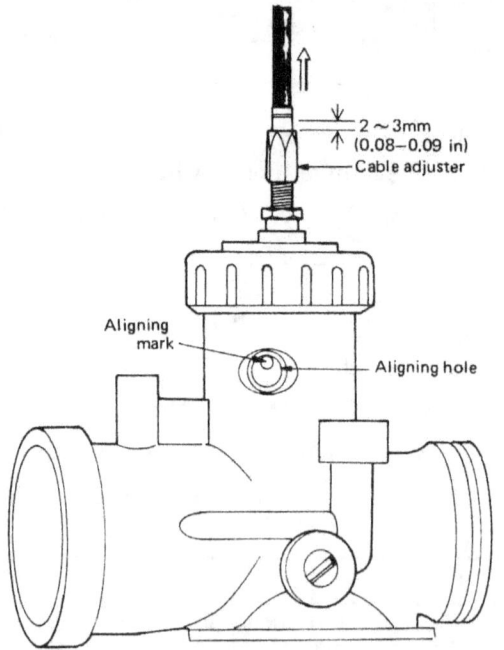

○ Screw pilot air adjusting screw of each carburetor all the way in and then back it out 1½ turns.

○ Start the engine and after sufficient warm-up adjust idling speed with the throttle stop screw. Idling adjustment is made with each cylinder actuated one by one by so turning the related throttle valve stop screw as to have a tachometer reading of 1,000 rpm in each case.

   Caution: In the case of one cylinder firing, the related throttle valve stop screw should be screwed in to a considerable extent to keep running.

○ After adjusting the carburettor so that each cylinder has a speed of 1,000 rpm independently, equally turn the throttle stop screws of three carburettors backward to set an idling speed at 1,000 rpm with three cylinders firing.

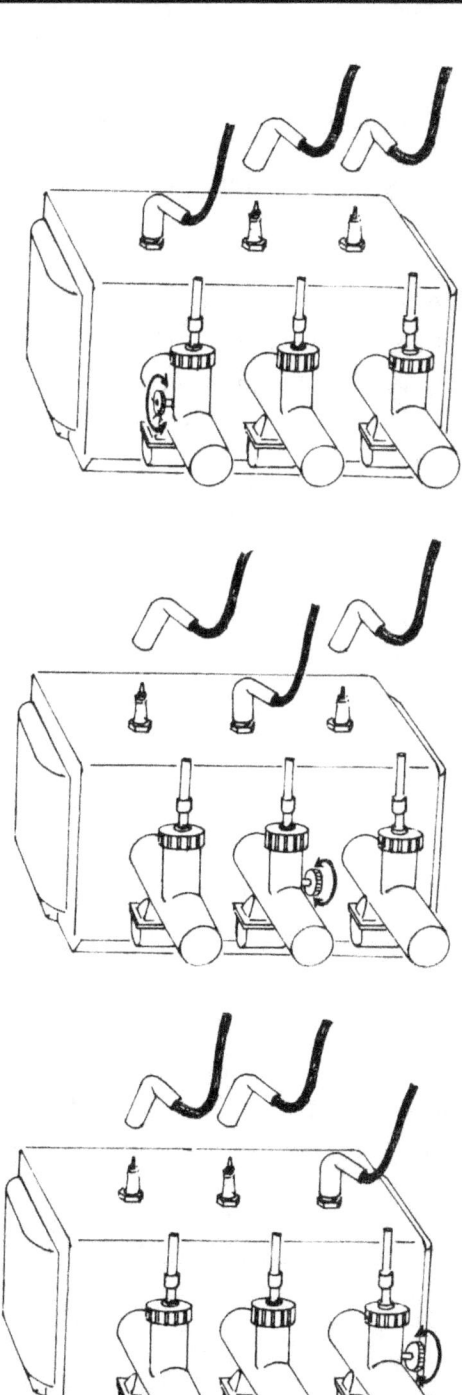

○ Finally turn the throttle cable adjuster under throttle grip to have a play of 0.5 ~ 1 mm (0.02 ~ 0.04 in) on throttle cable.

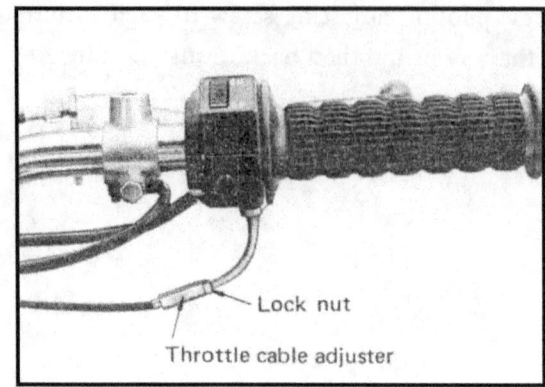

(2) Check whether a diaphragm type fuel cock or fuel pipe is clogged.

D. **In the case of insufficient air intake**

Check for air cleaner. Clean it by blowing compressed air if clogged.

E. **In the case of overheating**

The following are considered as major causes for overheating. Check each item according to the instruction. The thermometer gives warning for overheating by pointing to the red zone. When it occurs, stop the motorcycle immediately leaving the engine at idling. Disconnect a brown wire from the thermostat on the cylinder head to actuate electric fan and wait until the thermometer reading goes down, then remove a radiator cap by wrapping it with waste cloth after confirming that the red button on the cap was pressed for releasing the vapor.

(1) Check cooling solution level because the lack of cooling solution is most likely.
  − Checking cooling solution −
  In a pressure forced circulation type cooling system of GT750, cooling solution rarely gets low. However, check-up is necessary since it does get low when there is any leakage or some other defects. See page 8.

(2) In the case of defective thermostat.
  Operating temperature range of thermostat
  Valve begins to open at: 82°C (179.6°F)
  Valve fully opens at: 95°C (203.0°F)

  − Checking thermostat −
  Immerse thermostat into water in a container and warm it up stirring up the water to see if it functions at the operating temperatures as above.

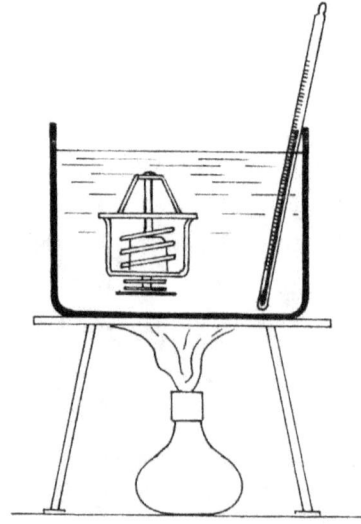

(3) In the case of defective water pump.

Unless water pump properly operates, cooling solution does not circulate within the cooling system. If the sealing incorporated in the water pump is defective, cooling solution or motor oil leaks out from the bottom of the engine.

The water pump assembly which incorporate the sealing, bearing and housing will be supplied as a replacement, and each inner parts will not be available.

In order to exhaust the transmission oil and/or cooling solution which might have soaked through the oil seal, water sealing seat and/or "o" ring, the breather pipe is connected from the top of water pump body to the crankcase bottom.

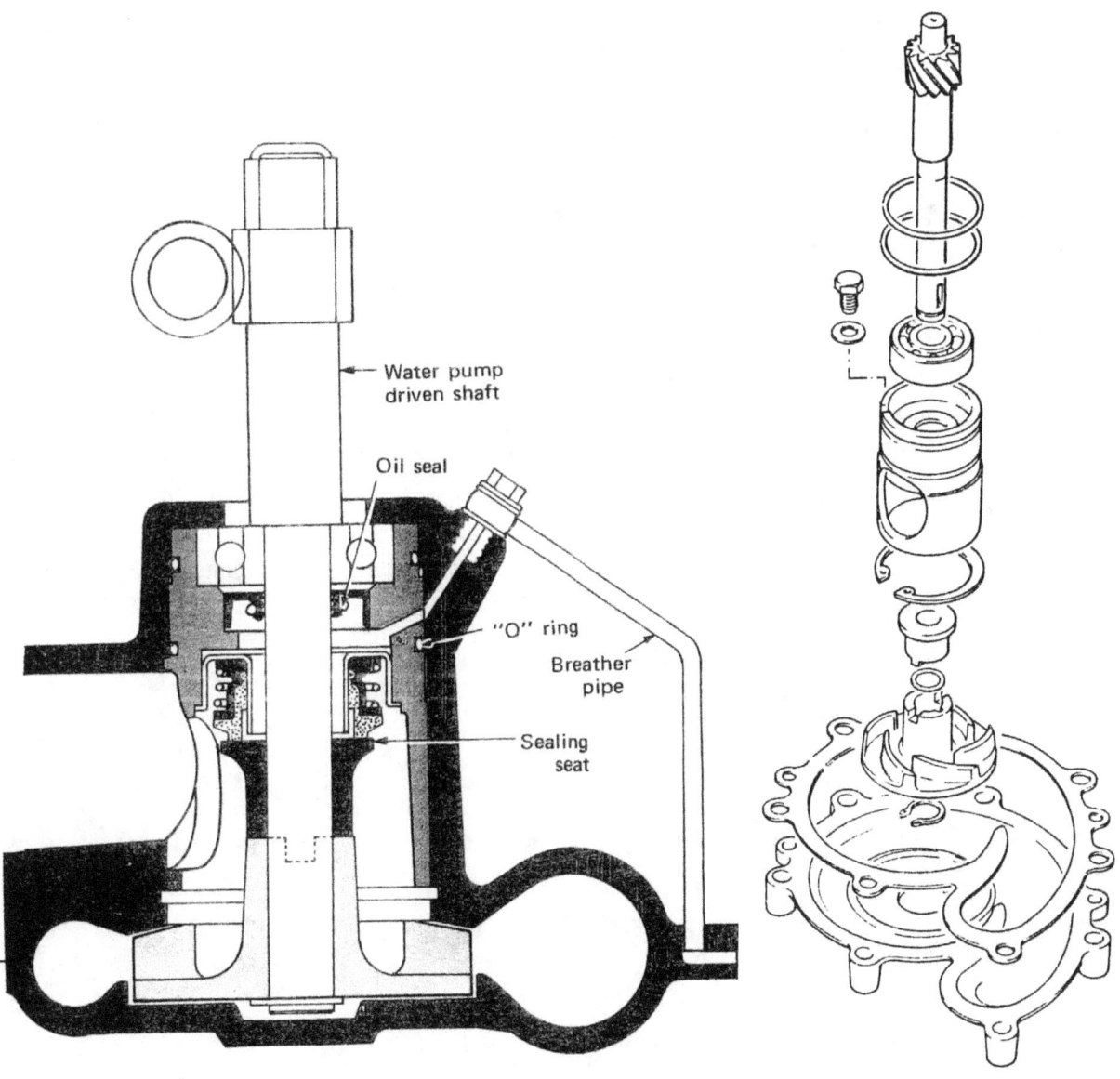

(4) Since radiator is made of aluminum material, heat radiation is large and it weighs less and well withstands vibrations and pressures. Check radiator, as a leakage might occur at an accident such as overturning.

A clogged radiator core caused by deposition of foreign substances through the use of cooling water or coolant of inferior quality would also be prone to overheating. Another example is when mud or insects stick on the radiator fins or a stone hits radiator and deforms the fins, then cooling effect of radiator is significantly lowered. Therefore, clean the fin and repair it if necessary.

— Inspection of radiator —

Remove the radiator and fill it up with water. Measure the quantity and compare with that of a new radiator. If the difference is over 20%, replace with new radiator since radiator does not function if it is clogged 20% of the total capacity.

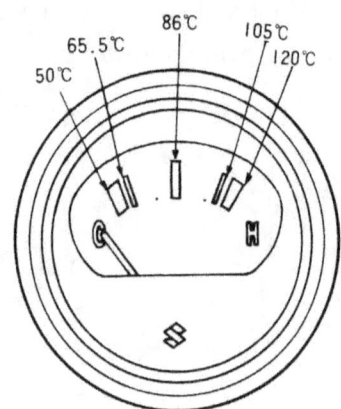

(5) Since improper ignition would also cause overheating, always adjust ignition timing as specified. See page 12.

(6) Without normal operation of cooling fan, overheating is likely to occur especially in crowded intracity driving at tropical district or in slow driving under a blazing sun. Cooling fan starts to operate when the thermometer points to a white line (105°C, 221°F) just before the red zone and stops as the temperature of cooling water goes down to around 100°C (212°F).

— Inspecting of Cooling fan —

Cooling fan starts to operate with ignition switch at its "ON" position, when brown colored wire, one of two wires from the thermostat laid on cylinder heads, is disconnected. In case the fan is not actuated by disconnecting brown colored wire, fan motor or thermo switch relay is defective. In case an actuating temperature deviates from the above figures, a thermo-switch is malfunctioning and needs to be replaced.

(7) Clogged cooling water passage also becomes a cause of overheating. Check connecting unions, etc. for possible choking.

2. HARD STARTING

GT750 engine is easily started by starting motor or by a kick. In case the starting is hard, the following are considered to be primary causes. Servicing must be made according to the procedures described below.

    A.   Defective fuel system
    B.   Defective ignition system
    C.   Defects inside the engine
    D.   Defective electrical system

A. In the case of defective fuel system

The following three cases are conceivable as defects in a fuel system.

(1) Malfunction of a carburetor starter system.

Check the starter system of each carburettor and blow off by compressed air for cleaning.

(2) Malfunctioning of a diaphragm type fuel cock

If engine starts with fuel cock at a "PRI" position and does not start at "ON" position, the fuel cock is malfunctioning and needs to be replaced.

(3) Unusual fuel flow due to clogging or deposition of dirt in fuel passage of each carburettor. Remove carburettor and clean thoroughly in cleaning solvent.

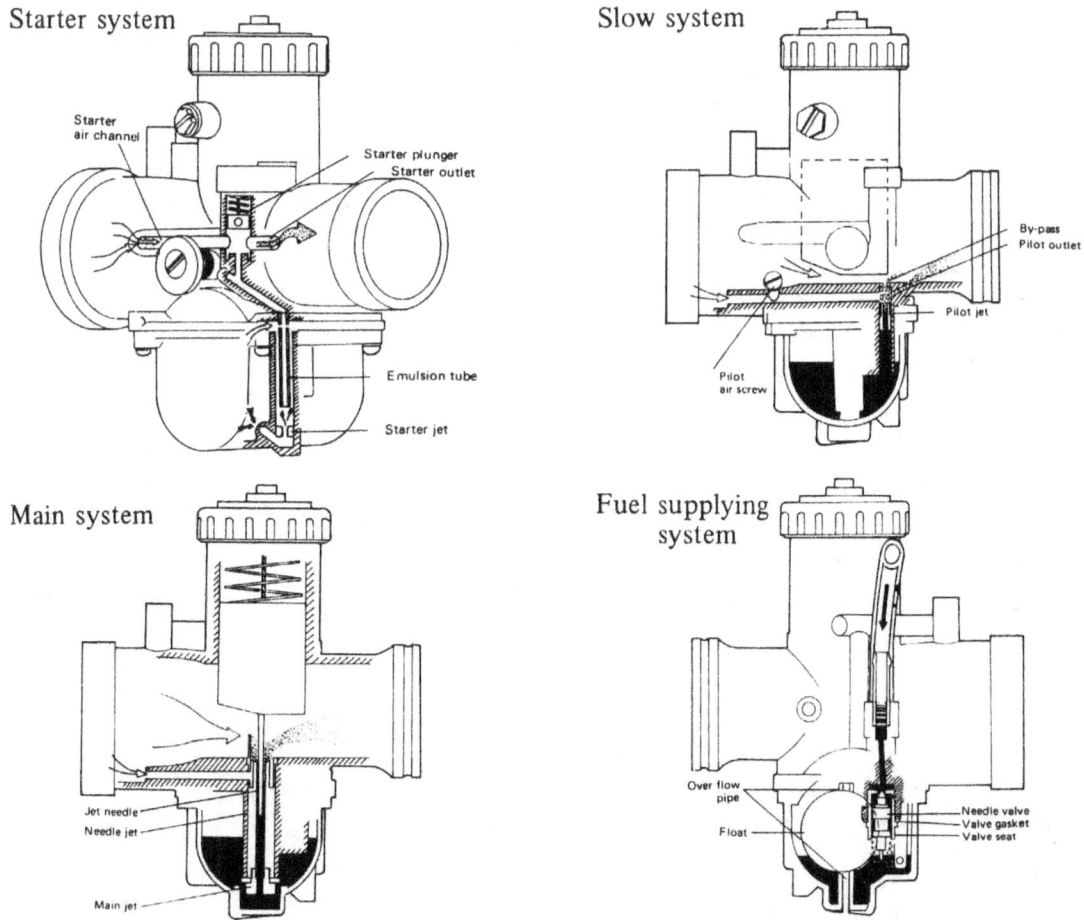

B. In the case of defective ignition system

(1) Check if contact points are burnt out or fouled. As a cause for burnt contact point, check for defective condenser or if dirt or grease sticks on the point surface.

(2) Improper point gaps often cause hard starting. Adjust point gap within the range of 0.3–0.4 mm (0.012–0.015 in).

(3) Wrong ignition timing may also be a cause.
See page 12 for adjustment of the ignition timing.

(4) Often experienced is a loose spark plug or a loose high tension cord. Fasten tightly at servicing or repair.
Hard starting sometimes occurs due to wet sprak plugs. When a spark plug tends to get wet, the malfunction of carburettor or defective spark plug is conceivable. Check the carburettor and replace if necessary with a new plug.

(5) Defective ignition coil sometimes causes hard starting. Check ignition coil with an electro tester.

C. In the case of defect inside the engine

When a cause of defects is traced inside of the engine, the following are considered to be primary causes directly associated with hard starting. However, before overhauling the engine, check it by measuring compression at each cylinder by means of compression gauge for any defect which can be detected by doing so.

When using compression gauge, each cylinder should be measured under the same conditions, which calls for engine rotation by the starting motor, with throttle fully opened but with spark plugs removed.

(1) Excessive wear in pistons, piston rings and cylinders lowers the compression, thereby impairing normal firing. The wear of these parts, however, is only recognizable after substantial mileage and never brings up problems at an early stage of operation.
Refer page 12 for inspection.

(2) Compression gets low similarly when the crankshaft oil seal is defective.
If the result of compression measurement is not in order without any substantial wear being observed, overhaul the engine and replace crankshaft with a new assembly.

(3) It is also important to check for loose cylinder head. Loosened cylinder head or leakage from cylinder head gasket causes not only hard starting but corrosion at the passage of cooling system due to sulphurous acid gas contained in combustion gas.

D. In the case of a defective electrical system

GT750 is equipped with an alternator which has high generating and charging performance over a wide range of speed and a (trouble-free) starting motor of high durability. However, please check the following in the case of hard starting.

(1) When starting motor becomes inoperative, wear of brush, rare short-circuit of field coil, ground or defective commutator would occur.

– Examining starting motor –
See page 26.

(2) Discharged battery also causes hard starting.
Possible defects are in alternator, regulator or rectifier.

– Detection of the cause of discharged battery –
Consult page 27 for detecting the cause of discharged battery.

(3) Check if battery is damaged.

4. CLUTCH AND TRANSMISSION SYSTEM

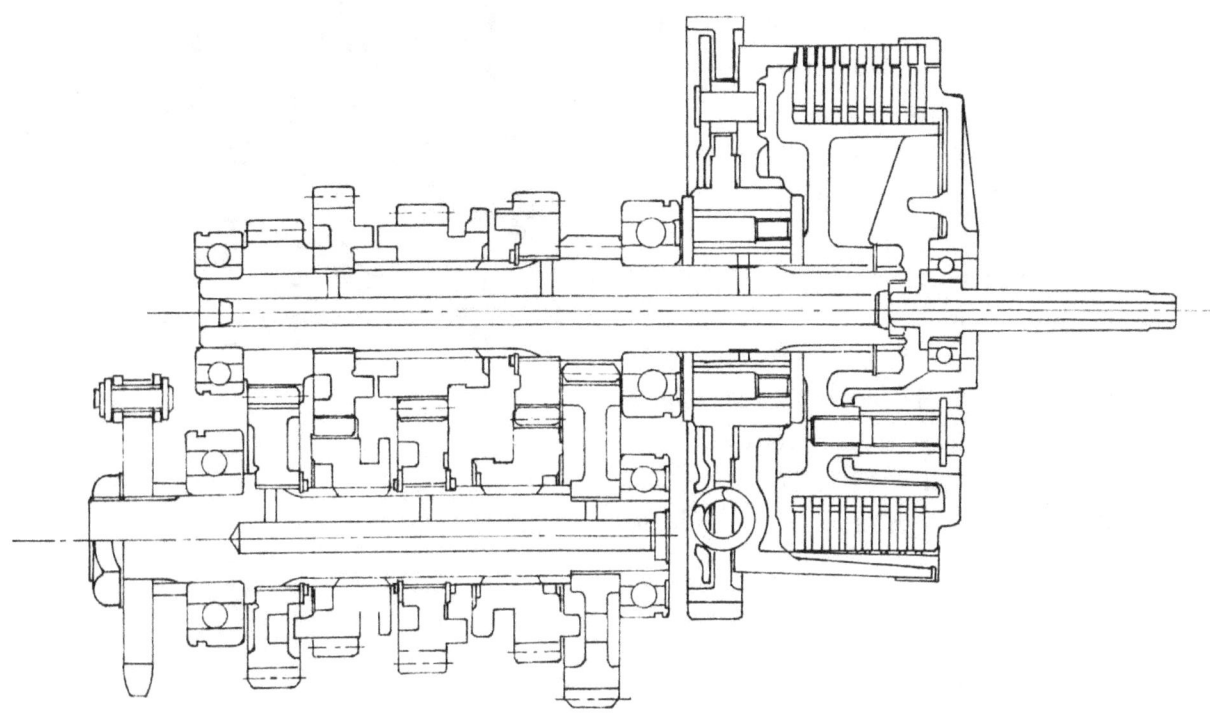

1. CLUTCH SYSTEM

As possible sources for troubles, the following two items are considered.

A. Clutch disc wear and slippage thereby

B. Unusual noise from clutch

If these occur, servicing should be provided according to the following procedures.

A. **In the case of clutch disc excessive wearing at early stage and slippage**

(1) Remove oil level screw from clutch cover and check if transmission oil level is as specified. Standard transmission oil capacity is 2500 cc (0.66/0.54 gal US/Imp.).
Use SAE 20W/40 oil of superior quality.

Caution: 2200 cc of transmission oil is indicated on the clutch cover to be required. This is because that transmission chamber of this engine is so large and devided with so many walls that the transmission oil may not come out of drain hole in a short time and may remain about 200–300 cc in it when draining the oil. Therefore, pour 2200 cc (0.58/0.48 gal US/Imp.) of transmission oil when exchanging it so that the total amount will be in the vicinity of 2500 cc, whereas the total 2500 cc of new oil is required when over-hauling the engine.

(2) Check if clutch adjustment is properly made and adjust if needed.

– Adjusting Clutch –

Clutch adjustment is made in two stages, i.e. adjustment of a play in clutch cable and that of clutch release mechanism.

Firstly, after loosening clutch cable adjuster on the clutch cover with sufficient play between cable and the adjuster, check the amount of a longitudinal play of clutch release shaft. If the play is too large, loosen release shaft adjusting nut to make the play in the vicinity of 0.5 mm (0.018 in), then fix by tightening the double nuts. Secondly, adjust clutch cable adjuster on the clutch lever to allow for a play of 3–4 mm (0.12–0.16 in) at the bottom of clutch lever.

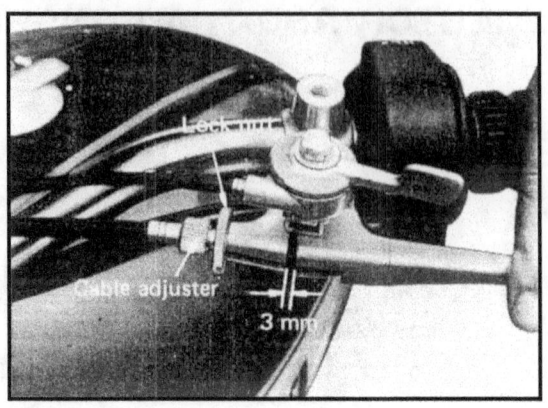

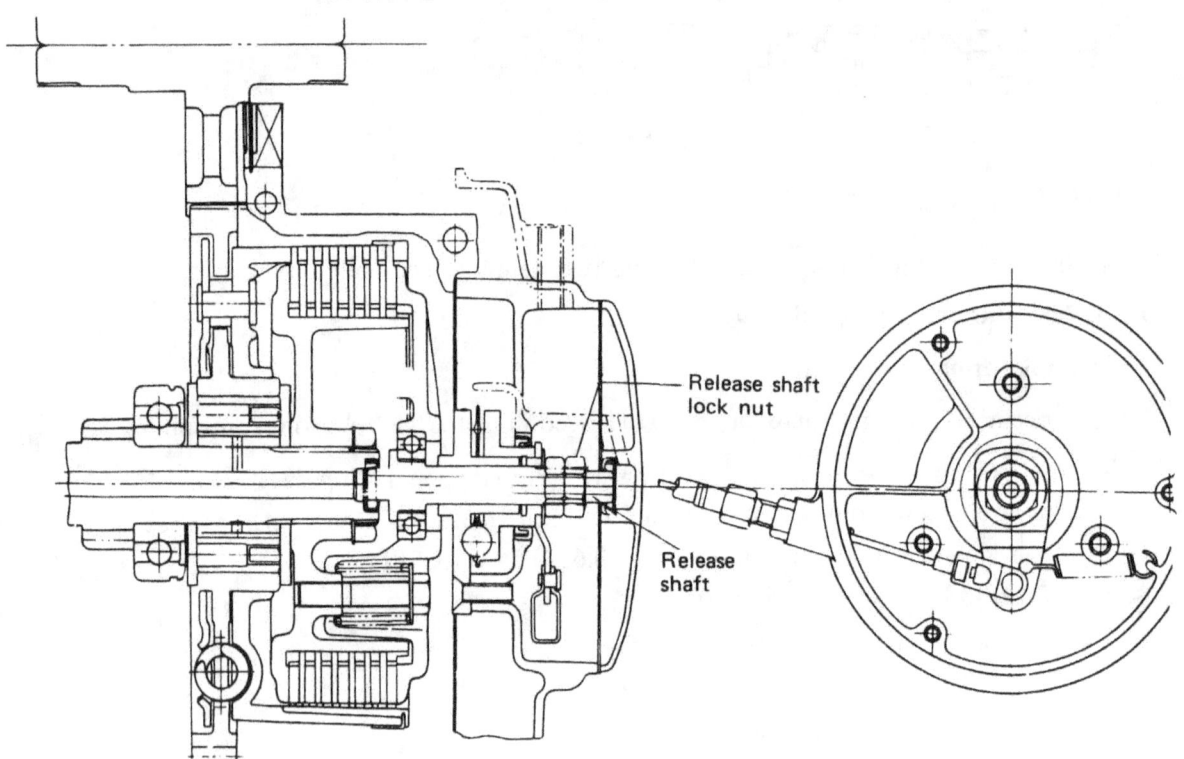

When demounting the clutch remove sleeve hub nut using clutch sleeve hub holder (special tool 09926–53110). Subsequent to the removal of clutch plates, take off sleeve hub and primary driven gear spacer and bushing by drawing, then remove the primary driven gear by drawing it backward.

B. **In the case of unusual noise from clutch**

(1) In case the noise from the engine does not decrease even though the clutch is disengaged by operating clutch lever, it is likely that the clutch is generating the noise. In that case, demount the clutch and check whether a proper play exists or whether an abnormal wear of a primary gear or excessive backlash is observed.

(2) If the noise dies away, the noise is from the transmission so check the gears.

2. TRANSMISSION SYSTEM

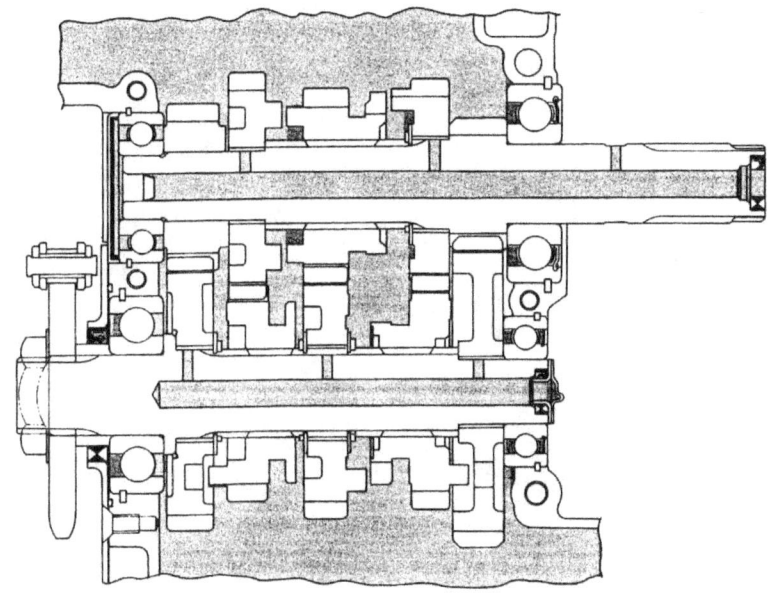

Transmission system of GT750 is of a similar type to TS125 and TS185. At an overhaul and assembly, the following two points should be kept in mind and be observed.

(1) Since the second drive gear is assembled by press-fit, apply Suzuki Lock Super 103Q (available as spare part) inner surface of gear before assembly.
The press fit should be made so as to have 109.4–109.5 mm (4.307–4.311 in) from low gear end to the end of second drive gear.

(2) Removal of a second drive gear from the countershaft is allowable only twice. At the third removal, replace with a new counter-shaft assembly.

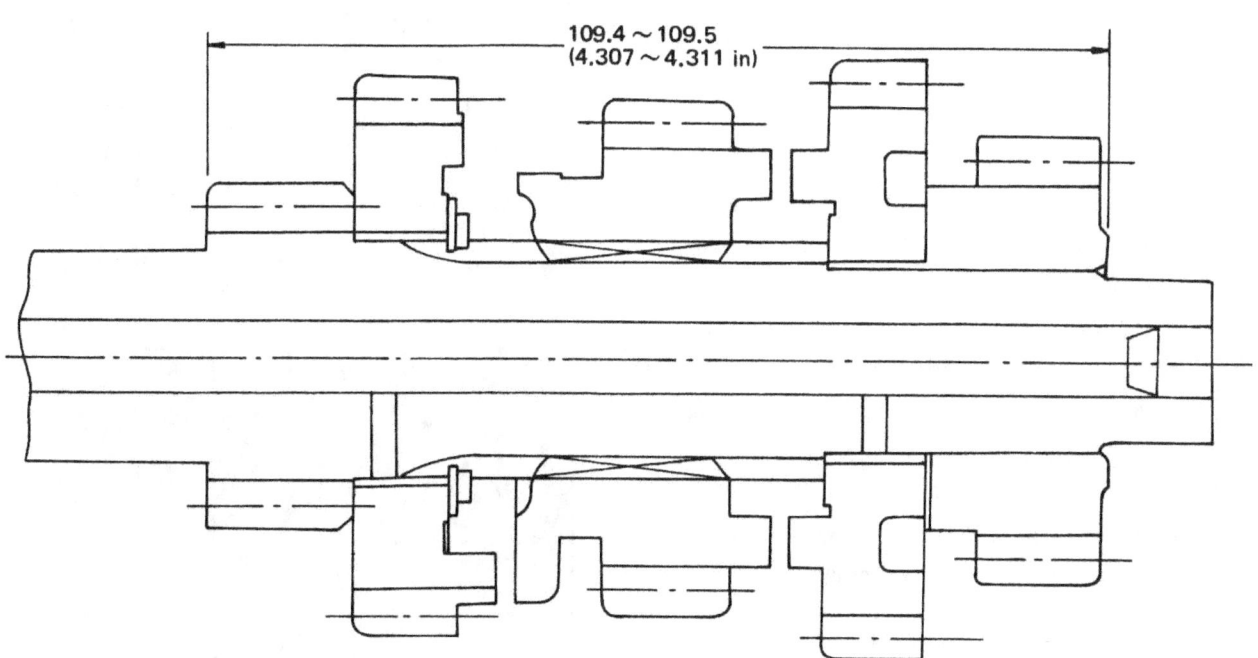

5. LUBRICATION SYSTEM

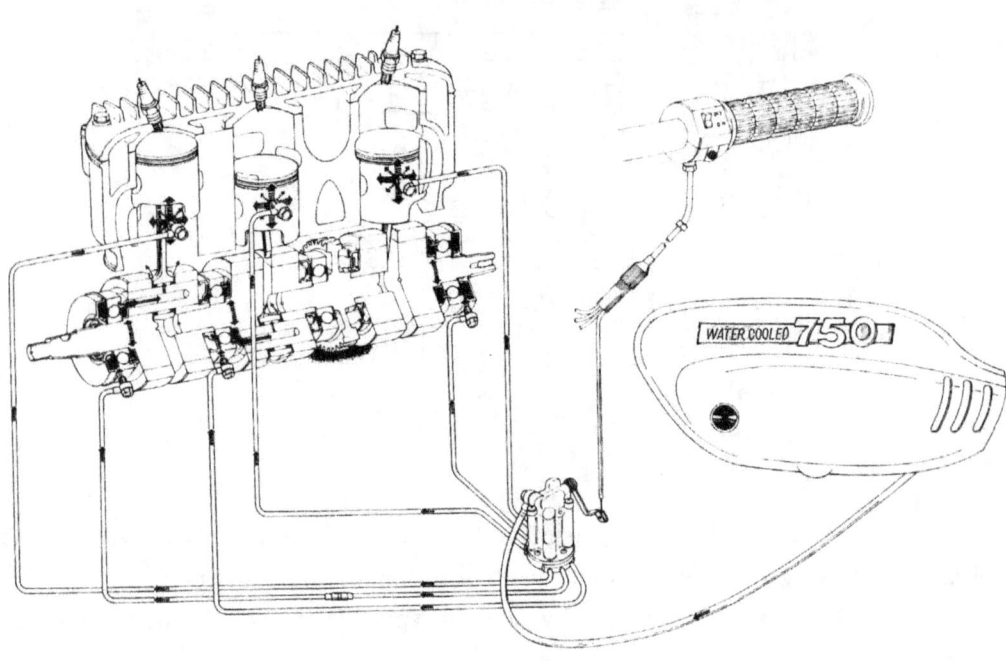

Lubrication system of GT750 is of a type separately lubricating each cylinder and crankshaft with a six-outlet oil pump.

Servicing must be made according to the procedures described below.

A. Adjusting oil pump

Remove aligning hole plug on the carburetar mixing chamber body, then adjust oil pump by turning cable adjuster so that a score on the oil pump lever aligns with the marking on the body when an aligning mark on the side of throttle valve comes on upper end of the hole as the throttle grip gradually winds up.

The oil pump is of non-overhaul type similar to previous ones and once disassembled it will be excluded from warranty items.

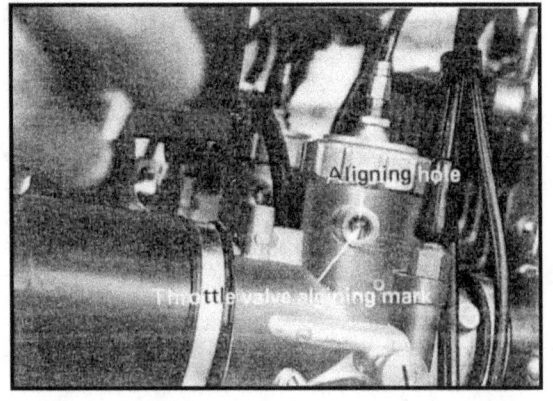

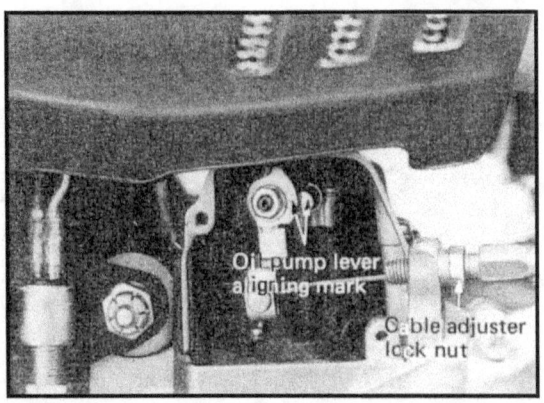

B. **Expelling Air**

Confirm that no air is locked in the pipe. Drive it off from the pipe if it exists.

C. **Arrangement of Oil Pipes**

The arrangement of oil pipes from crankcase to cylinder is as shown in the figure. Make sure to have correct piping.

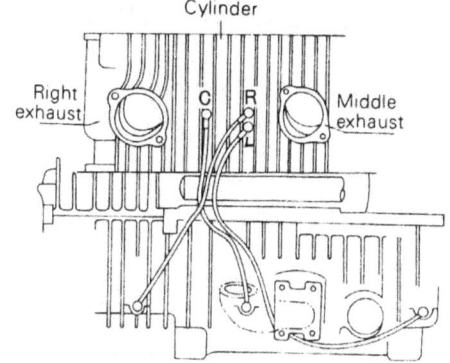

6. ELECTRICAL SYSTEM

1. ENGINE ELECTRICAL SYSTEM

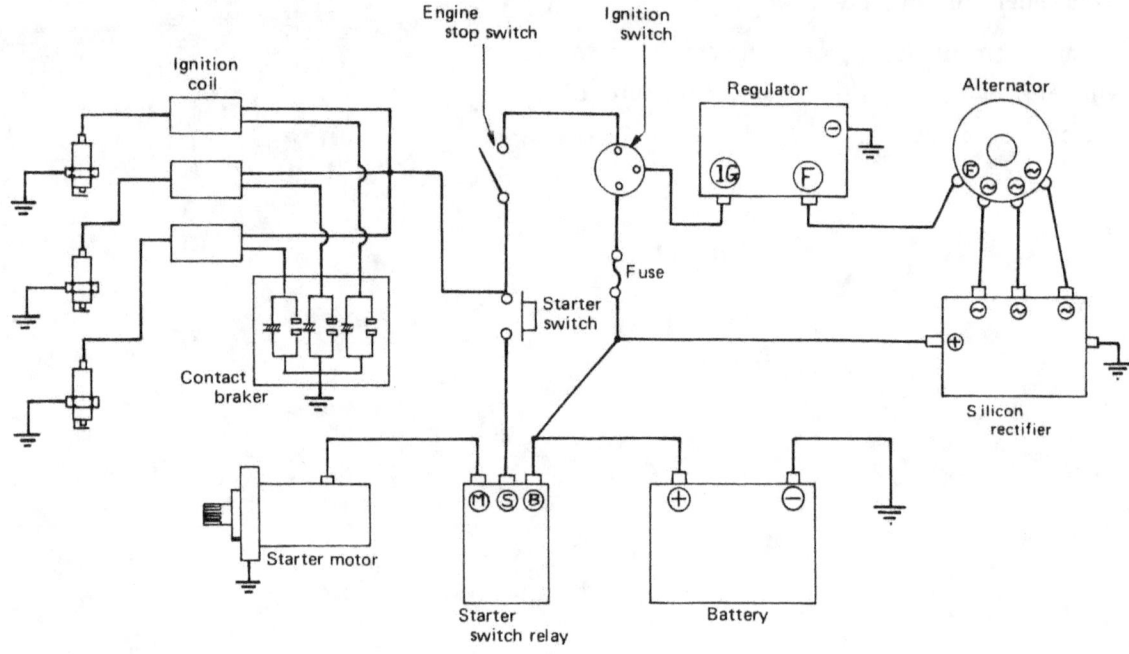

The wiring diagram of an engine electrical system is shown above.

The following are simple check and adjustment procedures. Please consult Service Manual for other servicings for electrical system.

A. **Starting system**

Examine in the following manner if something is wrong with the starting system.

− Checking starting motor −

(1) When the starting motor is not functioning, check before everything, terminals of the starting motor relay and battery for poor contact.

(2) In case all terminals are properly connected with fair contact, check whether the starting motor relay clicks by pressing starter button.

If it does click but the starting motor is inoperative, remove cylinders and take off the starting motor from crankcase for overhauling. Check degree of wear of brushes and commutator and replace the brush if its length is less than 10 mm (0.39 in). Also check the commutator for short circuit or ground.

(3) Starting motor relay rarely fails, but in case no trouble is detected through foregoing checks, examine contact points with the cap removed from the starting motor relay. This relay clicks when starter button is pressed to "ON". However, even if a click is heard, the one with burnt contact points does not allow large current to flow and thereby causes hard starting.

(4) Engine stop switch is furnished for the purpose of turning off the engine in emergencies such as overturning or other accidents. As shown in the wiring diagram, the starting motor is not actuated while the engine stop switch is off.

B. **Charging system**

GT750 will scarcely experience an excessive discharge of battery under normal conditions since it is equipped with an alternator.
If anything unusual occurs, check the silicon rectifier and voltage regulator, according to the following procedure.

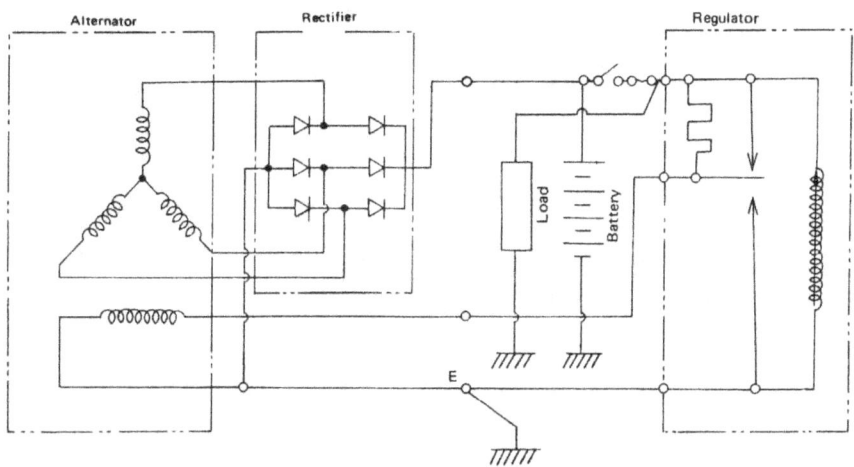

— Checking alternator —

(1) To demount the alternator, loosen the brush holder screws first while firmly pressing brush holder and then remove or otherwise the brush would spring up and the wire comes off.

(2) Pull out rotor with rotor remover (special tool No. 09930–33110)

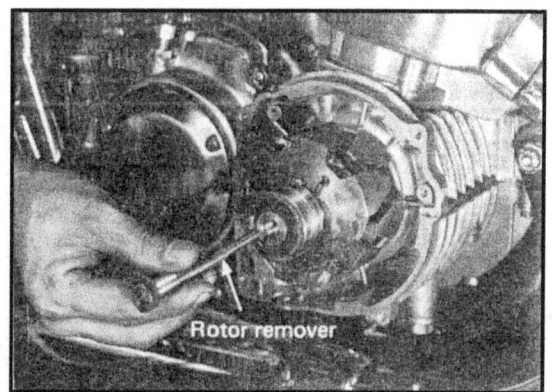

(3) Check stator coil for insulation

If there is conduction between each of lead wires of stator coil and stator core, the stator coil is judged defective. If the conduction between each pair of lead wires does not exist, the coil has a open circuit and needs to be replaced.

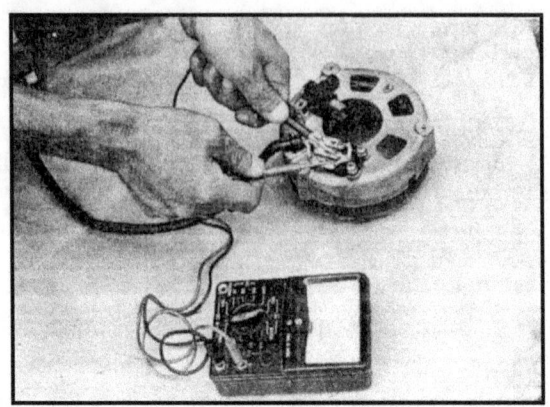

(4) Examine rotor coil for open circuit or ground.

An open circuit is tested by checking the conduction between each slip ring. The existence of conduction in this case means no open circuit.

Ground test is to check the conduction between the slip ring and the rotor core. The existence of conduction means a necessity for replacing the rotor.

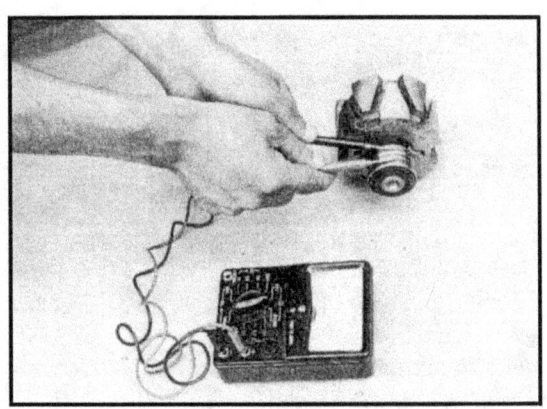

C. **Silicon rectifier**

– Inspecting silicon rectifier –

Wiring is shown in the figure. Measure the resistance between each terminal. If the silicon rectifier is in good condition, less resistance is measured in the normal direction (for example, Yellow → Red) and no current flows in the inverse direction.

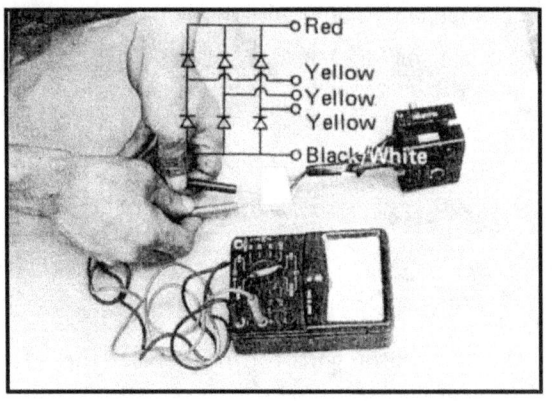

normal direction (current flows)

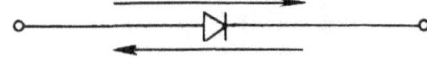

inverse direction (current doesn't flow)

D. **Voltage regulator**

Measure the resistance between "IG" and "F" terminals.

The resistance should be none.

Then, connect the voltmeter between "B" and "E" terminals and check if the voltage is within 13.5 to 14.5 volts at about 3,000 rpm.

Be sure to use a fully charged battery on this test.

2. BODY ELECTRICAL SYSTEM

A. Electric cooling fan

Cooling fan starts to operate when the thermometer points to a white line (105°C) just before the red zone. If inoperative at this temperature, check it in the following manner.

— Inspecting cooling fan —

Remove the brown wire from thermo switch attached to the thermostat case of the cylinder head. Cooling fan is OK if it operates by doing so with an ignition switch on. If it does not, the fan or the thermo switch relay is defective. Further, if the fan operates by connecting it to the battery, the thermo switch relay is defective and needs to be replaced.

B. Battery

In mounting the battery on the frame after charging it, or when a new battery is installed, never fail to clamp the battery breather pipe on the correct position on the frame, with the breather pipe clamps (A) and (B) located each frame cross member as illustrated below.

If the breather pipe is mistakenly clamped near the drive chain, the battery solution (sulphuric acid) will splash on the drive chain from the end of the pipe. It will crack the chain link plates in a short time due to chemical reaction, and may cause a serious accident.

Caution: (1) Replace the drive chain with new one immediately if the drive chain gets wet with the battery solution when repairing or charging it.

(2) When using the new battery, be sure to cut the end of the breather pipe.

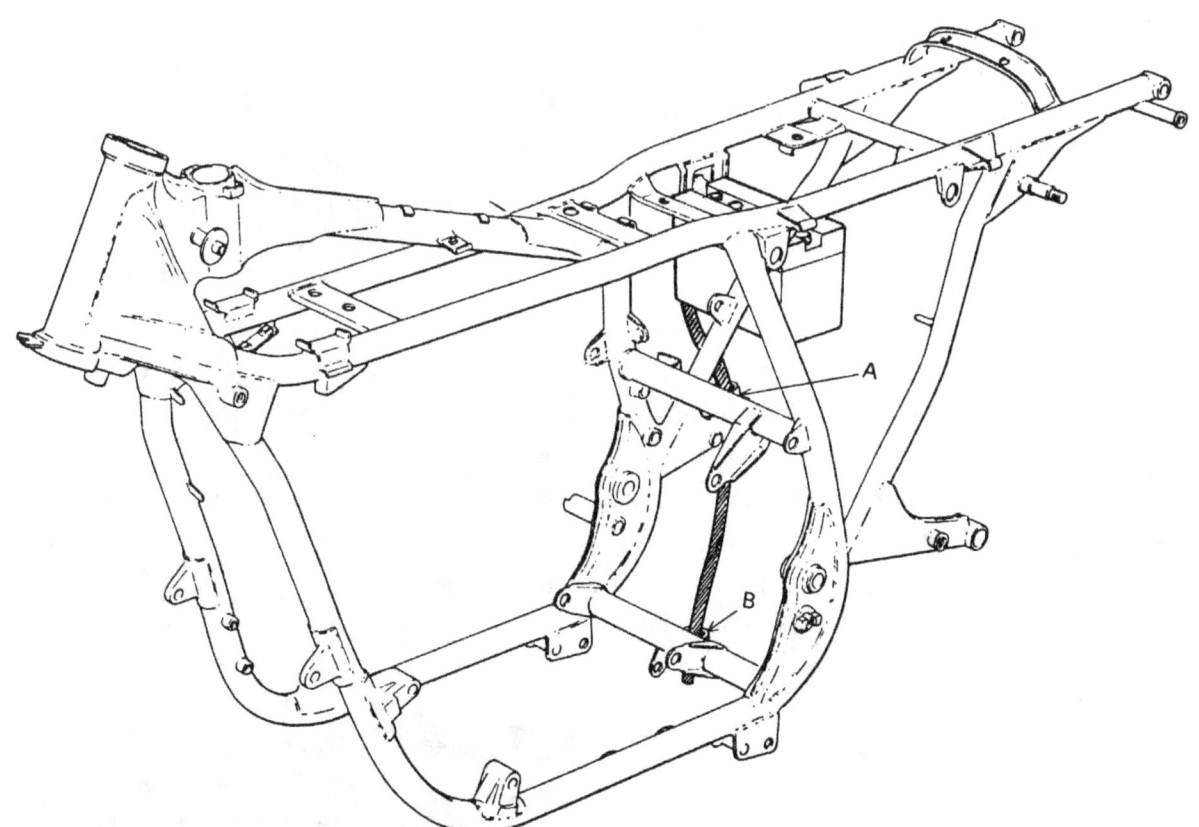

※ Other electrical equipments are of the same type as previous models.

7. BODY

1. FRONT FORK

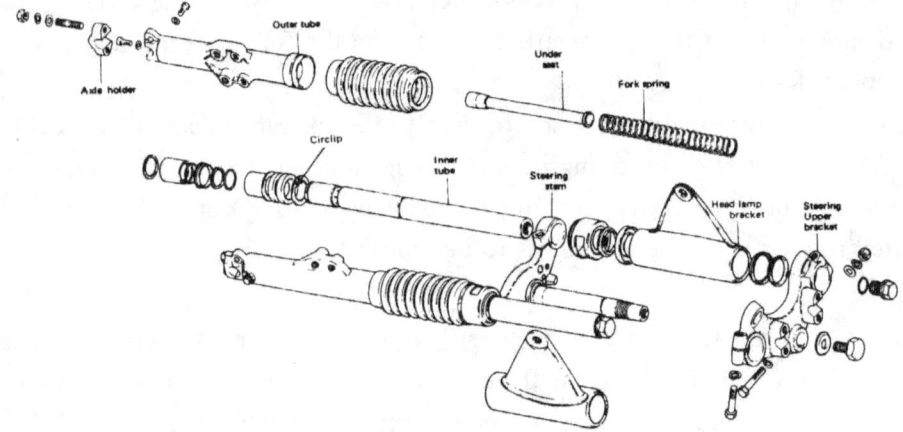

The following procedure should be followed at overhauling and repair.
(1) Remove the front axle by loosening the axle holder at the bottom part of a fork outer tube first.
(2) After pulling out an inner circlip as shown in the Figure using circlip remover (special tool No. 09900–06103), an outer tube is removable by pulling the outer tube downward while the inner tube staying at body side.
(3) Feed 250 cc (0.53/0.44 pt. US/Imp) of motor oil 10W/30 to each front fork leg after assembly.

2. BRAKE

A. Front brake uses a large-sized double panel 4 leading shoe type with a drum of 200 mm (0.8 in) dia. A specified performance can not be expected if the adjustment is incorrect. Properly adjust brakes without failure since it greatly affects the safety.

 — Adjusting front brake —
(1) Slacken brake cable by cable adjustor "A", then loosen the connecting rod nut "B".
(2) Press the cam shaft 1st lever "C" in the arrowed direction, turn connecting rod until the 2nd lever "D" can not move, then tighten to fix. If the second lever can still be moved to the right direction, adjustment is not made properly.
(3) After having both right and left sides adjusted in the same manner, turn the adjusters of the brake lever at handle bar and adjuster "A" to allow for an adequate play as well as to set the equalizer on the brake lever perpendicular to the lever even when the brake is operating.

B. **Rear brake is of the same type as previous models**

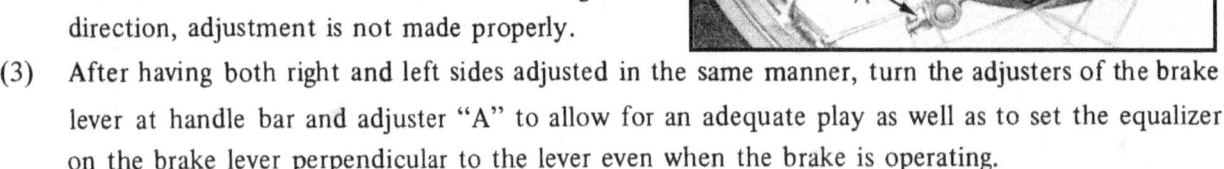

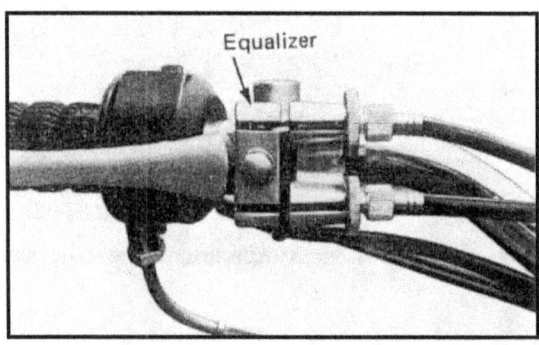

3. DRIVE CHAIN

GT750 adopts a flaring type of joint for the drive chain from the strength point of view. Therefore, chain joint tool (special tool No. 09900-21802) must be used either to cut or joint the chain. The drive chain assembly and chain joint are available as replacement parts. Please note that new joint is definitely required once the chain is cut and never cut the same place twice.

Follow the instruction given with the tool when using chain joint tool

Proper lubrication and adjustment of the drive chain prolong its service life and ensure smooth power transmission to the rear wheel. Poor maintenance will cause rapid wear or damage to the drive chain. Therefore, the drive chain must be checked and serviced after the first 800 km (500 miles) of operation and every 800 km (500 miles) thereafter, and lubrication is indespensable before the motorcycle is operated at sustained high speeds, or under conditions of frequent rapid acceleration.

— Inspecting and adjusting drive chain —

* Place the motorcycle on its center stand with transmission in neutral. Check the drive chain and sprockets for any of the following conditions:

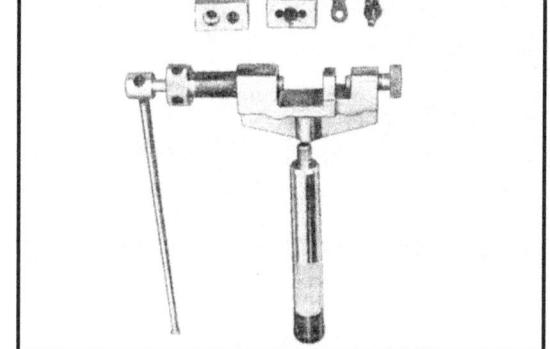

Drive chain	Sprockets
○ Damaged Rollers	○ Excessively Worn Teeth
○ Loose Pins	○ Broken or Damaged Teeth
○ Dry or Rusted Links	○ Loose sprockets nuts
○ Kinked or Binding Links	
○ Excessive Wear	
○ Improper Adjustment	

* Measure the distance between a span of 20 pins, from pin center to pin center, with the chain held taut and any stiff joints straightened in order to determine if the chain is worn beyond its service limit. The distance of the new drive chain is 301.7 mm (11 7/8"), and if the distance exceeds 308.0 mm (12 1/8"), the chain is worn and must be replaced.

301.7 mm (11 7/8 in)

* Check drive chain slack at the middle of the two sprockets by moving the chain up and down with fingers. Adjust the chain slack to 15–20 mm (0.6–0.8 in).

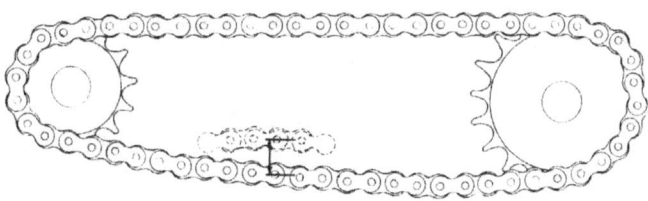

15–20 mm (0.6–0.8 in)

8. SERVICE DATA

Items to be checked	Data
Engine	
Cylinder head	
tightening torque 8 mm stud bolt	180 ~ 220 kg·cm
10 mm stud bolt	300 ~ 400 kg·cm
warpage	limit : 0.04 mm (0.001 in)
Cylinder bore	
diameter	standard 70.000 ~ 70.015 mm (2.7559 ~ 2.7564 in)
out-of-round	limit 0.05 mm (0.002 in)
taper wear	limit 0.05 mm (0.002 in)
Piston diameter	standard 69.950 ~ 69.965 mm (2.7539 ~ 2.7545 in)
	over size (0.5) 70.450 ~ 70.465 mm (2.7736 ~ 2.7742 in)
	over size (1.0) 70.950 ~ 70.965 mm (2.7793 ~ 2.7939 in)
Piston ring	
end gap	standard 0.15 ~ 0.35 mm (0.006 ~ 0.014 in)
side clearance	standard 0.030 ~ 0.095 mm (0.0012 ~ 0.0037 in)
Crankshaft	
bend	limit 0.05 mm (0.002 in)
connecting rod axial movement at small end	limit 3 mm (0.118 in)
Oil pump	
delevery amount of oil	4.8 ~ 6.7 cc in 2 min. at crankshaft 2,000 ± 100 rpm with control lever fully opened
VM 32 SC carburetor setting	MJ #102.5 (R & L) #100 (M), JN 5F16-3 NJ P-4 (R & L) P-3 (M), PJ #30, AS 1½
Compression	
pressure	7.5 kg/cm² (106.3 lb/in²) at 300 rpm
corrected ratio	6.7 : 1
Electrical equipment	
Spark plug	NGK B-7ES or ND W22ES
Ignition timing	
angle	standard $24°^{+2}_{-2}$ B.T.D.C.
piston distance before T.D.C.	3.64 mm (0.143 in) for R & L cylinders
	3.42 mm (0.136 in) for M cylinder
Condenser capacity	standard 0.22 μF ± 10%
Battery	type 12N 14-3A, 12V 14Ah
Alternator out-put	280W
Voltage regulator	regulated voltage 13.5 ~ 14.5V at 3,000 rpm

Items to be checked	Data	
Suspension & Tire		
Tire		
front size	specified size 3.25–19" 4PR	
rear size	specified size 4.00–18" 4PR	
pressure	normal riding	continuous high speed riding
front	1.6 kg/cm^2 (22.7 lb/in^2)	1.8 kg/cm^2 (25.6 lb/in^2)
rear solo riding	1.8 kg/cm^2 (25.6 lb/in^2)	2.0 kg/cm^2 (25.6 lb/in^2)
dual riding	2.0 kg/cm^2 (25.6 lb/in^2)	2.0 kg/cm^2 (25.6 lb/in^2)
replacement	when remaining depth of tread become less than 1.6 mm (0.063 in) for front, 2.0 mm (0.079 in) for rear tires.	
Wheel rim		
face-run-out	limit 3 mm (0.12 in)	
Front fork		
oil amount	250 cc (0.528/0.440 pt, US/Imp) for each leg	
oil quality	10W/30 motor oil	
Brake system		
front brake adjustment	20 ~ 30 mm (0.79 ~ 1.8 in) of distance between brake lever and throttle grip when brake acts.	
Rear brake adjustment	20 ~ 30 mm (0.79 ~ 1.18 in) of play at the end of brake pedal	

PERIODICAL INSPECTION CHART

The chart below indicates time when inspections, adjustments and maintenance are required based on the distance the motorcycle runs, that is first 1,000 km (750 mi), and every 3,000 km (2,000 mi), 6,000 km (4,000 mi) and 12,000 km (8,000 mi) thereafter. According to the chart, advise users to make the motorcycle checked and serviced at your shop. See the appropriate section for instructions on making the inspection.

Service \ Mi / Km	750 Mi / 1,000 Km	Every 2,000 Mi / Every 3,000 Km	Every 4,000 Mi / Every 6,000 Km	Every 8,000 Mi / Every 12,000 Km
Oil Pump	Check operation, adjust control lever adjusting marks	Check operation, adjust control lever adjusting marks		
Spark Plug	Clean	Clean and adjust gap	Replace	
Gearbox Oil	Change	Change		
Throttle, Brake Clutch and Oil Pump Cables	Adjust play	Adjust play	Lubricate	
Carburetor	Adjust with throttle valve screw and pilot air screw	Adjust with throttle valve screw and pilot air screw		Overhaul and clean
Contact Point Breaker Ass'y	Check contact point gap and ignition timing.	Check contact point gap and ignition timing. Lubricate contact breaker cam oil felt.		Replace contact point
Cylinder Head and Cylinder	Retighten cylinder head nut	Retighten cylinder head nut		
Battery	Check and service electrolyte solution	Check and service electrolyte solution		
Fuel Cock	Clean fuel strainer		Clean fuel strainer	
Drive Chain	Wash, then adjust and lubricate	Wash, then adjust and lubricate	Wash, then adjust and lubricate	
Brakes	Adjust play	Adjust play		
Air cleaner		Clean		
Throttle Grip			Grease	
Clutch	Adjust	Adjust		
Steering stem	Check play, re-tighten stem nuts		Check play, re-tighten stem nuts	
Muffler		Remove carbon		
Tire		Check the tire tread condition		
Bolts and Nuts	Retighten	Retighten		

NOTICE

This manual originally included 5 additional pages after the 'PERIODICAL INSPECTION' page.

Those 5 pages consisted of 2 wiring diagrams, 2 technical drawings plus an exploded view of the engine/gearbox assembly.

However, as these pages are identical to those found to the rear of the 'SERVICE MANUAL' they have been omitted as they represent unnecessary duplication.

SUZUKI MOTOR CO., LTD.

SUZUKI SERVICE MANUAL

MODEL

GT750
DISC BRAKE

FOREWORD

The purpose of this service manual is to provide a detailed description on the construction, operating principles, and adjusting and operating methods of the hydraulic disc brakes which have been recently adopted to Models GT125, GT185, GT250, GT380, GT550 and GT750.

To ensure a safe operation of these models capable of high-speed performance, an adequate maintenance of the brakes is vital. This manual is presented in the simplest possible manner so that the materials included are easily comprehensive to you. We hope that correct maintenance of these disc brakes will be facilitated most effectively by utilization of this manual.

Because this manual has been compiled on the models of the motorcycles available as of December, 1973, it is possible that the contents of this manual may not necessarily correspond to the motorcycles delivered to you due to possible changes of their specifications.

International Service Department

$ SUZUKI MOTOR CO ,LTD

December, 1973

FEATURES OF DISC BRAKE

Compared with the conventional drum-type brakes, the hydraulic disc brake has the following features:

- *Heat radiation from the friction surfaces is quite effective since the discs rotate in direct contact with the air. Therefore, stable brake power can always be provided, even if the disc brake is used repeatedly at high speeds.*

- *A brake lever stroke remains always constant since none of the disc brake parts is subjected to any deformation due to elevated temperatures.*

- *Replacement of pads is simple and no troublesome adjustment is required.*

- *Steady brake performance is ensured, since, even if the disc is wet during running in rainy weather or on muddy road, the restoring ability of brake power is excellent due to the extreme pressure characteristics for pushing pads.*

- *It has a smooth operation, since it has little portion to be mechanically abrased.*

INDEX

1. SPECIFICATION AND SERVICE DATA 4
2. TROUBLE SHOOTING 5
3. OUTLINE OF HYDRAULIC DISC BRAKE 6

   3-1 General 6
   3-2 Operation of Master Cylinder 7
   3-3 Operation of Caliper 8

4. INSPECTION AND REPAIR 9

   4-1 Brake Fluid and Its Handling 9
   4-2 Inspection and Replacing Method of Pads 10
   4-3 Master Cylinder, Brake Hose and Brake Pipe 13
   4-4 Caliper 19
   4-5 Brake Disc 22
   4-6 Periodic Replacement Parts 23

5. TIGHTENING TORQUE 24
6. SPECIAL TOOLS FOR DISC BRAKE 25

   6-1 Special Tools 25
   6-2 Necessary Materials 25

1. SPECIFICATION AND SERVICE DATA

Item	GT125 GT185 S.T.D. figure	GT125 GT185 Limit	GT250 GT380 S.T.D. figure	GT250 GT380 Limit	GT550 S.T.D. figure	GT550 Limit	GT750 S.T.D. figure	GT750 Limit
Disc thickness, front brake	5.00 mm (0.197 in.)	under 4.00 mm (0.157 in.)	7.00 mm (0.276 in.)	under 6.00 mm (0.236 in.)	7.00 mm (0.276 in.)	under 6.00 mm (0.236 in.)	7.00 mm (0.276 in.)	under 6.00 mm (0.236 in.)
Disc runout front brake	max. 0.1 mm (0.004 in.)	over 0.3 mm (0.012 in.)	max. 0.1 mm (0.004 in.)	over 0.3 mm (0.012 in.)	max. 0.1 mm (0.004 in.)	over 0.3 mm (0.012 in.)	max. 0.1 mm (0.004 in.)	over 0.3 mm (0.012 in.)
Outer diameter brake disc	250 mm (9.843 in.)		275 mm (10.827 in.)		295 mm (11.614 in.)		295 mm (11.614 in.)	
Inner diameter, master cylinder	14.00 to 14.04 mm (0.551 to 0.553 in.)	over 14.05 mm (0.553 in.)	14.00 to 14.04 mm (0.551 to 0.553 in.)	over 14.05 mm (0.553 in.)	14.00 to 14.04 mm (0.551 to 0.553 in.)	over 14.05 mm (0.553 in.)	15.87 to 15.91 mm (0.625 to 0.626 in.)	over 15.92 mm (0.627 in.)
Piston diameter, master cylinder	13.96 to 13.98 mm (0.550 to 0.551 in.)	under 13.94 mm (0.549 in.)	13.96 to 13.98 mm (0.550 to 0.551 in.)	under 13.94 mm (0.549 in.)	13.96 to 13.98 mm (0.550 to 0.551 in.)	under 13.94 mm (0.549 in.)	15.83 to 15.85 mm (0.623 to 0.624 in.)	under 15.81 mm (0.622 in.)
Inner diameter caliper cylinder	38.18 to 38.20 mm (1.503 to 1.504 in.)	over 38.22 mm (1.504 in.)	38.18 to 38.20 mm (1.503 to 1.504 in.)	over 38.22 mm (1.504 in.)	38.18 to 38.20 mm (1.503 to 1.504 in.)	over 38.22 mm (1.504 in.)	38.18 to 38.20 mm (1.503 to 1.504 in.)	over 38.22 mm (1.504 in.)
Piston diameter caliper cylinder	38.15 to 38.18 mm (1.502 to 1.503 in.)	under 38.10 mm (1.500 in.)	38.15 to 38.18 mm (1.502 to 1.503 in.)	under 38.10 mm (1.500 in.)	38.15 to 38.18 mm (1.502 to 1.503 in.)	under 38.10 mm (1.500 in.)	38.15 to 38.18 mm (1.502 to 1.503 in.)	under 38.10 mm (1.500 in.)
Effective diameter, front brake disc	199 mm (7.835 in.)		224 mm (8.819 in.)		244 mm (9.606 in.)		244 mm (9.606 in.)	
Effective brake lining area	19cm² × 2 pcs. (2.95 in² × 2 pcs.)		19cm² × 2 pcs. (2.95 in² × 2 pcs.)		19cm² × 2 pcs. (2.95 in² × 2 pcs.)		19cm² × 4 pcs. (2.95 in² × 4 pcs.)	
Type, front brake	Right-hand, hydraulic, single disc brake						Right-hand, hydraulic, double disc brake	
Type, caliper	Floating caliper, single cylinder							

2. TROUBLE SHOOTING

Symptom and possible cause	Countermeasure
1. Insufficient brake power	
1) Leakage of brake fluid from hydraulic system	Repair or replace
2) Worn pads	Replace
3) Oil adhesion on engaged surface of pads	Clean disc and pads
4) Worn disc	Replace
5) Instruded air in hydraulic system	Bleed air
2. Brake squeaking	
1) Carbon adhesion on pad surface	Repair surface with sandpaper
2) Tilted pad	Modify pad fitting
3) Damaged wheel bearing	Replace
4) Loosened front-wheel axle	Tighten with regular torque
5) Worn pads	Replace
6) Intruded foreign substance into brake fluid	Replace brake fluid
7) Clogged return port of master cylinder	Disassemble and clean master cylinder
3. Excessive brake lever stroke	
1) Intruded air into hydraulic system	Bleed air
2) Worn brake lever cam	Replace brake lever
3) Insufficient brake fluid	Replenish fluid to normal level; bleed air
4) Improper quality of brake fluid	Replace by proper one
4. Leakage of brake fluid	
1) Insufficient tightening of connection joints	Tighten with regular torque
2) Cracked pipe	Replace
3) Worn piston and/or cup	Replace piston and/or cup

3. OUTLINE OF HYDRAULIC DISC BRAKE

3-1 General

The hydraulic disc brake adopted in Suzuki's models GT125, GT185, GT250, GT380, GT550 and GT750 consists of four main portions, i.e., brake discs mounted on a front wheel hub, a master cylinder for pressurizing, a brake hose line for fluid pressure, and a caliper which presses pads to brake disc by means of hydraulic pressures.

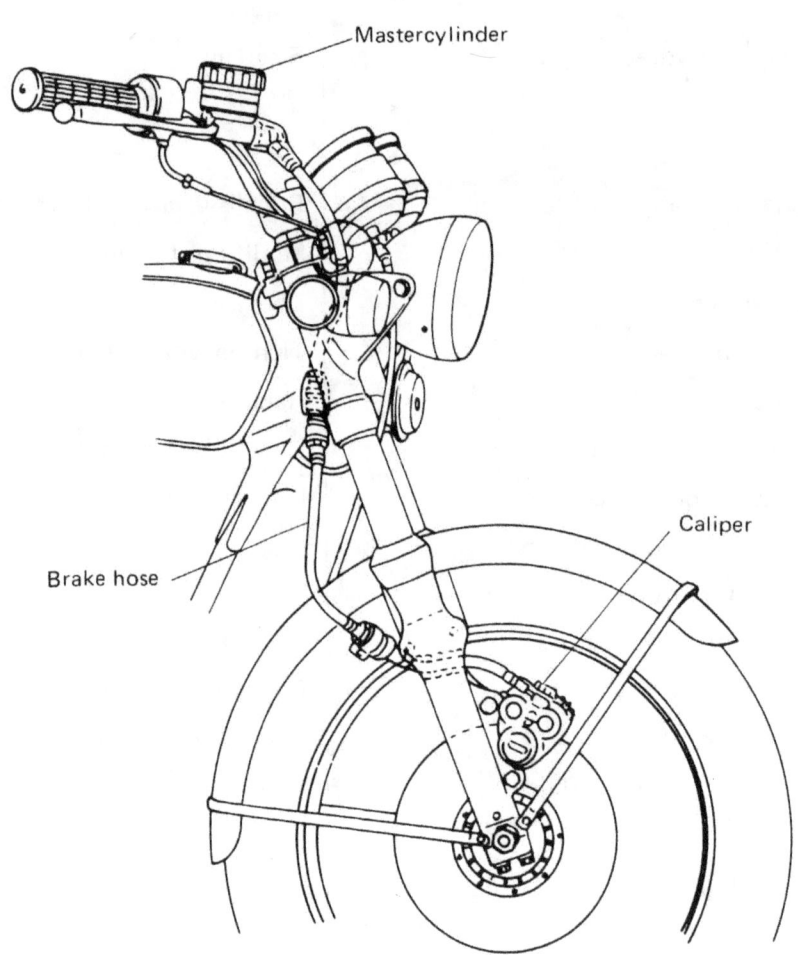

Fig. 3-1-1

3-2 Operation of Master Cylinder

3-2-1 Squeezing brake lever

The piston ③ is pushed in the direction of arrow by the brake cam ② when the brake lever is squeezed. The primary cup ④ also moves together with the piston and when it closes the return port ⑤ which is provided at the master cylinder body, brake fluid in front of the primary cup begins to be pressurized and delivered to the caliper by opening the check valve ⑥ with its pressure.

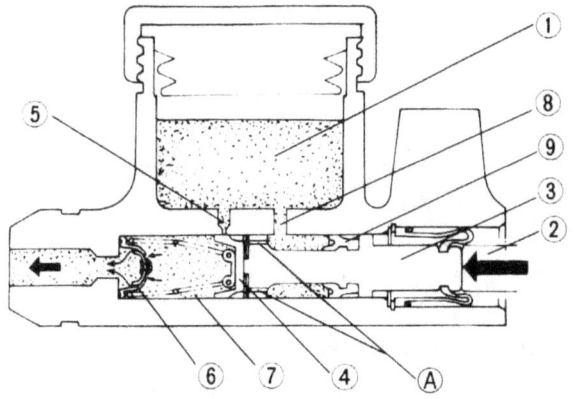

1 Reservoir	6 Check valve
2 Brake lever cam	7 Spring
3 Piston	8 Inlet port
4 Primary cup	9 Secondary cup
5 Return port	

Fig. 3-2-1

3-2-2 Releasing brake lever

As soon as the brake lever is released, the piston is pushed back by the spring ⑦. Because the brake fluid from the caliper may not return to the master cylinder immediately due to its flow resistance, hydraulic pressure inside the cylinder is reduced momentarily and fluid flows from the reservoir to the front section of the primary cup through the inlet port ⑧, three small holes Ⓐ on the piston flange and the circumference of the primary cup.

Then high pressure brake fluid from the caliper releases the check valve body from its contact with the outlet part allowing to have the clearance for a fluid passage. A small amount of the fluid returns from the caliper to the master cylinder through the clearance thus made by the movement of the check valve body.

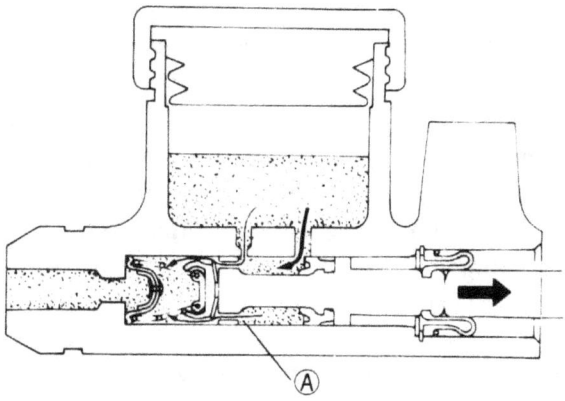

Fig. 3-2-2

3-2-3 After completing return stroke of brake lever

A large amount of the brake fluid having been delivered to the caliper returns to the reservoir through the clearance behind the check valve base and the return port on the master cylinder body.

As the brake fluid from the caliper returns to the reservoir, hydraulic pressure in the brake hose is reduced gradually and the spring tension surmounts the hydraulic pressure of the brake hose resulting in closing the clearance behind the check valve base. However, some fluid pressure still remains in the brake hose because of the initial tension of the spring. Brake fluid continues to flow into the reservoir through a small notch provided around the periphery of the check valve body and the return port. The master cylinder completes its operation when residual pressure in the brake hose vanishes completely.

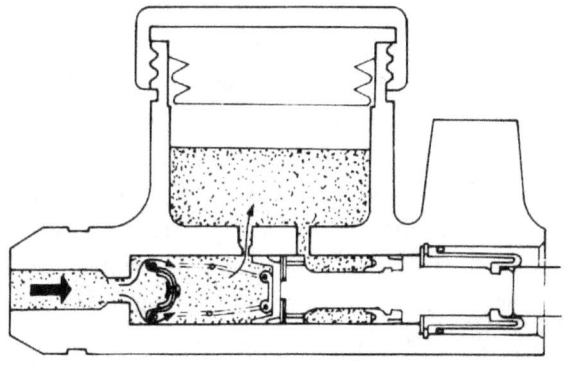

Fig. 3-2-3

3-3 Operation of Caliper

3-3-1 Squeezing brake lever

Brake fluid from the master cylinder delivered under pressure flows into the caliper cylinder through inlet portion Ⓐ of the caliper and pushes piston ① in the direction of arrow.

The pushed piston moves together with the pad No.1 (moving side) ② in this direction until it can not move any further forward due to the pad No.1 hitting brake disc ③.

As soon as the pad No.1 touches the brake disc so that the piston may not move any further, the caliper body floating on the caliper axle is pushed in reverse direction by the fluid pressure in the cylinder and moves in the right side direction as shown in Fig. 3-3-2.

Since the pad No.2 (stationary side) ④ is mounted to the caliper body, the disc is subjected to a powerful braking force with pads Nos.1 and 2 depressing the disc from opposite directions respectively.

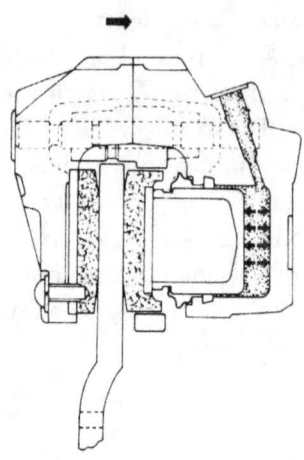

Fig. 3-3-2

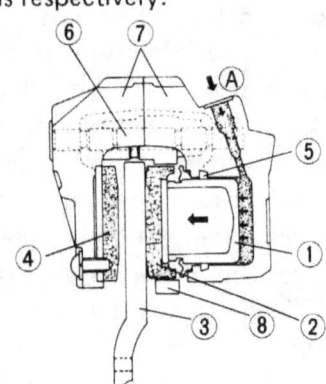

1 Piston	5 Piston seal
2 Pad No. 1	6 Caliper axle
3 Brake disc	7 Caliper body
4 Pad No. 2	8 Caliper holder

Fig. 3-3-1

3-3-2 Releasing brake lever

When the brake lever is released and fluid pressure in the caliper cylinder vanishes, the piston moves in the direction of arrow in Fig. 3-3-3, being pushed by piston seal ⑤ which was pressed onto the piston by fluid pressure and is now restoring its original shape with fluid pressure released. Therefore, the pads pressed to the disc part from the disc since the piston moves as much as the piston seal displacement, thus setting the brake disc free.

3-3-3 Self adjusting of clearance between pads and disc

If the traveling distance of piston exceeds the displacement of the piston seal, the piston is moved as far as the braking stroke while the piston slides between itself and the piston seal, whereas a return stroke of the piston due to the piston seal restoration after brake release is always constant and the returned position of the piston relatively varies with the wear of pads.

Consequently, clearance between the pads and the piston, or between the pads and the brake disc is always kept constant regardless of the condition of pad wear.

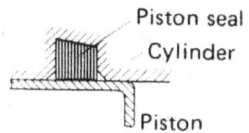

When brake lever is released

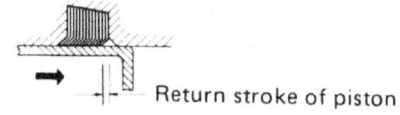

When brake lever is squeezed

Fig. 3-3-3

4. INSPECTION AND REPAIR

4-1 Brake Fluid and Its Handling

4-1-1 Inspecting brake fluid level

Be sure to check brake fluid level in the reservoir. In inspecting brake fluid, first mount your motorcycle firmly onto the center stand with its handlebar kept straight up without fail. If the level is found to be lower than the level mark ① provided on the reservoir, replenish the reservoir with one of the brake fluid graded below.

Spacification & Classification	Remarks
DOT 3	in U.S.A.
DOT 4	in U.S.A.
SAE J1703a	
SAE J1703b	
SAE J170c	
SAE 70R3	A classification in obsolete specification of SAE J70b.

Note: Since the brake system of these motorcycles is filled with a glycol base brake fluid by the manufacturer, do not use or mix different types of fluid such as silicone-based and petroleum-based fluid for refilling the system, otherwise damage sustained will be serious.

Do not use any brake fluid taken from old or used, or unsealed containers.

Do not squeeze the brake lever while the reservoir cap is removed, otherwise brake fluid will sometimes spout out. Do not put the removed reservoir cap on the speedometer or tachometer. Brake fluid will damage the paint surface and instrument gauge lenses.

Take due care especially so that water may not enter brake fluid on rainy day particularly during replacement or in handling a brake fluid container, because brake fluid has hygroscopic property, and its boiling point falls excessively if water is mixed with it.

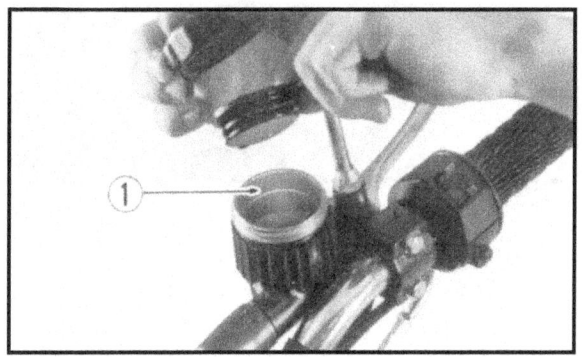

(All "K" models)   Fig. 4-1-1

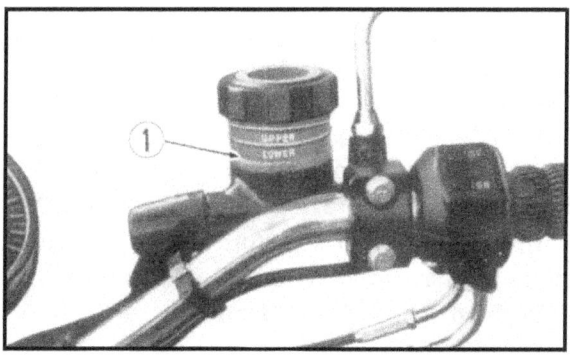

(All "L" models)   Fig. 4-1-2

4-1-2 Air bleeding from brake system

If the brake lever travel becomes excessive or the lever feels a soft or spongy feeling, you must carry out air bleeding from the brake system in the following procedure:

It is best if two persons perform this.

1) Attach the bleeder tube to the bleeder valve after removing the bleeder valve dust cap as shown in Fig. 4-1-3. A transparent tube is useful in finding air bubble expelled from the system.
2) The tube must be submerged in a clean container partially filled with brake fluid.
3) Fill the reservoir with the aforementioned brake fluid.

Note: Keep at least one half full of fluid in the reservoir during the bleeding procedure.

Fig. 4-1-3

4) Screw in the cap on the reservoir to prevent a spout of brake fluid and entry of dust.
5) Allow the pressure in the hydraulic system by squeezing rapidly the brake lever several times and then holding the lever tight.
6) Unscrew (open) the bleeder valve by one half turn and squeeze the lever all the way down. Do not release the lever until the bleeder valve is screwed in (closed) again.
7) Repeat steps 5) and 6) until air bubbles disappear in the bleeder tube or container and screw in (close) the bleeder valve securely.
8) Remove the tube and install the bleeder valve dust cap.
9) Check the fluid level in the reservoir and replenish if necessary, after the bleeding operation has been completed.
10) Reinstall the diaphragm and the diaphragm plate and tighten the reservoir cap securely.

Caution: Do not reuse the brake fluid drained from the system.

For model GT750, bleed air at first from the left-hand side caliper and then from the right according to the aforementioned procedure.

4-1-3 Changing brake fluid

Boiling point of brake fluid falls considerably with absorption of moisture which may take place during a long period of use. Therefore, it is recommended to exchange old brake fluid with new one periodically.

Exchange interval: One year

On changing brake fluid, extreme attention should be paid so as not to mix any foreign materials because they would block the return port of the master cylinder resulting in the brake dragging or squeaking.
When brake fluid is to be changed, perform the following procedure.
1) Attach a bleeder tube to the bleeder valve. Drain out old brake fluid by squeezing the brake lever with the bleeder valve opened until the brake fluid disappears in the bleeder tube.
2) After old brake fluid is drained out from the system completely, carry out the same procedure as described in "4-1-2 Air bleeding".

4-2 Inspection and Replacing Method of Pads

4-2-1 Inspection of pads

Check worn condition of the friction pads. If any of the friction pads is worn out up to the red limit line ① marked on its circumference, replace it following the procedure of "4-2-2" or "4-2-3".

Caution: Wash mud and dust off around the front wheel and/or caliper prior to the replacing operation.

Fig. 4-2-1

4-2-2 Replacing of pads for models GT125, GT185, GT250, GT380 or GT550

1) Set up the center stand and load at the rear portion to let the front wheel free.
2) Remove the front wheel assembly.
3) Unscrew the pad fastening screw, and take off pad No. 2 (stationary side).

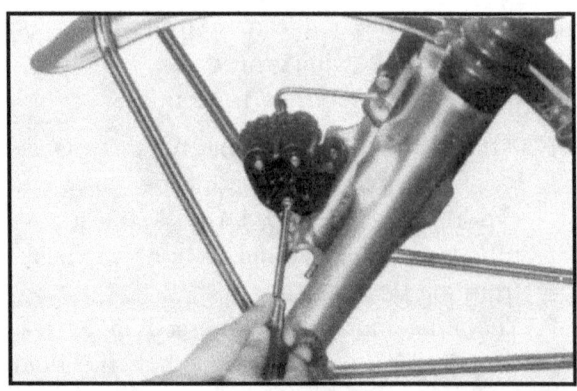

Fig. 4-2-2

4) Squeeze the brake lever two or three times gradually to force out pad No. 1 by fluid pressure while observing the motion of pad.

Fig. 4-2-3

5) Apply "Brake Pad Grease", which is provided as a component of Pad Set as shown in Fig. 4-2-4, onto the periphery and back plate of pad No. 1 as illustrated in Fig. 4-2-5 in a very thin layer.

Caution: *Do not use another grease.*
Apply grease thinly so as not to flow out, otherwise resulting in reduced brake performance.

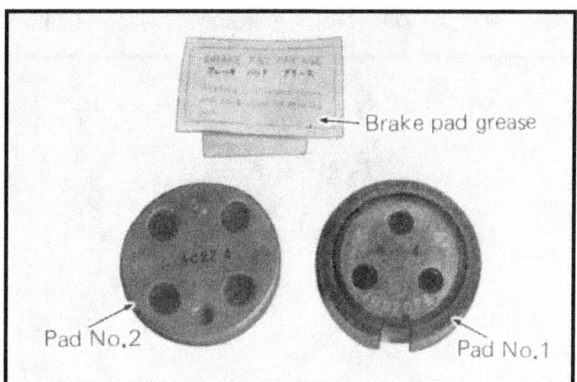

Fig. 4-2-4

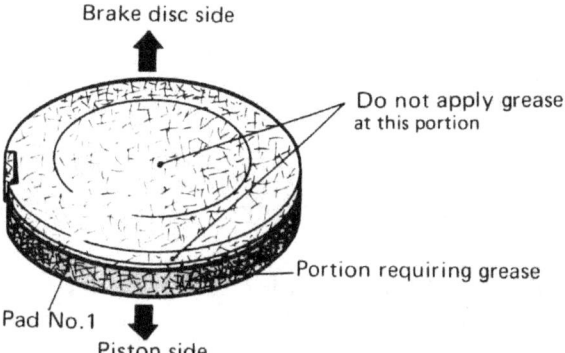

Fig. 4-2-5

Note: *The pad set supplied as a repair part is classified into three types according to the shape of Pad No. 1. The following table shows part numbers and the shapes of Pad No. 1. When replacing this part, refer to this table and be careful not to assemble erroneously.*

Shape of pad	Parts No.	Model to which pad is applicable
Flat	59100-36830	GT125L, GT185L
Indentification mark "A" Depth 1.5mm (0.06 in.)	59100-18840	Models GT250L, GT380L, GT550L and GT550K with engine serial numbers 32292 and thereafter, and models GT750L and GT750K with engine serial numbers 38591 and thereafter.
Depth 2.8 mm (0.11 in.)	59100-31830	Models GT250K, GT380K and GT550K with engine serial numbers 32291 and before, and model GT750K with engine serial numbers 38590 and before.

6) Push in pad No. 1 into the caliper holder.

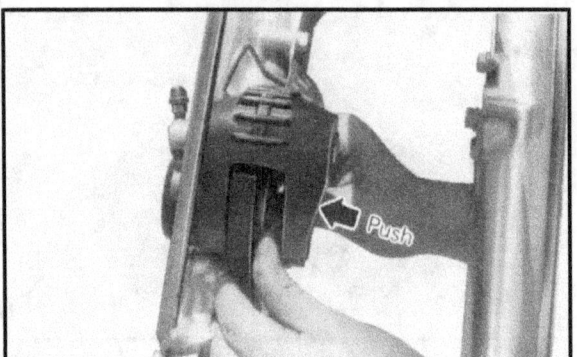

Fig. 4-2-6

7) Mount pad No. 2 to the caliper body.

Caution: Do not apply any grease to the pad No. 2, and take care not to mount it inclined.

8) Install the front wheel assembly to the front fork.
9) Squeeze the brake lever two or three times to confirm its operation, and bleed air if necessary.

4-2-3 Replacing of pad for model GT750

1) Take off the left brake pipe cover ① and pipe guide ②.

Fig. 4-2-7

2) Loosen the two left caliper fitting bolts ③.

Fig. 4-2-8

3) Detach the left caliper with the brake pipe connected and fix it on the front fork by string or hold it unmoved so as not to bend the brake pipe.

Fig. 4-2-9

4) Take off the front wheel assembly.
5) Mount the removed left caliper to the front fork
6) Insert a spacer ④ between pads Nos. 1 and 2 of the right caliper to stop piston movement and clip it with an elastic rubber ring ⑤ to prevent it from falling.

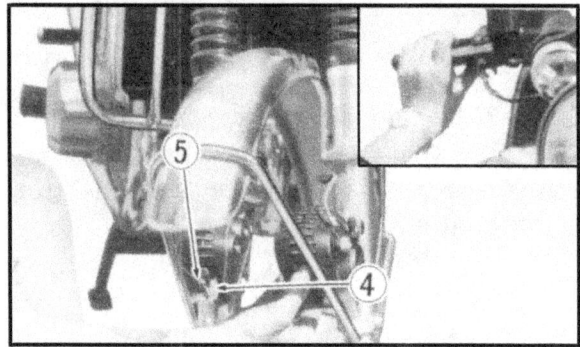

Fig. 4-2-10

7) Replace pads Nos. 1 and 2 of the left caliper in the same manner as for models GT125, GT185, GT250, GT380 and GT550.
8) Remove the spacer from the right caliper, and insert it in the left caliper.
9) Replace pads Nos. 1 and 2 of the right caliper.
10) Take off the left caliper and hold it.
11) Install the front wheel assembly to the front fork.
12) Mount the left caliper to the front fork.
13) Mount the left brake pipe cover and guide.
14) Squeeze the brake lever two or three times to confirm its operation, and bleed air if necessary.

Note: When replacing the front tire or repairing puncture, it is necessary to remove the left caliper before removing the front wheel assembly.

4-3 Master Cylinder, Brake Hose and Brake Pipe

4-3-1 General

Always check the master cylinder, brake hose and the brake pipe for operation and leakage of brake fluid since they are very important parts for safe riding.
If any abnormal condition is found, repair or replace. Though every part is made of material rigidly selected under high degree quality control, periodically replace the master cylinder piston cup and its related parts in order to always keep the motorcycle in its best condition.

Index No.	Description
1	Master cylinder assembly
2	Check valve
3	Spring
4	Primary cup
5	Secondary cup
6	Piston
7	Stop plate
8	Circlip
9	Boot
10	Boot plate
11	Boot stopper
12	Diaphragm
13	Diaphragm plate
14	Reservoir cap
15	Washer
16	Bolt
17	Master cylinder boot
18	Union bolt
19	Washer
20	Front brake hose
21	Brake hose guide
22	Grommet
23	Brake pipe
24	Brake hose guide
25	Grommet
26	Brake hose
27	Grommet

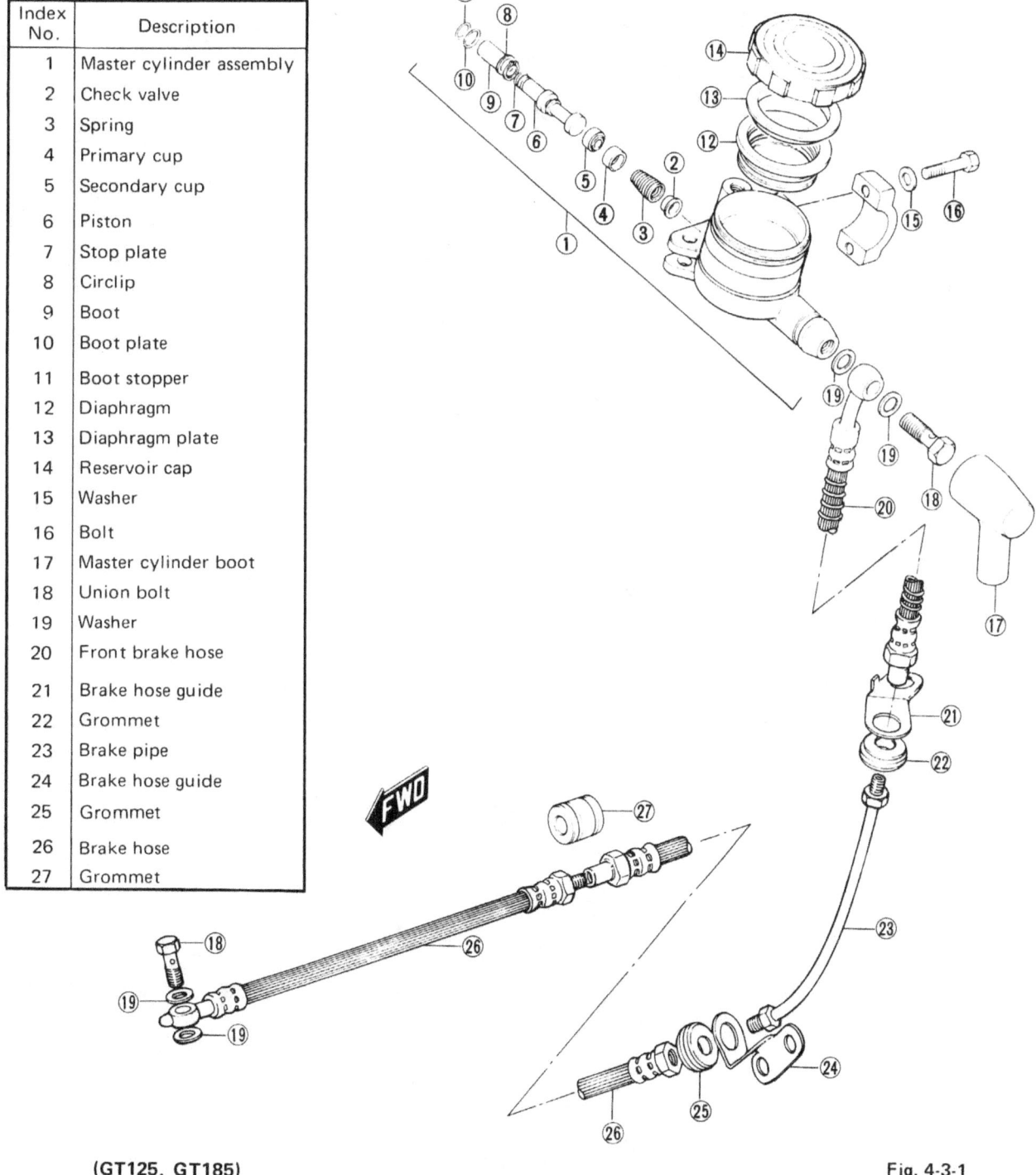

(GT125, GT185)　　　　　　　　　　　Fig. 4-3-1

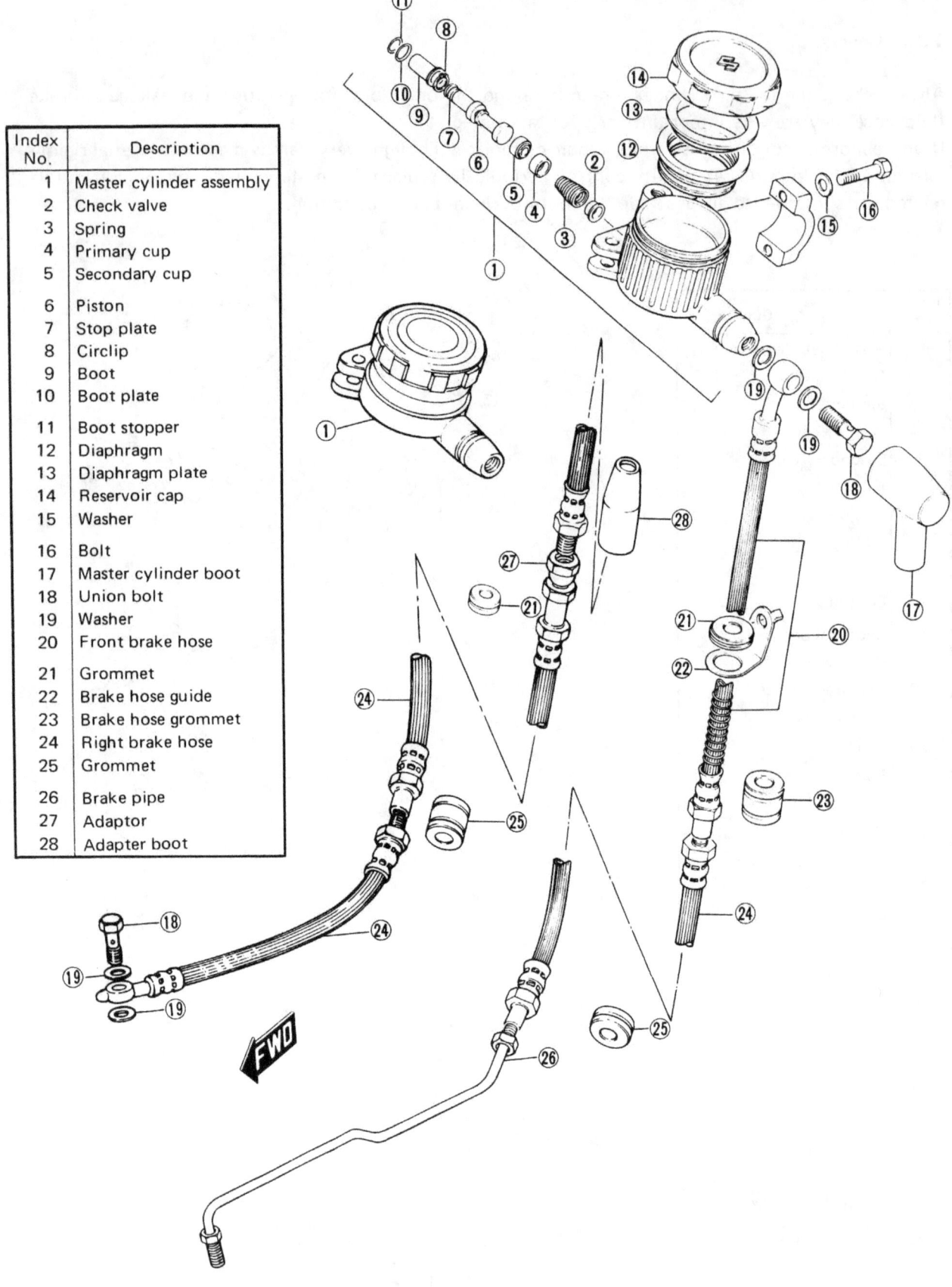

Index No.	Description
1	Master cylinder assembly
2	Check valve
3	Spring
4	Primary cup
5	Secondary cup
6	Piston
7	Stop plate
8	Circlip
9	Boot
10	Boot plate
11	Boot stopper
12	Diaphragm
13	Diaphragm plate
14	Reservoir cap
15	Washer
16	Bolt
17	Master cylinder boot
18	Union bolt
19	Washer
20	Front brake hose
21	Grommet
22	Brake hose guide
23	Brake hose grommet
24	Right brake hose
25	Grommet
26	Brake pipe
27	Adaptor
28	Adapter boot

(GT250, GT380 & GT550) Fig. 4-3-2

Index No.	Description
1	Master cylinder assembly
2	Check valve
3	Spring
4	Primary cup
5	Secondary cup
6	Piston
7	Plate stop
8	Circlip
9	Boot
10	Boot plate
11	Boot stopper
12	Diaphragm
13	Diaphragm plate
14	Reservoir cap
15	Bolt
16	Washer
17	Master cylinder boot
18	Union bolt
19	Washer
20	Grommet
21	Brake hose guide
22	Front brake hose
23	RH & LH brake hose
24	Three way joint
25	Grommet
26	RH brake pipe
27	LH brake pipe
28	Adapter
29	Adapter boot

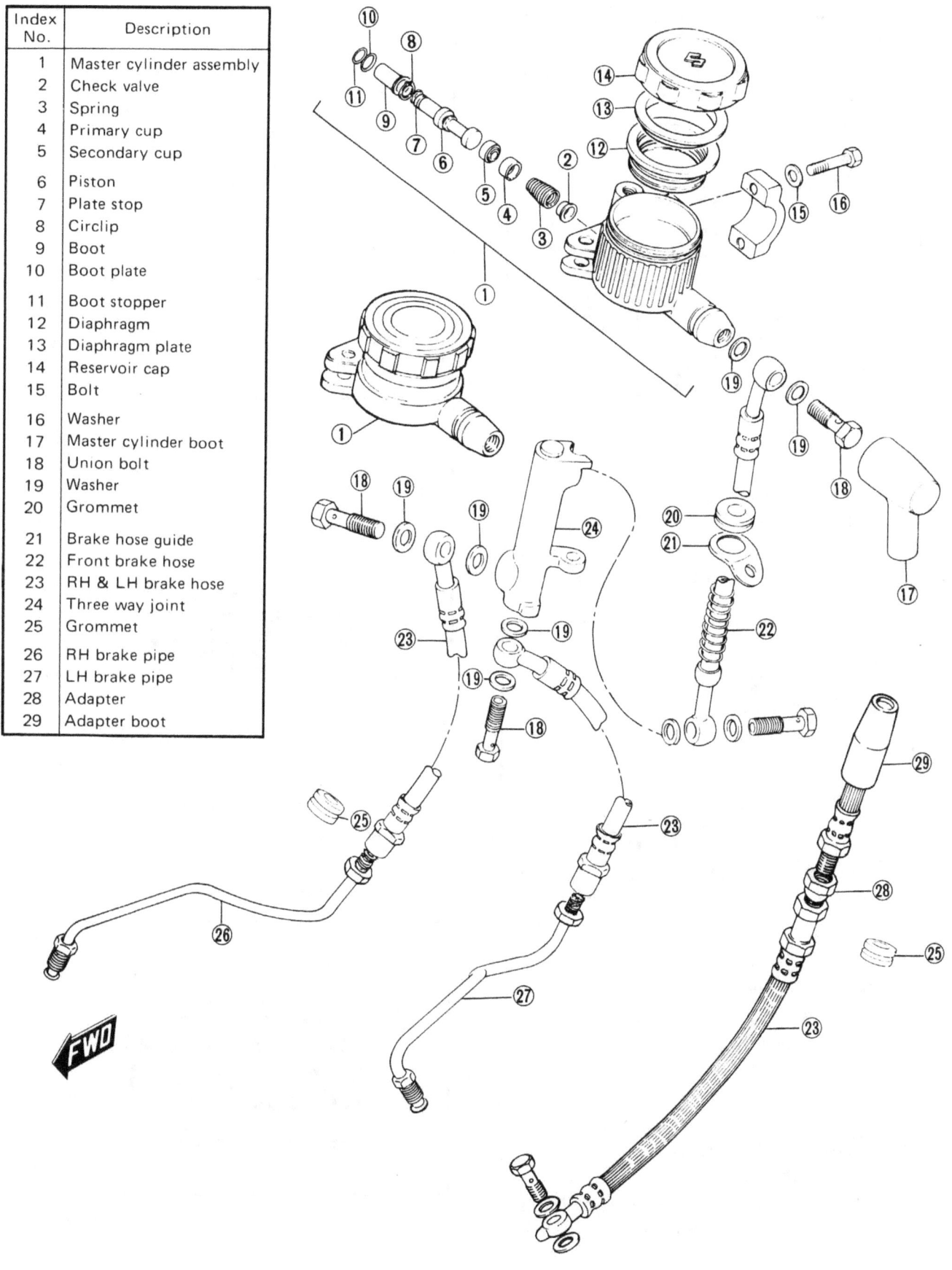

(GT750) Fig. 4-3-3

4-3-2 Removing master cylinder

1) Remove the stop switch from the master cylinder (only for U.S.A. and Canadian specifications).

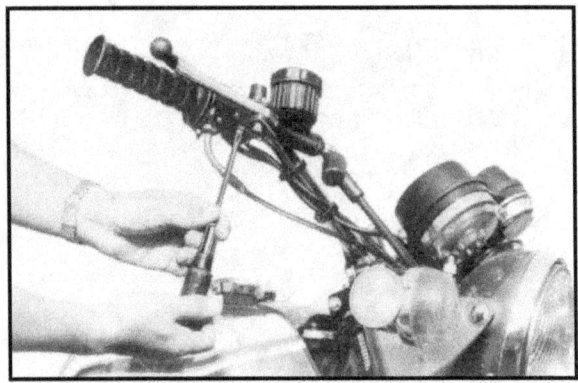

Fig. 4-3-3

2) Put a piece of rag beneath the union bolt on the master cylinder to catch drops of brake fluid. Unscrew the union bolt and disconnect the connection between the brake hose and the master cylinder.

Fig. 4-3-4

3) Unscrew two master cylinder fastening bolts and remove the master cylinder body from the handlebar.
4) Empty brake fluid out of the reservoir.

4-3-3 Disassembling master cylinder

1) Remove the brake lever.
2) Remove the boot stopper while taking care not to damage the boot and then remove the boot.

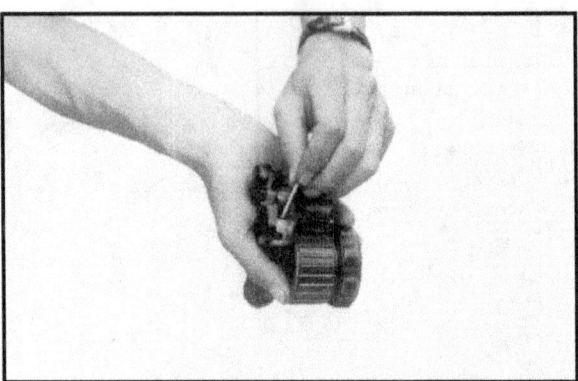

Fig. 4-3-5

3) Remove the circlip with the special tool (Circlip remover ① 19920 - 73110).

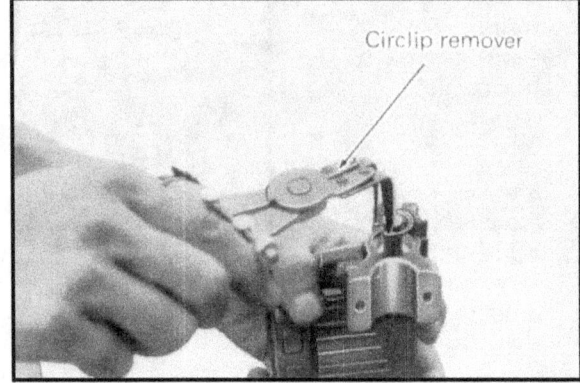

Fig. 4-3-6

4) Remove the piston, primary cup, spring and check valve.
5) Put the removed parts into a clean container and wash them in new brake fluid.

Caution: Never wash them in gasoline or petroleum; otherwise such fluid will damage rubber parts.

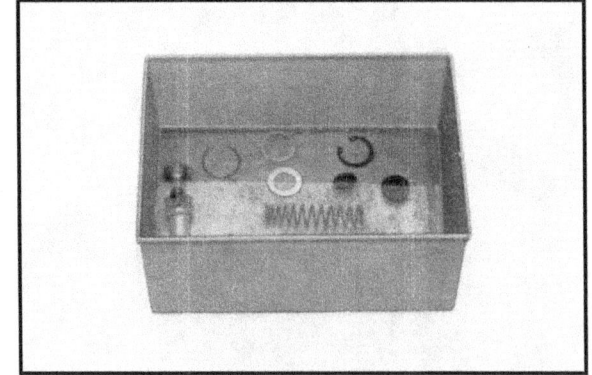

Fig. 4-3-7

4-3-4 Checking master cylinder

Replace the following parts with new one if any abnormality is found.

1) Master cylinder: Measure inner diameter of the master cylinder with an inside dial indicator.

Standard	Limit	Model
14.00 to 14.04 mm (0.551 to 0.553 in.)	Over 14.05 mm (0.553 in.)	GT125 GT185 GT250 GT380 GT550
15.87 to 15.91 mm (0.625 to 0.626 in.)	Over 15.92 mm (0.627 in.)	GT750

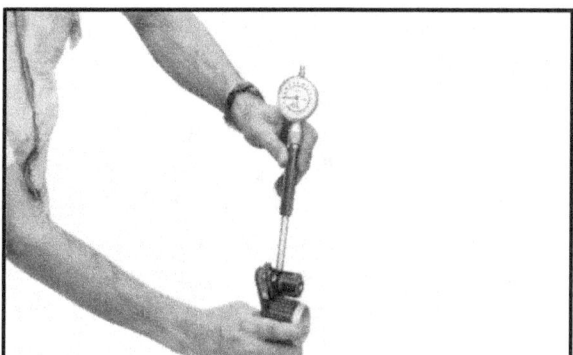

Fig. 4-3-8

2) Piston: Measure outer diameter of the piston.

Standard	Limit	Model
13.96 to 13.98 mm (0.550 to 0.551 in.)	Under 13.94 mm (0.549 in.)	GT125 GT185 GT250 GT380 GT550
15.83 to 15.85 mm (0.623 to 0.624 in.)	Under 15.81 mm (0.622 in.)	GT750

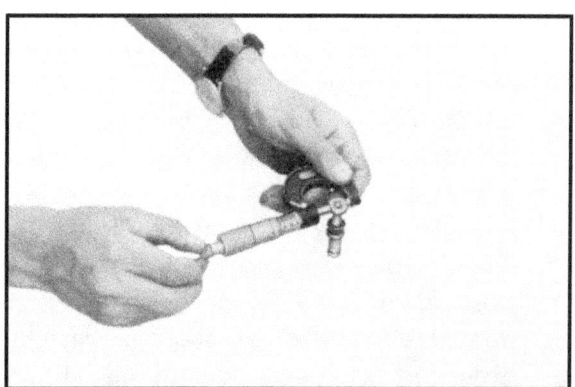

Fig. 4-3-9

3) Check valve: Inspect the check valve for operation.
4) O-ring (For models GT125L, GT185L, GT250L, GT380L, GT550L and GT750L):

Check the mating surfaces of the plastic reservoir and master cylinder proper for oil leaking.

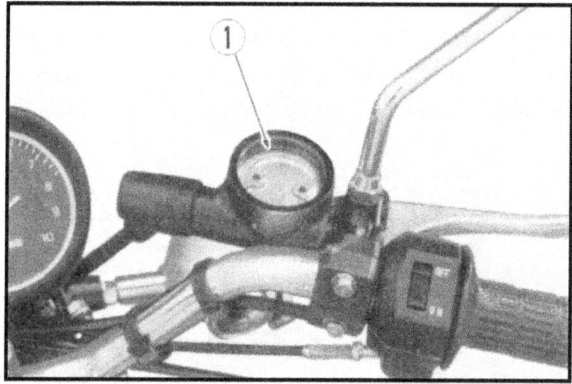

Fig. 4-3-10

4-3-5 Assembling master cylinder

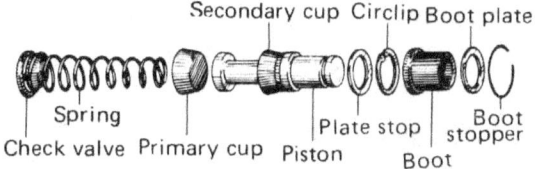

Fig. 4-3-11

Follow the removal procedures in the reverse order. When assembling them, pay attention to the following points.

1) Do not confuse the directions of assembling the primary cup. Refer to Fig. 4-3-11.
2) Replace a cotter pin of the brake lever pivot nut with new one and fit it securely.
3) Mount the master cylinder to the handlebar so that a gap between it and the switch box is about 2 mm (0.08 in.) and the reservoir becomes horizontal when the motorcycle is held on the center stand and steering is kept in a straight-on direction. Refer to Fig. 4-3-12.

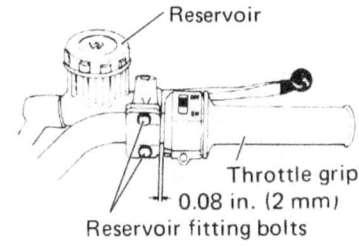

Fig. 4-3-12

4-3-6 Master cylinder identification mark

Cylinder bore of the master cylinder for model GT750 is larger than that for model GT125, GT185, GT250, GT380 or GT550. In order to easily distinguish the master cylinder for model GT750 from those for other models, an identification mark "D" is punched on the back of the reservoir.

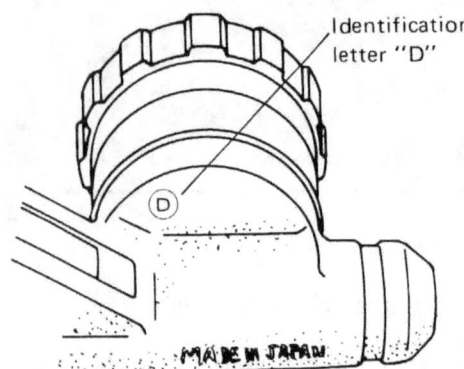

Fig. 4-3-13

4-3-7 Checking brake hose and pipe

Always check for the following items and replace immediately if any abnormality is found.
1) Damage to or swell of brake hose and/or pipe.
2) Traces of wear on the brake hose and/or pipe in contact with other parts.
3) Rusty brake pipe.
4) Fluid leakage at any joint of brake pipes and/or hose.

Note: If leakage should be found at any joint, retighten the bolts and nuts to the specified tightening torque. (Refer to page 24.)

4-3-8 Assembling brake hose and pipe

When connecting the brake hose and pipe, pay attention to the following points.
1) Be sure to use new brake pipe at all times when the brake pipe is assembled, because the cut end of the used brake pipe has been flared along the shape of the caliper inlet or the brake hose outlet as shown in Fig. 4-3-14. If the used pipe is reinstalled as it is, the air-tightness of the connection decreases, causing the brake fluid leakage.

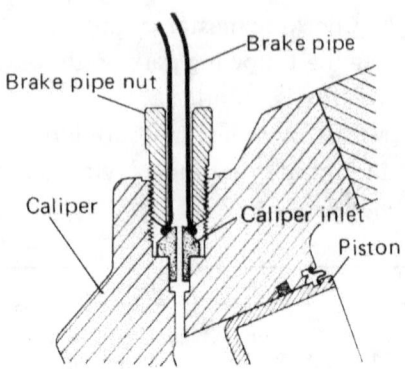

Fig. 4-3-14

2) When tightening two brake hose adapters, make sure that the hoses are free and not twisted. For models GT125L, GT185L, GT250K, GT380K, GT550K and GT750K which use brake pipe rather than hose, tighten the brake pipe adapter last of all. For models GT250L, GT380L, GT550L, and GT750L, first of all, remove twist from the hose, and then, tighten the hose joint with the brake hose adapter shown in Fig. 4-3-15.

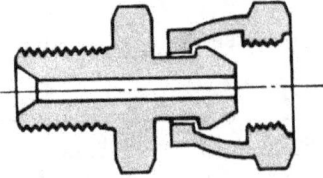

Fig. 4-3-15

3) When connecting the brake pipe to the caliper body, screw the nut in with your fingers to prevent stripping the threads, and then tighten it with a wrench to the specified torque.
4) Check that there is a generous space between each of them and the fuel tank, the front fork or other parts, and correct if any abnormality is found. Check that the hose or pipe does not contact any other parts particularly when the handlebar is turned fully to the right or left or when the front fork is brought down to the bottom.
5) After the assembling, check for no brake fluid leakage at any connection while holding the brake lever tightly.

4-4 Caliper

4-4-1 General

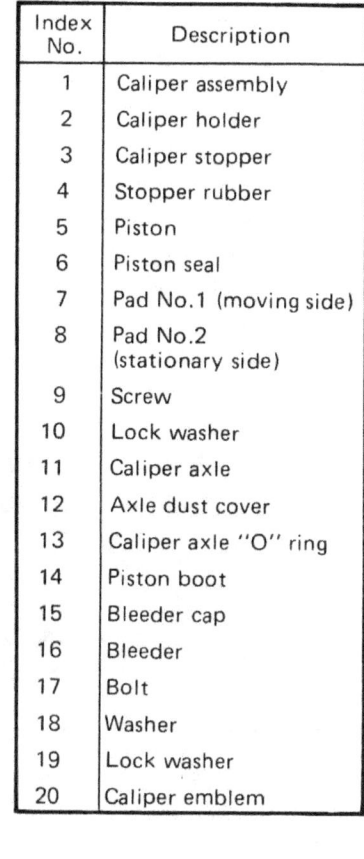

Index No.	Description
1	Caliper assembly
2	Caliper holder
3	Caliper stopper
4	Stopper rubber
5	Piston
6	Piston seal
7	Pad No.1 (moving side)
8	Pad No.2 (stationary side)
9	Screw
10	Lock washer
11	Caliper axle
12	Axle dust cover
13	Caliper axle "O" ring
14	Piston boot
15	Bleeder cap
16	Bleeder
17	Bolt
18	Washer
19	Lock washer
20	Caliper emblem

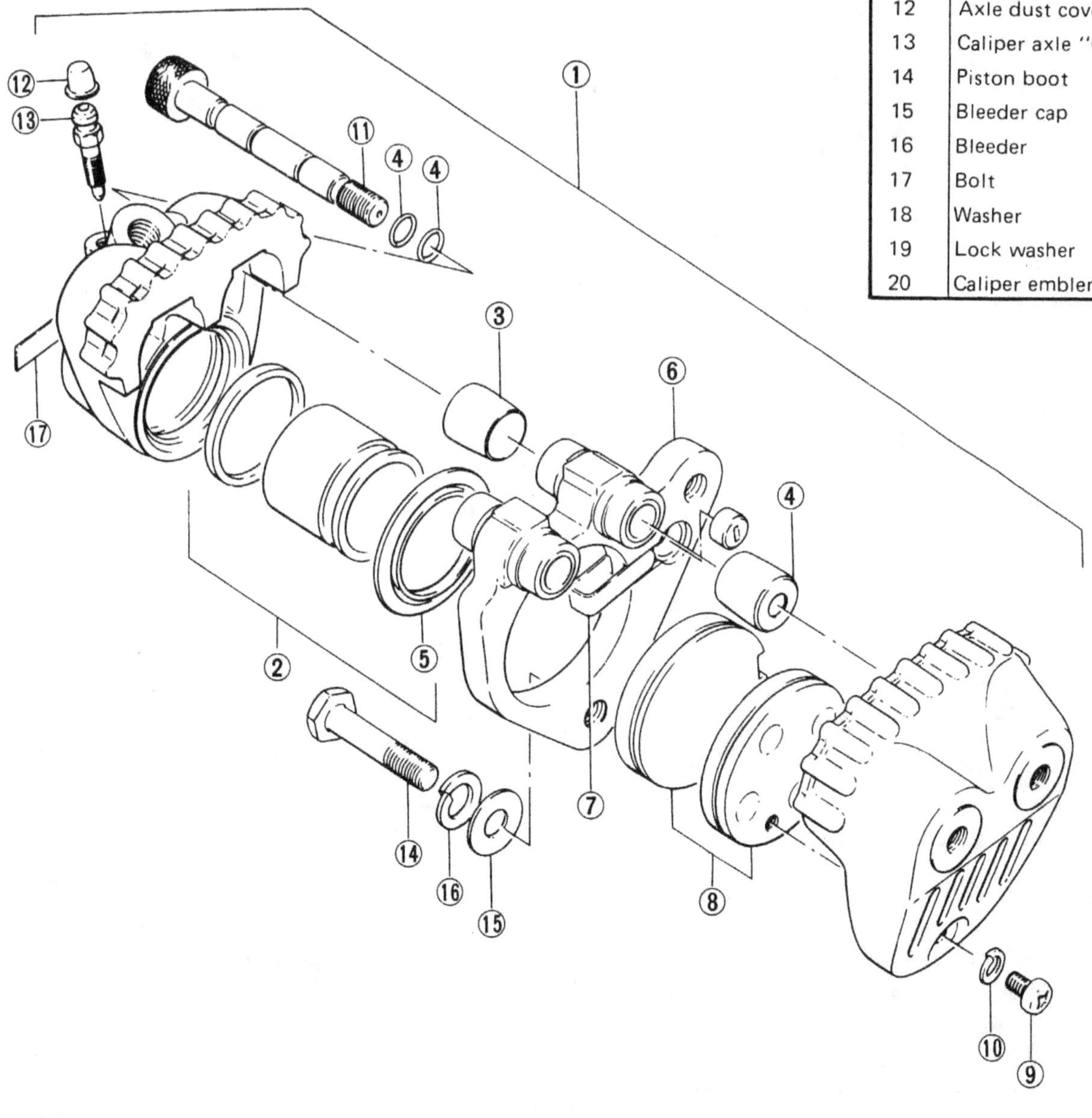

Fig. 4-4-1

4-4-2 Removing
1) Unscrew the brake pipe nut and caliper fastening bolts.
2) Pull out the caliper body from the disc plate.

4-4-3 Disassembling
1) Unscrew the caliper axle bolts with a special tool (8 mm hexagon L-type wrench 09900-06904) and separate the inner caliper body from the outer body.

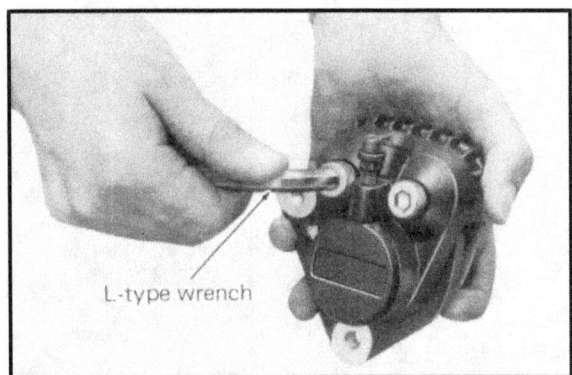

Fig. 4-4-2

2) Remove the caliper holder.
3) Remove "O" rings on the caliper axle.
4) Remove the caliper axles.
5) Remove the piston boot.
6) Push out the piston with compressed air while holding it with finger to prevent it from blowing out.

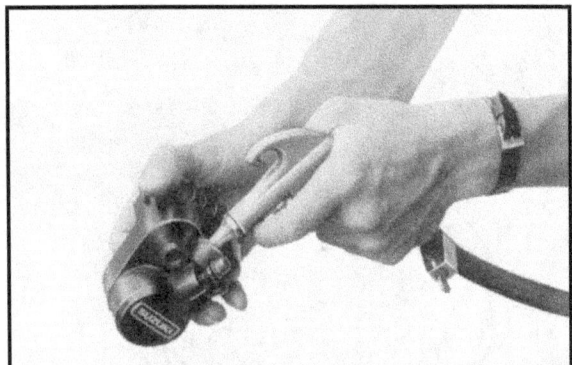

Fig. 4-4-3

7) Remove the piston seal as shown in Fig. 4-4-4.
8) Wash the piston, piston boot, piston seal and "O" rings of the caliper axles with new brake fluid. See Fig. 4-4-5.

Caution: Never use gasoline or petroleum; otherwise rubber parts will be damaged.
Do not wash the pads and also take care that brake fluid is not splashed onto the pads.

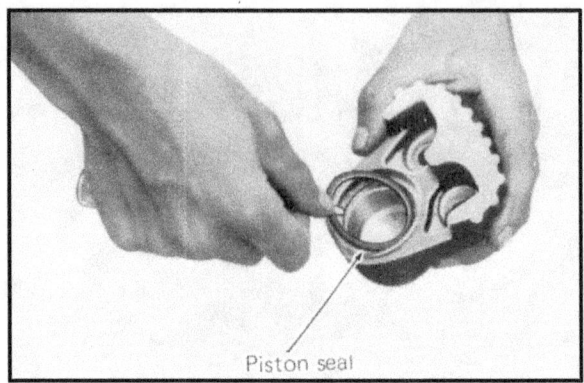

Fig. 4-4-4

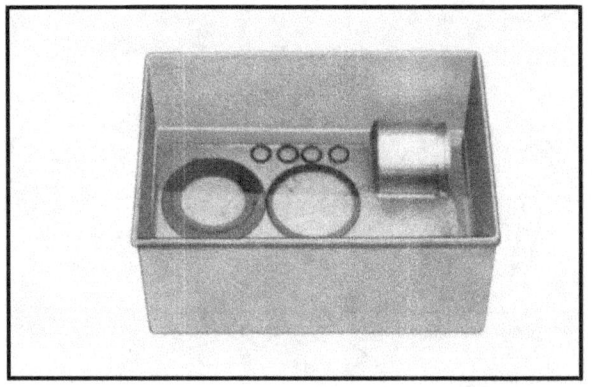

Fig. 4-4-5

4-4-4 Checking
When disassembling the caliper, check the following points and replace if any abnormality is found.

1) Cylinder: Its inner diameter is not worn out of its limit.

Standard	Limit	Model
38.18 to 38.20 mm (1.503 to 1.504 in.)	Over 38.22 mm (1.504 in.)	GT125 GT185 GT250 GT380 GT550 GT750

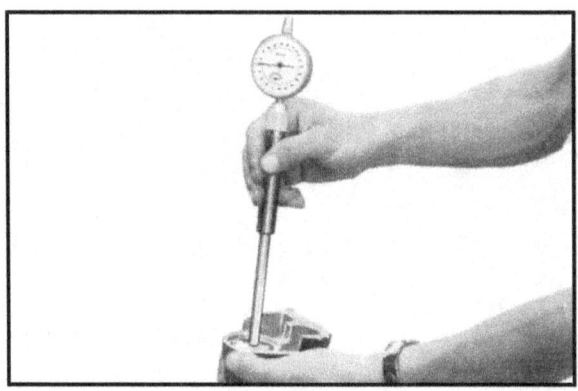

Fig. 4-4-6

2) Piston: Its outer diameter is not worn out of its limit.

Standard	Limit	Model
38.15 to 38.18 mm (1.502 to 1.503 in.)	Under 38.10 mm (1.500 in.)	GT125 GT185 GT250 GT380 GT550 GT750

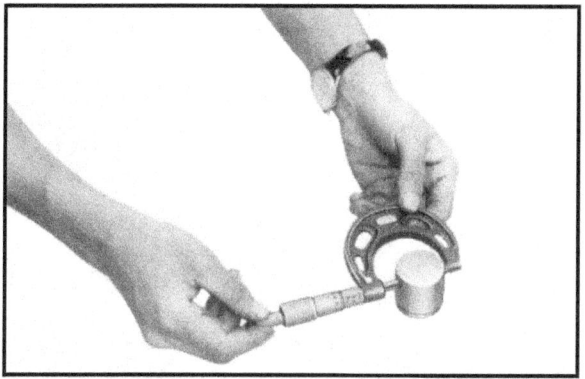

Fig. 4-4-7

3) Piston seal: No damage nor excessive wear
4) Piston boot: No damage nor settling
5) Pads Nos. 1 and 2: Not worn out of its limit (refer to "4-2-1 Inspecting of Pads").
6) Caliper body: No crack

4-4-5 Assembling

Follow the removal procedure in the reverse order. When assembling them, pay attention to the following points.

1) Apply "Suzuki Caliper Axle Grease" with property of high heat resistance onto the caliper axle.

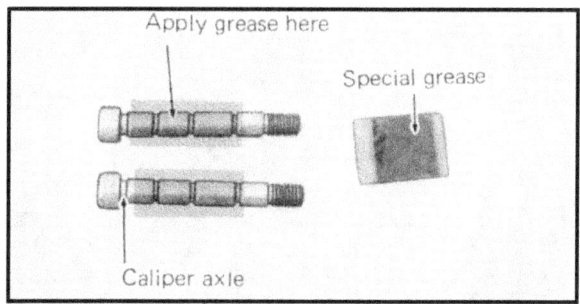

Fig. 4-4-8

2) Apply a generous amount of brake fluid onto the inner surface of the cylinder and periphery of the piston and then assemble.
3) Do not assemble the piston seal with it inclined or twisted. See Fig. 4-4-9.

4) In installing the piston, push it slowly into the cylinder while taking care not to damage the piston seal.

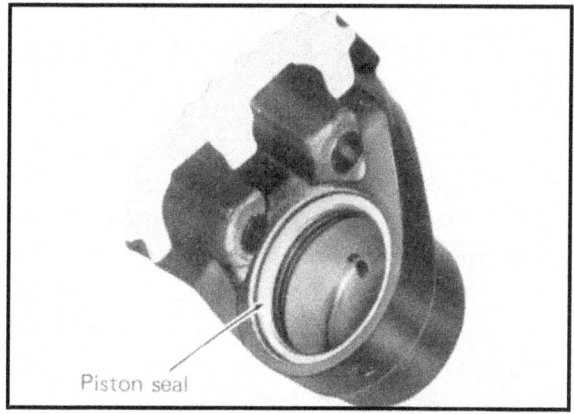

Fig. 4-4-9

5) Apply "Suzuki Brake Pad Grease" shown in Fig. 4-4-10 onto the periphery of pad No. 1 (refer to "4-2-2 Replacing of Pads").

Fig. 4-4-10

6) Bleed air after assembling (refer to "4-1-2 Air bleeding from brake system").
7) After bleeding air, check for brake fluid leakage while holding the brake lever tightly.
8) After a test run, check the pads and brake disc do not press each other excessively by turning the front wheel by hand.

4-5 Brake Disc

4-5-1 General

The brake disc, made of stainless steel having excellent heat-resistance and abrasion-proof properties, is fastened to the front hub with six high tensile strength bolts.

4-5-2 Checking

1) Runout of the brake disc should not be greater than the limit. Measure brake disc runout with a dial indicator as shown in Fig. 4-5-1. If the runout is over the limit on the largest periphery of the disc plate, check whether the cause lies in the front wheel bearing or the brake disc itself, and replace defective parts.

Standard	Limit	Model
0.1 mm (0.004 in.)	0.3 mm (0.012 in.)	GT125 GT185 GT250 GT380 GT550 GT750

Fig. 4-5-2

Fig. 4-5-1

2) Thickness of the brake disc should not be less than the limit. Measure its worn portion with a micrometer as shown in Fig. 4-5-2 and replace the brake disc if the thickness is less than the limit.

Standard	Limit	Model
5.00 mm (0.197 in.)	Under 4.00 mm (0.157 in.)	GT125 GT185
7.00 mm (0.276 in.)	Under 6.00 mm (0.236 in.)	GT250 GT380 GT550 GT750

3) Surface of the brake disc should be free from oil. Take care that no oil is adhered on the brake disc surface, since oil adhesion there is very dangerous. If oil is placed on the disc by mistake, wipe off the oil with a soft waste-cloth soaked with alcohol.

4) The brake disc fitting bolts should be securely tightened to the specified torque and should be secured with lock washers.

Fig. 4-5-3

4-6 Periodic Replacement Parts

The component parts of the master cylinder assembly and the caliper assembly may be worn and deteriorated in function in long period of use. However, it is generally difficult to foresee how long each component will further work with proper function thereafter, since deterioration of function much depends upon usage of brake by individual motorcycle.

Then, from safety points of view, the following is defined as periodic replacement parts in order to prevent unforeseen trouble caused by wearing of component.

Replace all the following parts at a time with Suzuki genuine parts sets.

Exchange interval: Two years

1. Components of master cylinder assembly
   (Use Suzuki Genuine parts: Master cylinder cup set)

1 Primary cup	6 Boot plate
2 Spring	7 Boot
3 Piston	8 Stop plate
4 Check valve	9 Boot stopper
5 Circlip	

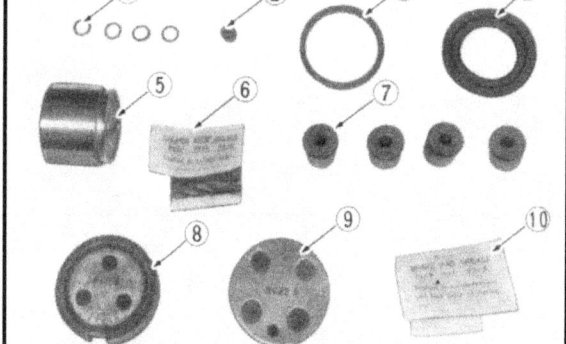

Fig. 4-6-1

2. Component of caliper assembly
   (Use Suzuki Genuine parts: Pad and piston set)

1 "O" ring	7 Axle shaft dust cover
2 Stopper	8 Pad No. 1
3 Piston seal	9 Pad No. 2
4 Boot	10 Suzuki Brake Pad Grease
5 Piston	
6 Suzuki Caliper Axle Grease	

Fig. 4-6-2

Note: Pad and piston set includes two kinds of grease packed in pouch. Grease in the pouch printed "Caliper Axle Grease" should be used for the caliper axle and printed "Brake Pad Grease" for the pad No. 1.

Caution: Be sure to wash all component parts in the above sets with clean brake fluid before installing them into the master cylinder or caliper.

5. TIGHTENING TORQUE

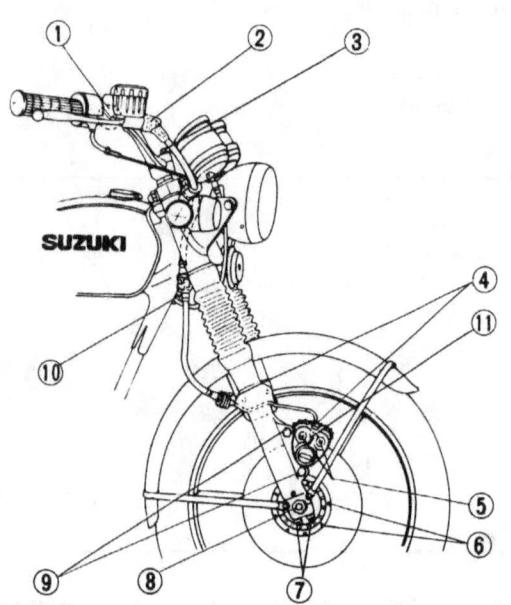

Fig. 5-1-1

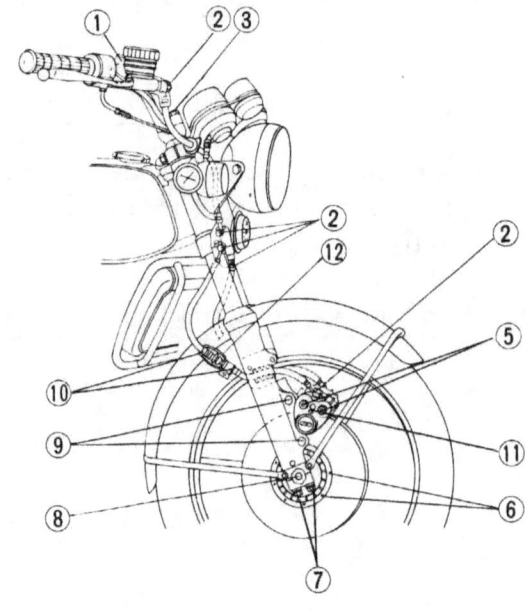

Fig. 5-1-2

Item No.	Description	Bolt-and nut diameter	Tightening torque	
		mm	kg-cm	ft-lb
1	Master cylinder clamp bolt	6	50 to 80	3.6 to 5.8
2	Union bolt	10	150 to 250	11 to 18
3	Handlebar clamp bolt	8	120 to 200	9 to 14
4	Brake pipe nut	10	130 to 180	9.5 to 13
5	Caliper axle bolt	10	250 to 350	18 to 25
6	Brake disc fitting bolt	8	150 to 250	11 to 18
7	Front axle holder nut	8	150 to 250	11 to 18
8	Front axle shaft nut	12	360 to 520	26 to 38
9	Caliper fitting bolt	10	250 to 400	18 to 29
10	Brake hose joint	10	250 to 350	18 to 25
11	Bleeder bolt	7	60 to 90	4.3 to 6.5
12	Adaptor	10	250 to 300	18 to 22

6. SPECIAL TOOLS FOR DISC BRAKE

6–1 Special tools

The following special tools are necessary for disassembling and reassembling disc brakes. Please use these special tools to ensure your operation.

Part No.	Description	Used for
09920–73110	Special circlip opener	Disassembling master cylinder
09900–06904	8 mm hexagon L-type wrench	Disassembling caliper

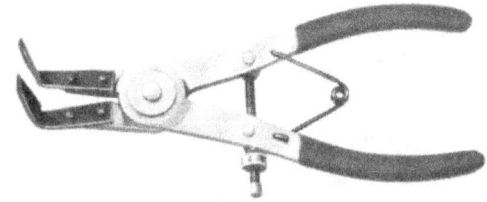

Special circlip opener   Fig. 6-1-1

8 mm hexagon L-type wrench   Fig. 6-1-2

6–2 Necessary materials

The two types of grease shown in the following table are applied to the moving parts when overhauling the disc brake. These grease feature their high lubrication and pressure withstanding performances even at a high temperature, and further, they do not affect rubber parts. When overhauling the disc brake, do not use other grease but these two types only.

Part No.	Description	Use
99000–25100	Suzuki brake pad grease	Lubrication of pad No.1
99000–25110	Suzuki caliper axle grease	Lubrication of caliper axle

Suzuki brake pad grease   Fig. 6-2-1

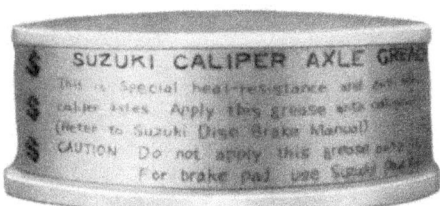

Suzuki caliper axle grease   Fig. 6-2-2

SUZUKI MOTOR CO., LTD.

SUZUKI SERVICE MANUAL

MODEL

BS40 CARBURETOR

FOREWORD

This manual is published for the information and use of the personnel who are concerned in the maintenance of the BS40 Carburetors used on the GT750L. The manual applies only to the carburetors and is prepared for use with the manuals published for the motorcycles. It has its own index and contains a description of the major components and their functions as well as maintenance.

All information, illustrations and specifications contained in this manual are based on the products manufactured before Nov., 1974. Any changes, deletions or additions to this manual will be followed by the Service Bulletin.

Feb., 1974

SUZUKI MOTOR CO., LTD.

INDEX

SUZUKI BS TYPE CARBURETOR FOR GT750

CHAPTER 1   DESCRIPTION 1
   1. Operation 2
   2. Specifications 7
   3. Troubleshooting Guide 8
   4. Special Tools and Adhesive 9

CHAPTER 2.   REPAIR AND ADJUSTMENT 10
   1. Disassembly 10
   2. Inspections 11
   3. Assembly and Adjustment 13
   4. Carburetor Adjustment 16

CHAPTER 1. DESCRIPTION

The Model BS40 Carburetor currently used on the Suzuki GT750L is an automatic variable-venturi carburetor which is controlled by vacuum caused by engine suction. It includes an independent starter system and a forced throttle-return system which consists of a pull cable on the return side and linkage to force the throttle valve to the closed position.

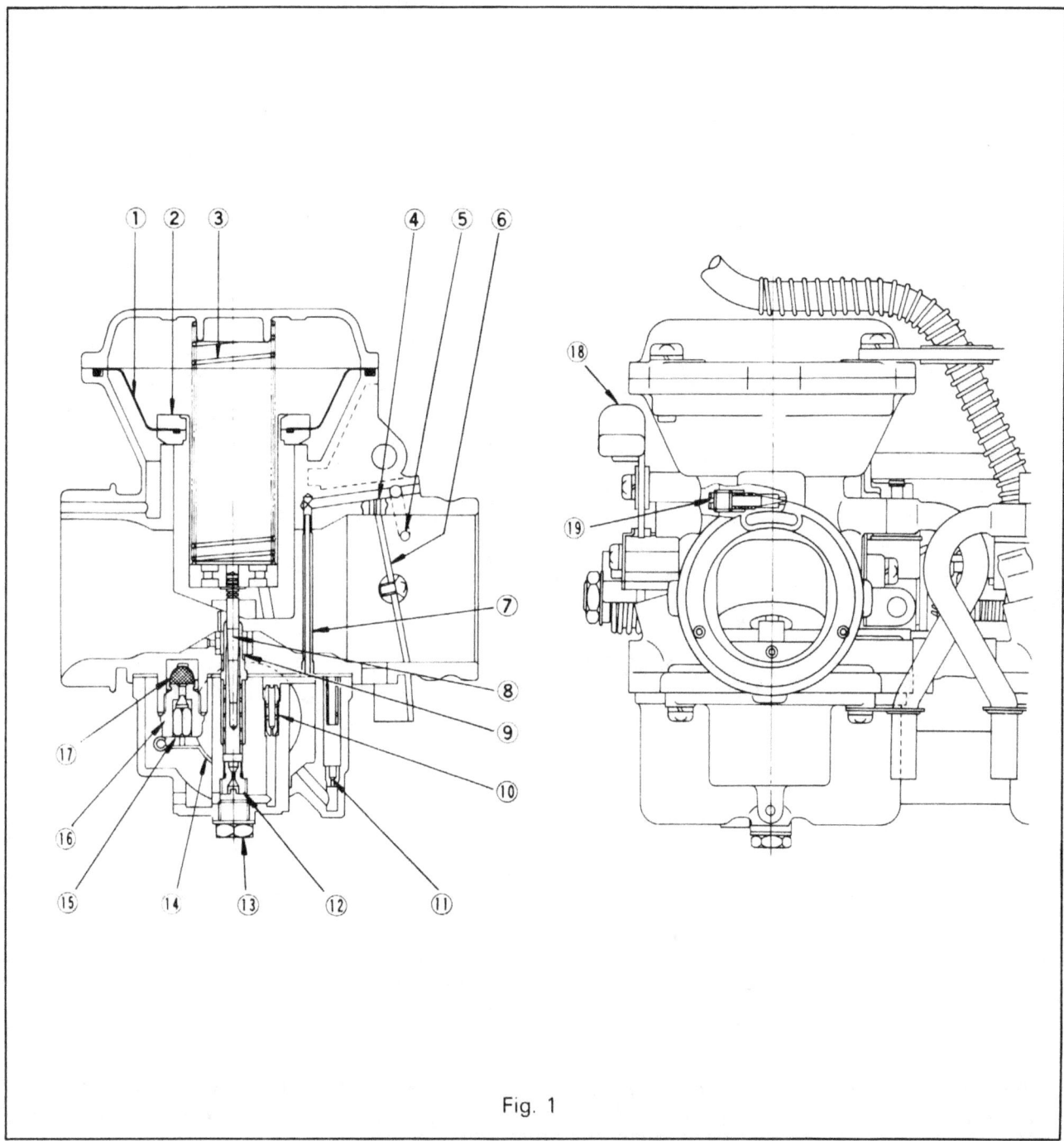

Fig. 1

1. Diaphragm
2. Piston valve
3. Piston valve spring
4. Bypass
5. Pilot outlet
6. Throttle valve
7. Pilot pipe
8. Jet needle
9. Needle jet
10. Pilot jet
11. Starter jet
12. Main jet
13. Drain plug
14. Float
15. Needle valve
16. Valve seat
17. Fuel strainer
18. Choke lever
19. Pilot screw

1. Operation

a) Forced throttle-return system

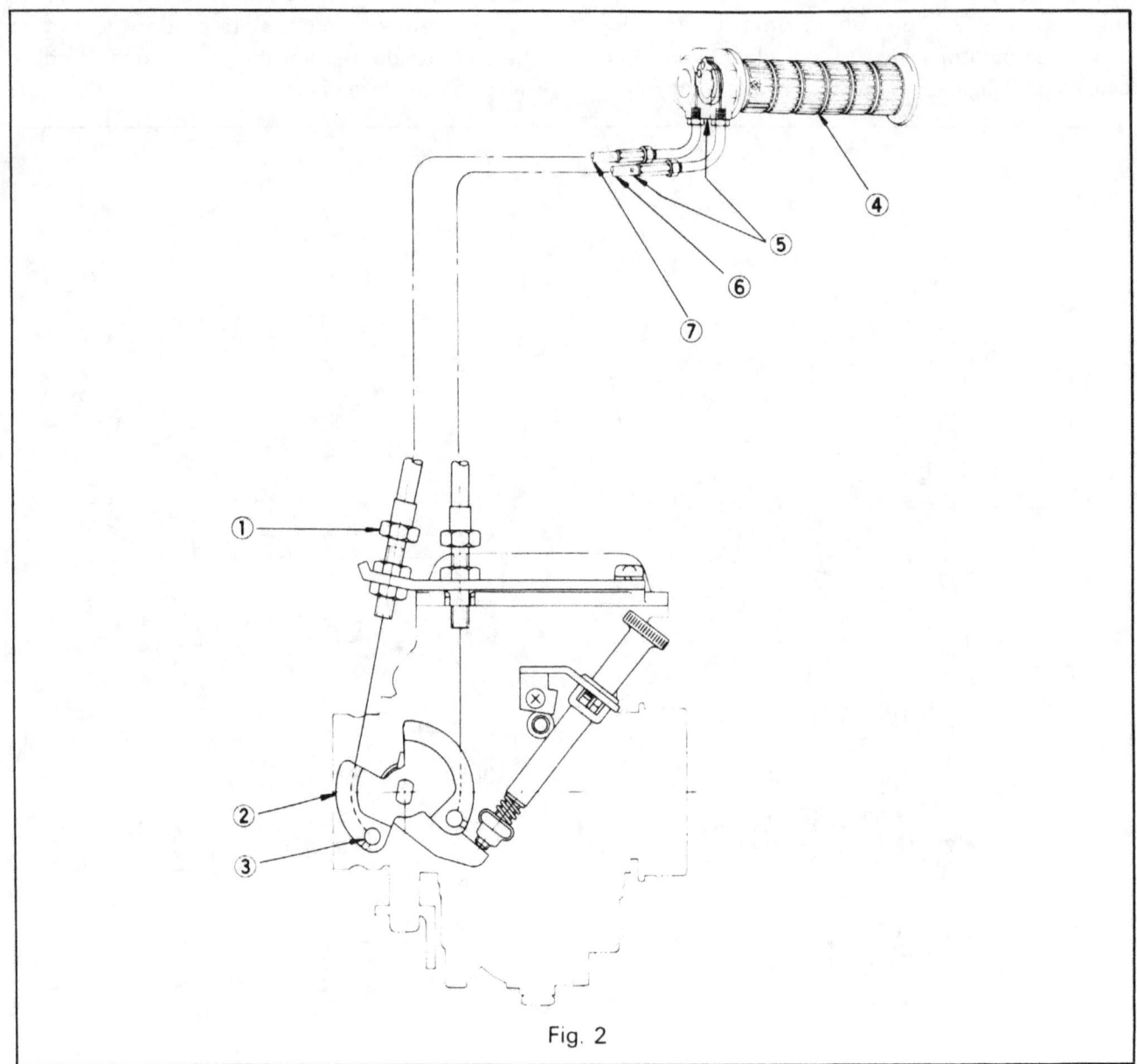

Fig. 2

1. Throttle cable adjuster
2. Pulley
3. Cable end
4. Throttle grip
5. Identification letter "R" (return side)
6. Throttle cable (return side)
7. Throttle cable (pull side)

The forced throttle-return system provides an added means of returning the throttle valve to the closed position. Fig. 1 shows an exaggerated view of the system to understand the operation that takes place when the system is operated.

When the throttle grip is turned inward, the pulley is pulled up by a pull side cable. The throttle valve is opened.

Now, when the grip is twisted outward, a spring produces some further closing of the throttle valve and spring-loads it in the closed position.

The system forces the throttle valve toward the closed position by a return side cable in case the valve has stuck or the spring broken.

b) Piston valve action

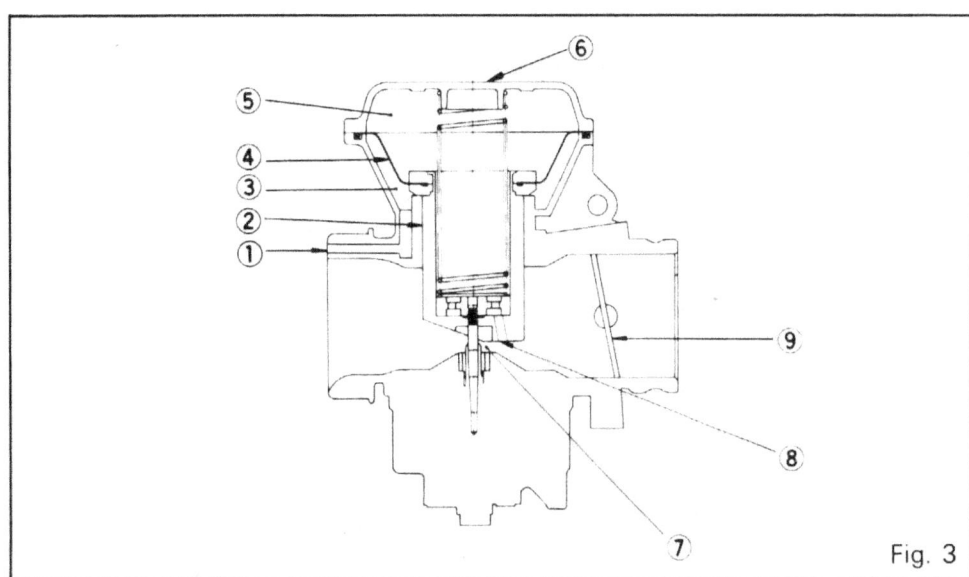

1. Inlet
2. Piston valve
3. Air chamber
4. Diaphragm
5. Vacuum chamber
6. Mixing chamber top
7. Venturi
8. Vacuum intake
9. Throttle valve

Fig. 3

Air from the air cleaner is drawn through the carburetor inlet, venturi, and throttle valve into the engine.

The throttle valve allows more or less air to flow through the air horn depending on which way the grip is twisted.

As air flows through the venturi, a partial vacuum is created. This vacuum is then admitted to the space above the diaphragm through a passage (vacuum intake) at the lower end of the piston valve.

Atmospheric pressure then acts on the diaphragm, lifting it up until an equilibrium is reached between the pressure and the tension of the piston valve spring.

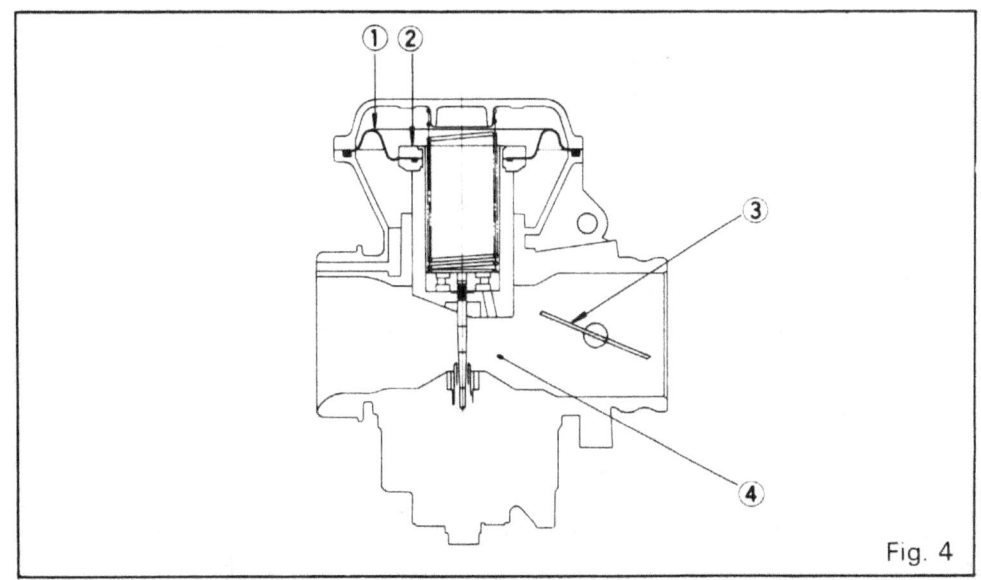

1. Diaphragm
2. Piston valve
3. Throttle valve
4. Venturi

Fig. 4

If the throttle is fully opened, the engine runs at its maximum speed; i.e., it draws the maximum amount of air through the carburetor. The speed of the air flowing through the venturi is also at the maximum, producing the maximum vacuum at the venturi. Under such condition, the piston valve is rested against the mixing chamber top, being prevented from taking further upward movement.

The diameter of the venturi will be at the maximum.

c) Slow system

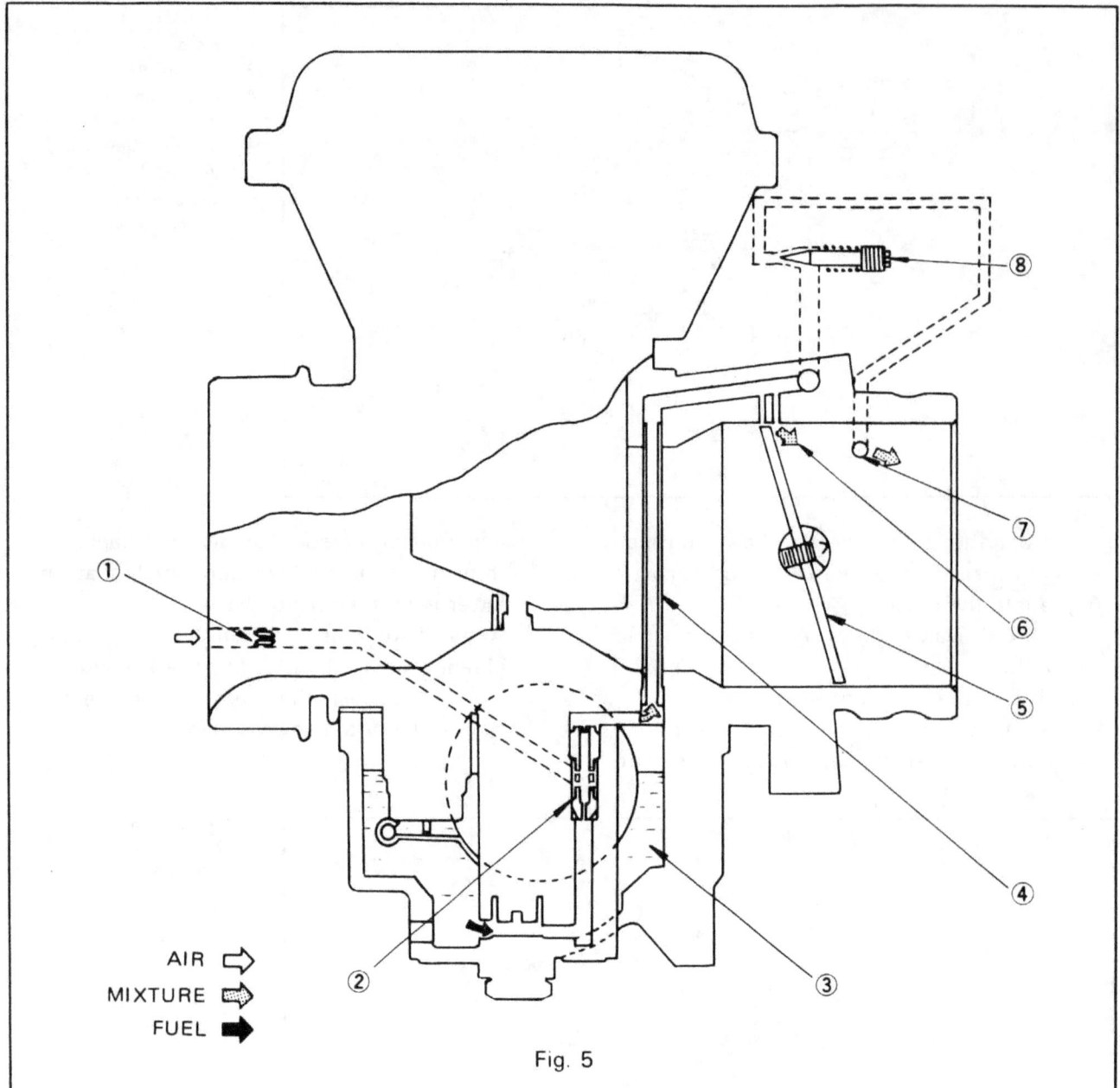

Fig. 5

1. Pilot air jet
2. Pilot jet
3. Float chamber
4. Pilot pipe
5. Throttle valve
6. Bypass
7. Pilot outlet
8. Pilot screw

When the throttle valve is closed or only slightly opened, the speed of air flowing through the air horn is low. As the result, there will be very little vacuum at the venturi to draw fuel from the needle jet.
The slow system supplies fuel during operation with the throttle closed or slightly opened.
The fuel from the float chamber is first metered by the pilot jet where it enters air flowing through the pilot air jet.
This rich mixture then goes up through the pilot pipe to the pilot screw. A part of the mixture is discharged out of the bypass port before it reaches the pilot screw. The remaining mixture, after metered by the pilot screw, will discharge out through the pilot outlet into the carburetor main bore.

d) Main system

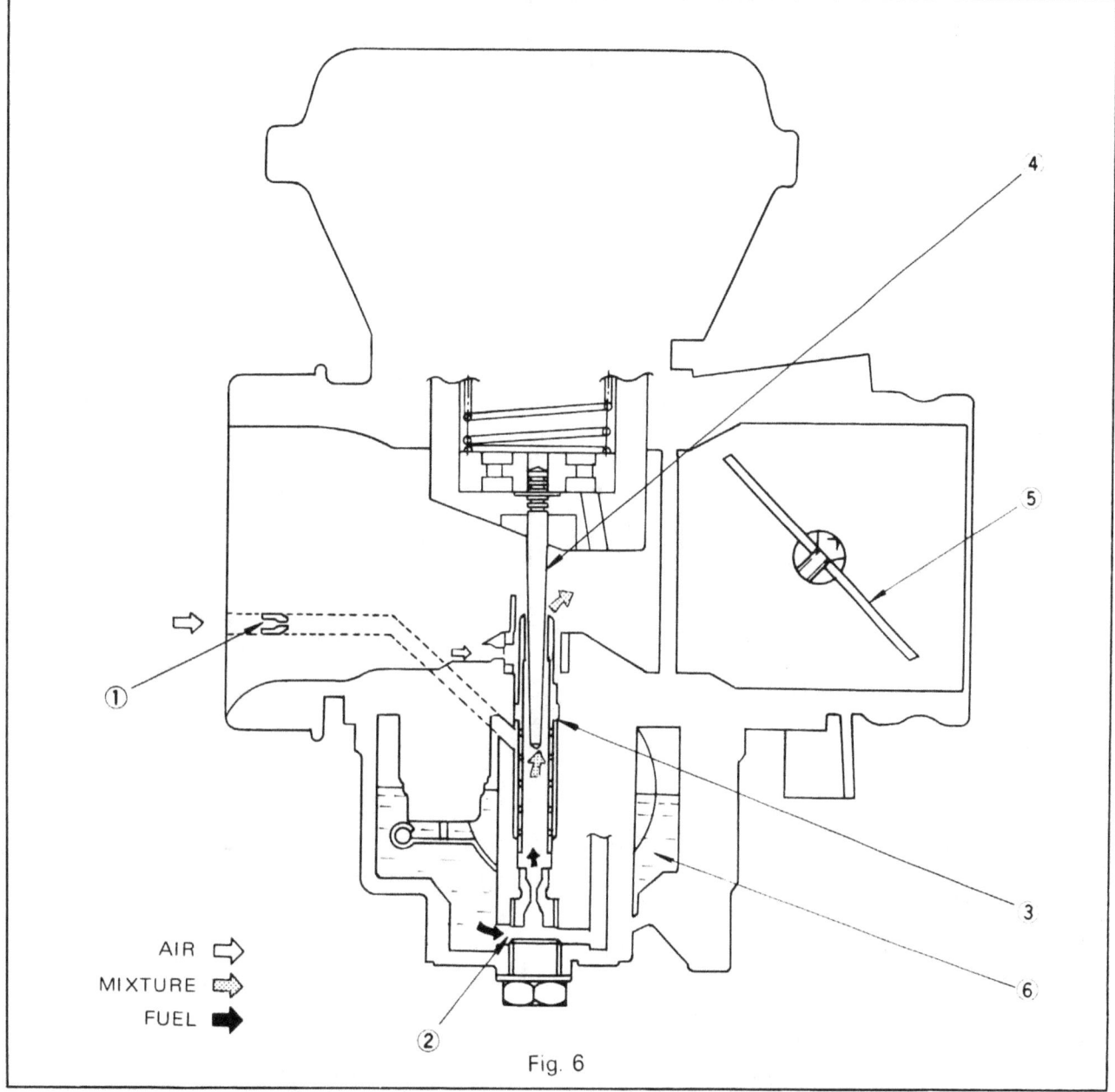

1. Main air jet
2. Main jet
3. Needle jet
4. Jet needle
5. Throttle valve
6. Float chamber

Fig. 6

When the throttle valve is opened, this gives rise to the speed of the engine. As a result, the vacuum at the venturi will be increased, causing the piston valve to move upward. Meanwhile, the fuel in the float chamber is metered by the main air jet, forming an emulsified fuel in the needle jet. The emulsified fuel then passes through the clearance between the needle jet and jet needle and is discharged into the venturi.

In the venturi, the emulsified fuel meets the main air stream and is drawn into the engine.

The fuel is given correct mixture proportions as it passes through the needle jet since the effective size of the needle jet depends on the throttle position.

e) Starter system

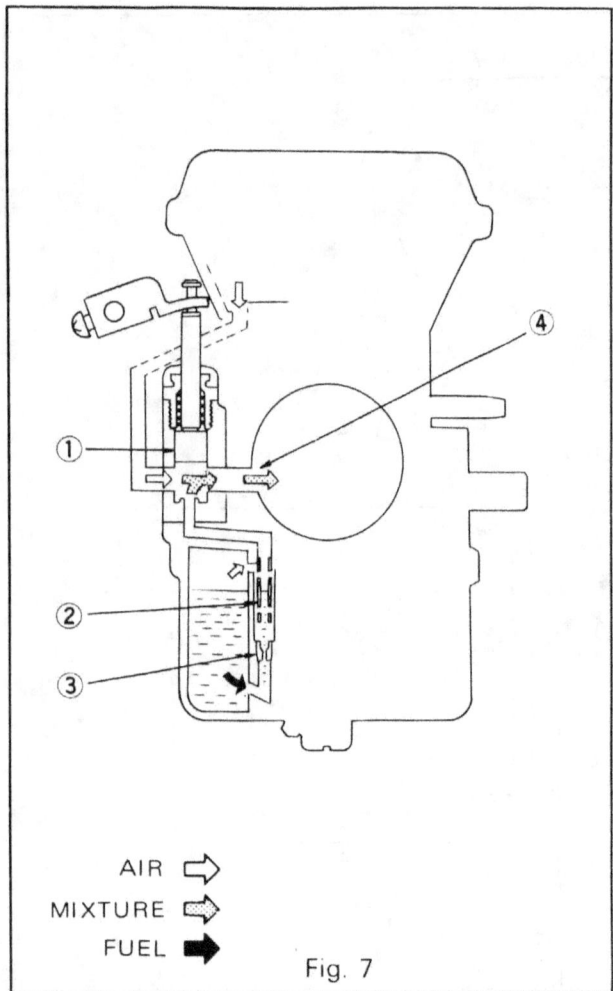

AIR ⇨
MIXTURE ⇨
FUEL ➡

Fig. 7

1. Starting plunger
2. Starter pipe
3. Starter jet
4. Starter outlet

Now, let us see how the starter system works. The carburetor includes an independent starter circuit consisting of a spring-loaded plunger linked to the choke lever at the left side of the carburetor body.
When the choke lever is pushed down, the starter plunger is pushed up. The action allows the fuel to bleed into the starter circuit.
The starter jet is supplied with fuel directly from the float chamber.
The fuel is first metered by the starter jet and passes into the starter pipe where it meets air in the float chamber.
This rich mixture, when it reaches the starter plunger, again enters air flowing through a passage from behind the diaphragm, providing correct air/fuel ratio for starting. Finally, it is discharged through the starter outlet into the engine directly.

f) Float system

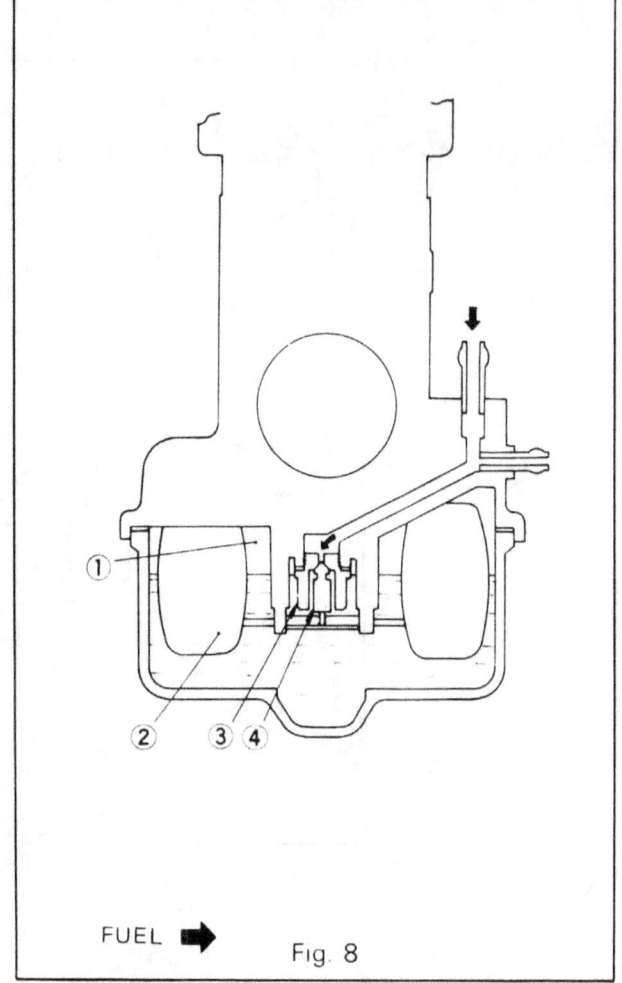

FUEL ➡

Fig. 8

1. Float chamber
2. Float
3. Valve seat
4. Needle valve

The float system consists of float, needle valve and valve seat, assembled to maintain a constant level of fuel in the float chamber. When the fuel enters the float chamber, this causes the float to move up. The valve is so designed that, if the float moves up, it is pushed up into the valve seat. This shuts off the fuel inlet so that no fuel can enter.
If the float level lowers, the float moves down; i.e., fuel can now enter since this releases the needle valve.
The same sequence of events takes place to maintain a constant level of fuel in the float chamber.

2. Specifications

Type		Automatically Variable Venturi Carburetor
Venturi Size		Equivalent to 32 mm
Main Jet	R & L	#110
	C	#107.5
Main Air Jet		0.5 mm
Pilot Jet		#47.5
Pilot Air Jet		1.0 mm
Throttle Valve		#120 (12.0°)
Bypass	No.1	0.8 mm
	No.2	0.9 mm
	No.3	1.0 mm
Bypass Pitch	No.1	3.98 mm
	No.2	4.95 mm
	No.3	5.90 mm
Pilot Outlet		0.7 mm
Jet Needle		4DN18 − 3rd
Needle Jet		Z − 0
Valve Seat		2.3 mm
Starter Jet		0.6 mm
Pilot Screw Opening		1/4
Float Level		27.6 mm

3. Troubleshooting Guide

Symptom	Probable Cause	Remedy
Erratic Idling or slow speed	1. Clogged or loose pilot jet	Clean or retighten
	2. Clogged pilot air jet	Clean
	3. Leaky float chamber gasket	Retighten or replace
	4. Carburetor balance out of adjustment	Adjust
	5. Improper float level	Adjust. Check needle valve and float; if necessary, replace
		Clean fuel strainer
	6. Pilot screw improperly adjusted	Adjust (1/4 turns)
	7. Clogged bypass hole	Clean
Improper part- and full-throttle operation	1. Clogged or loose main jet	Clean or retighten
	2. Clogged main air jet	Clean
	3. Needle jet O-ring broken	Replace
	4. Carburetor balance out of adjustment	Adjust
	5. Defective piston valve	Check diaphragm, piston valve and valve spring. Replace if necessary
	6. Improper float level	Adjust. Check needle valve and float; replace if necessary. Clean fuel strainer
Engine will not start (with choke lever operated)	1. Faulty starter plunger	Retighten starter rod screw. Check choke lever stop spring and, if necessary, replace
	2. Clogged or loose starter jet	Clean or retighten
	3. Leaky starter plunger body gasket	Retighten or replace

4. Special Tools and Adhesive

a) Throttle valve adjust tool
This tool is designed to adjust carburetor without removing it from the motorcycle. It is a combination of a 10mm box wrench and plain head screwdriver.

b) Thread Lock Cement
The thread lock cement is used to lock the starter rod screw.

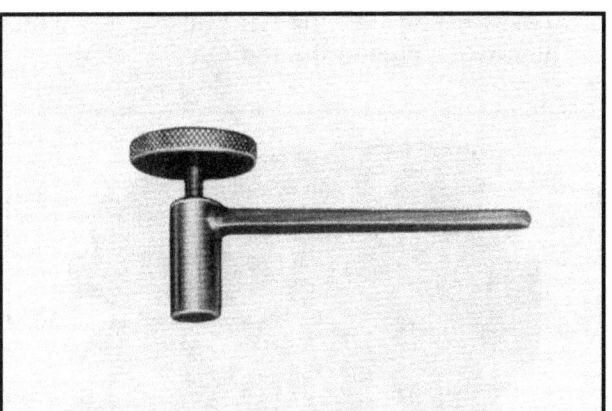

Fig. 9

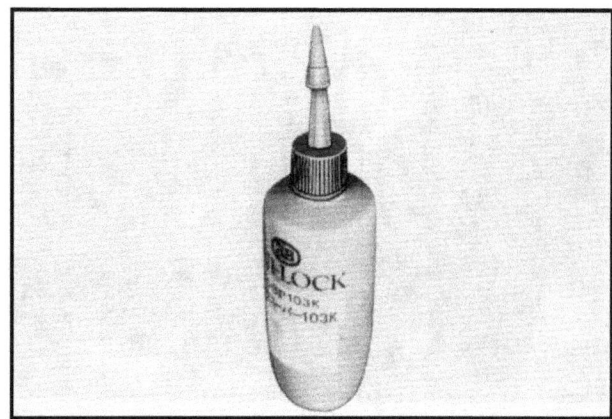

Fig. 10

Part Name	Throttle Valve Adjust Tool
Part No.	09913-13110

Part Name	Thread Lock Cement "103K"
Part No.	99000-32030

CHAPTER 2. REPAIR AND ADJUSTMENT

1. Disassembly

a) Remove the fuel hose and vacuum hose; take out the fuel tank. Remove the air cleaner.

1. Fuel hose 2. Vacuum hose Fig. 2-1

b) Loosen the throttle cable adjuster; free the cable end from the pulley.

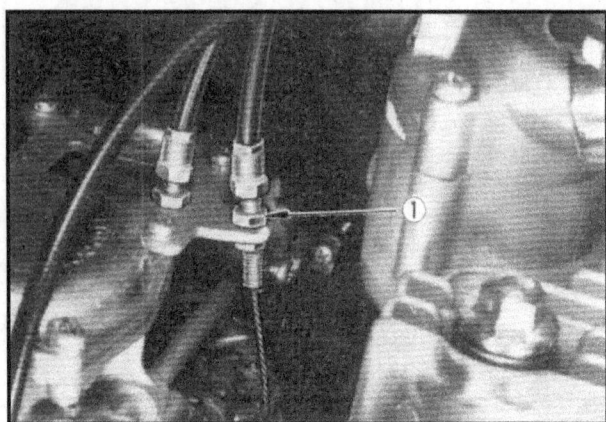

1. Throttle cable adjuster Fig. 2-2

c) Loosen the adjusting nut at the oil pump control rod. Disconnect the rod from the oil pump control lever.

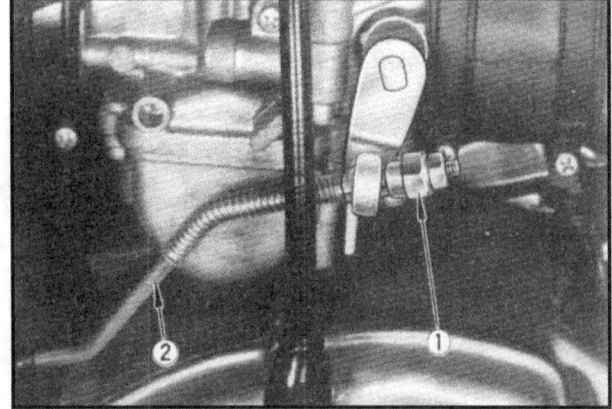

1. Adjusting nut 2. Oil pump control rod Fig. 2-3

d) Loosen the clamp at the carburetor inlet side; remove the carburetor.

e) Loosen a total of three screws at the starter rod. While pushing the rod toward the inside slightly, withdraw the starter rod. It is necessary to turn the rod in the arrow direction when pulling the rod out.

1. Starter rod 3. Choke lever
2. Starter rod screw

Fig. 2-4

f) Turn out the throttle valve adjust screw just enough to cause a clearance between the throttle valve lever and end of the screw.

1. Throttle valve adjust screw 2. Throttle valve lever

Fig. 2-5

g) Loosen the screws securing the carburetor upper bracket and L-shaped bracket at the bottom.

h) Remove the mixing chamber top and take out the piston valve spring and piston valve.

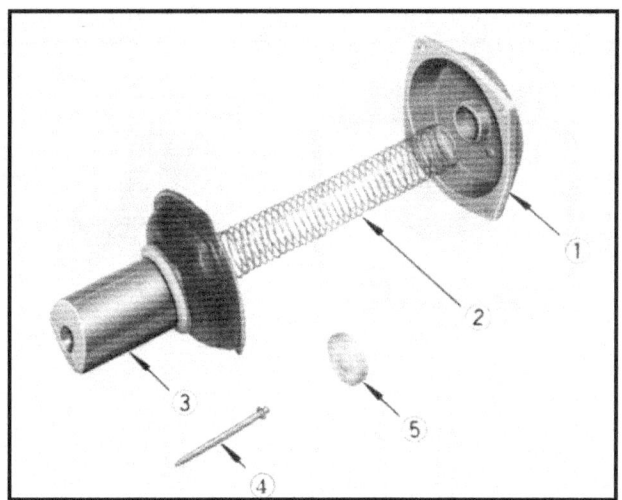

1. Mixing chamber top
2. Piston valve spring
3. Piston valve
4. Jet needle
5. Jet needle set plate

Fig. 2-6

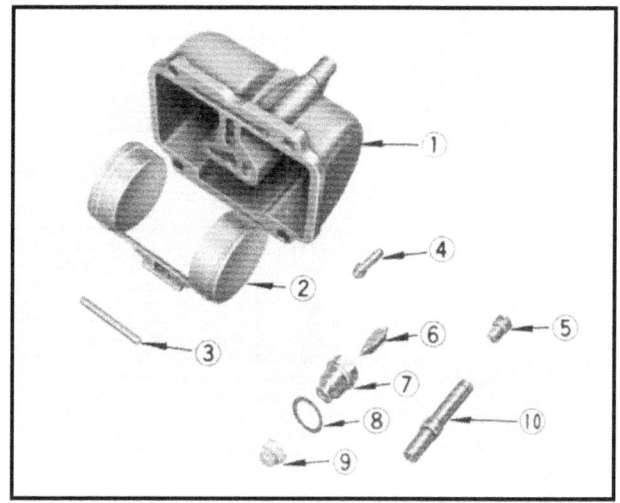

1. Float chamber
2. Float
3. Float arm pin
4. Pilot jet
5. Main jet
6. Needle valve
7. Valve seat
8. Valve seat gasket
9. Fuel strainer
10. Needle jet

Fig. 2-8

Note:

Place the piston valves in order in a part rack so that they can be placed back to their original locations or carburetors with which they were mated. Neglecting this caution could result in faulty piston valve.

i) Remove the drain plug at the bottom of the float chamber. With the use of a suitable screwdriver, turn off the main jet.

1. Float chamber   2. Drain plug   Fig. 2-7

j) Loosen the float chamber attaching screw. Remove the float chamber. Using a pair of pliers, remove the pin from the float arm. Take out the float and needle valve.
With help of a suitable screwdriver, turn off the pilot jet from the float chamber. Pull out by hand the needle jet from the carburetor body. After removing the valve seat, separate the fuel strainer from the seat.

2. Inspections

a) Piston valve

Examine the diaphragm and piston valve, particularly on its sliding surfaces. Replace the piston valve if the diaphragm is broken, or if its edge is weakened. Replace the carburetor as an assembled unit if the piston valve is scored or worn excessively.

b) Needle valve, valve seat and fuel strainer

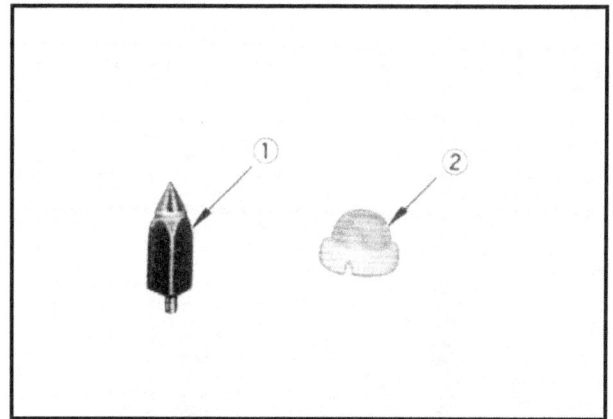

1. Needle valve   2. Fuel strainer   Fig. 2-9

Be sure that the tapered point of the needle valve is not worn. Replace the needle valve and valve seat as a matched set if the point is stepped. Be sure that all residue is washed from the strainer. Discard the strainer if broken.

c) Float level

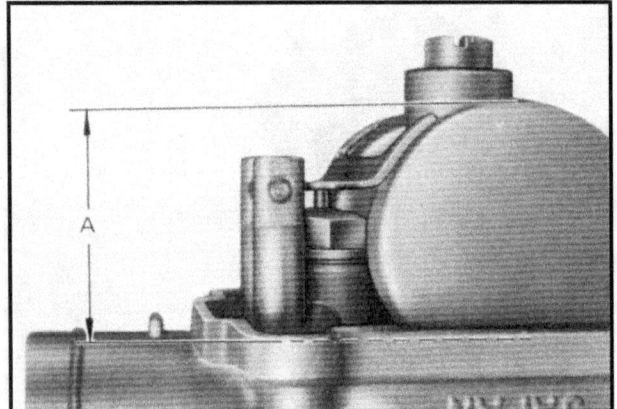

1. Float height   Fig. 2-10

Assemble the valve seat, needle valve and float in the float chamber. Tilt the chamber at 10° ~ 30° from vertical. Without disturbing the above setup, measure the distance between the chamber attaching face and top of the float (without thickness of gasket). Adjustment can be made by bending the float arm.

Standard float height	27.6 ± 1 mm (1.09 ± 0.04 in)

d) Piston valve spring

Check the tension of the piston valve spring. This can be made by compressing the spring to 68 mm (2.39 in). Springs that exceed the following limits should be replaced with new ones.

Spring length	Tension
68 mm (1.39 in)	100 ± 10 g (0.22 ± 0.02 lb)

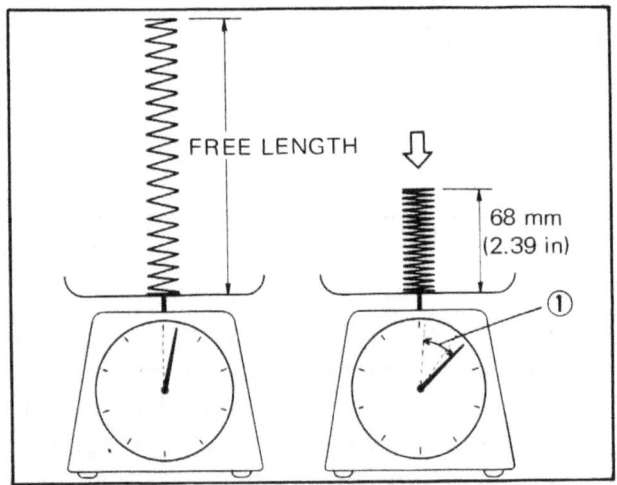

1. Spring tension   Fig. 2-11

e) Gasket and O-ring

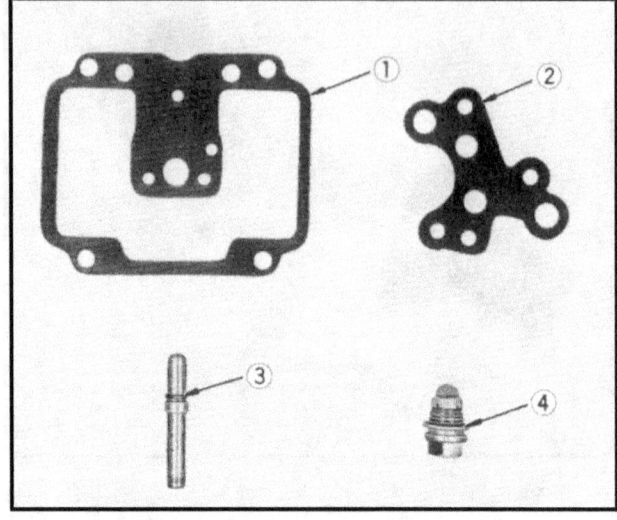

1. Float chamber gasket   3. Needle jet O-ring
2. Starter plunger body gasket 4. Valve seat gasket

Fig. 2-12

Examine all gaskets and O-ring, and make sure that they are in perfect condition. Broken or deteriorated gaskets or O-ring should be discarded, and new ones installed.

3. Assembly and Adjustment

Wash all parts in clean solvent and dry with compressed air.

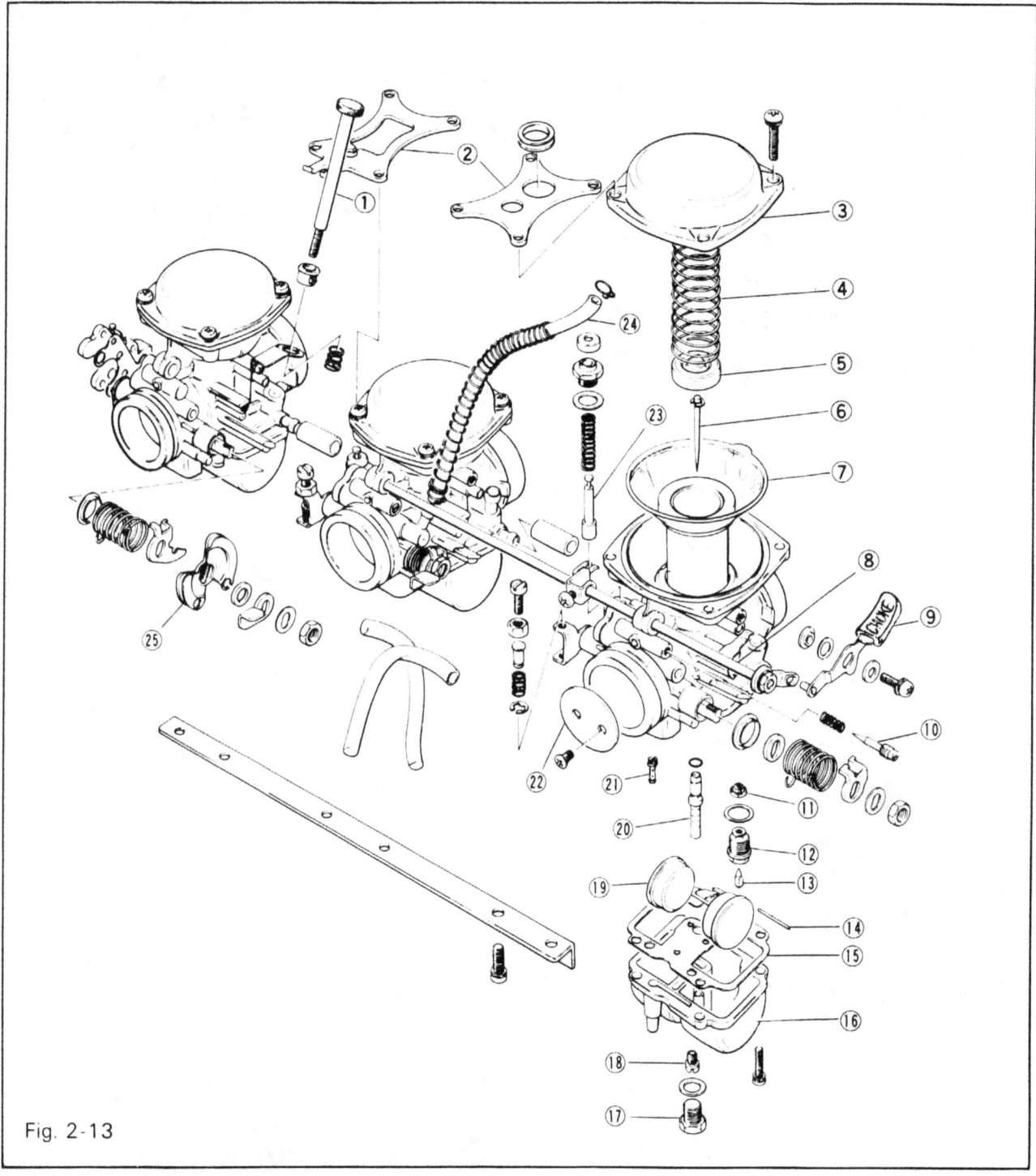

Fig. 2-13

1. Throttle valve stop screw
2. Bracket
3. Mixing chamber top
4. Piston valve spring
5. Jet needle set plate
6. Jet needle
7. Piston valve
8. Starter rod
9. Choke lever
10. Pilot screw
11. Fuel strainer
12. Valve seat
13. Needle valve
14. Float arm pin
15. Float chamber gasket
16. Float chamber
17. Drain plug
18. Main jet
19. Float
20. Needle jet
21. Pilot jet
22. Throttle valve
23. Starter plunger
24. Fuel hose
25. Pulley

a) Assemble the main jet, pilot jet and needle jet as they should.

b) Position the gasket on the carburetor body so that the holes indicated with arrow mark in the figure are opposite to the starter pipe.

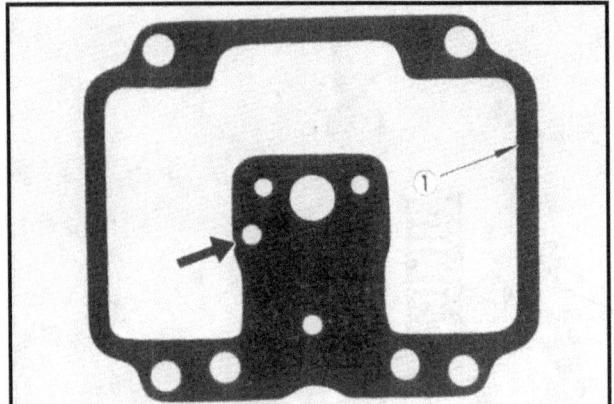

1. Mixing chamber gasket   Fig. 2-14

c) Insert the jet needle and jet needle set plate into place in the piston valve. Enter the valve in the carburetor body.
Press the edge of the diaphragm into place in the groove in the carburetor snugly. Make certain that the lug of the diaphragm is lined up with the notch cut in the carburetor before installation.

1. Lug   2. Notch   Fig. 2-15

d) Install the upper and lower brackets, and then tighten the screws.

e) With the starter plunger lever placed on the end of the plunger, run the starter rod starting with the left carburetor. Apply a coating of Thread Lock Cement, No. 99000-32030, to the threaded part of the starter rod screws and tighten the screws securely.

1. Starter rod screw   2. Starter rod   Fig. 2-16

f) Turn in or out the right side carburetor throttle valve stop screw until the highest point of the throttle valve is in line with the edge of No.1 bypass hole.

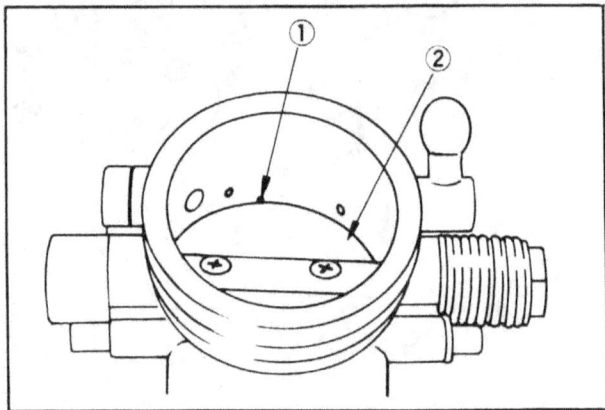

1. Bypass hole (No.1)   2. Throttle valve   Fig. 2-17

g) In like manner as above, turn in or out the throttle valve adjust screw at the center carburetor until the top of the throttle valve aligns with the edge of No. 1 bypass hole. Apply the same technique to the left carburetor.

1. Throttle valve adjust screw   Fig. 2-18

h) Gently turn in the pilot screw until they seat; then turn them out 1/4 turn each.

i) Install the carburetor in the reverse order of the removal.

j) Adjust the throttle cables (pull side and return side) so that the deflections are 3 ~ 5 mm (0.12 ~ 0.20 in) when a thumb pressure 100 ~ 200 g (0.22 ~ 0.44 lb) is applied between the cable adjuster and cable end.

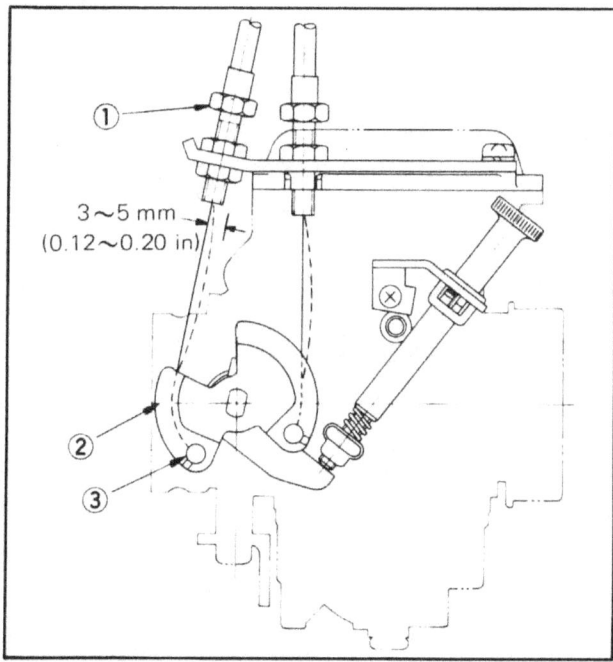

1. Throttle cable adjuster   3. Cable end   Fig. 2-19
2. Pulley

k) Start and warm up the engine for about five minutes. Turn out the throttle valve stop screw until the engine runs at 1,000 rpm.

l) Finally align the marking on the oil pump control lever with that on the oil pump. This can be done by turning in or out the adjust nut as necessary.

1. Aligning mark   Fig. 2-20

4. Carburetor Adjustment

Observe either of the following procedures when making a throttle-opening (balance) adjustment during periodic maintenance, etc.

Off-motorcycle adjustment:
    Follow the steps "f" thru "m" under Assembly in Chapter 3 above.

On-motorcycle adjustment:
    Proper procedure for adjustment of carburetor on motorcycle is as follows. However, carburetor should not be adjusted unless the following items or parts are properly adjusted.

- Contact breaker point gap
- Spark plug gap
- Ignition timing
- Pilot screw opening
- Throttle cable deflection

1. Start and warm up the engine for about five minutes.
2. Turn in the throttle valve stop screw so that the engine will run at about 3,000 rpm.
3. Ground the contact breaker points or remove the spark plug caps so that the center and left cylinders will not fire.
   Turn in or out the throttle valve stop screw at the right carburetor so that the engine will run at 1,000 rpm.

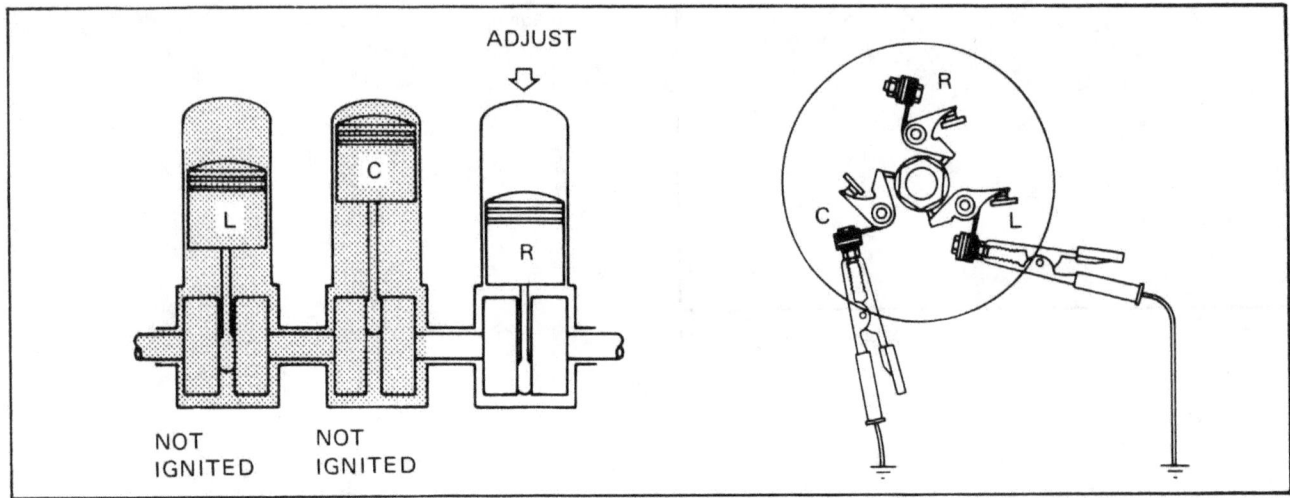

4. In like manner as above, disable the right and left cylinders. Using tool "Valve Adjust Tool No. 09913-13110", rotate the throttle valve adjust screw at the center carburetor until the engine runs at 1,000 rpm.

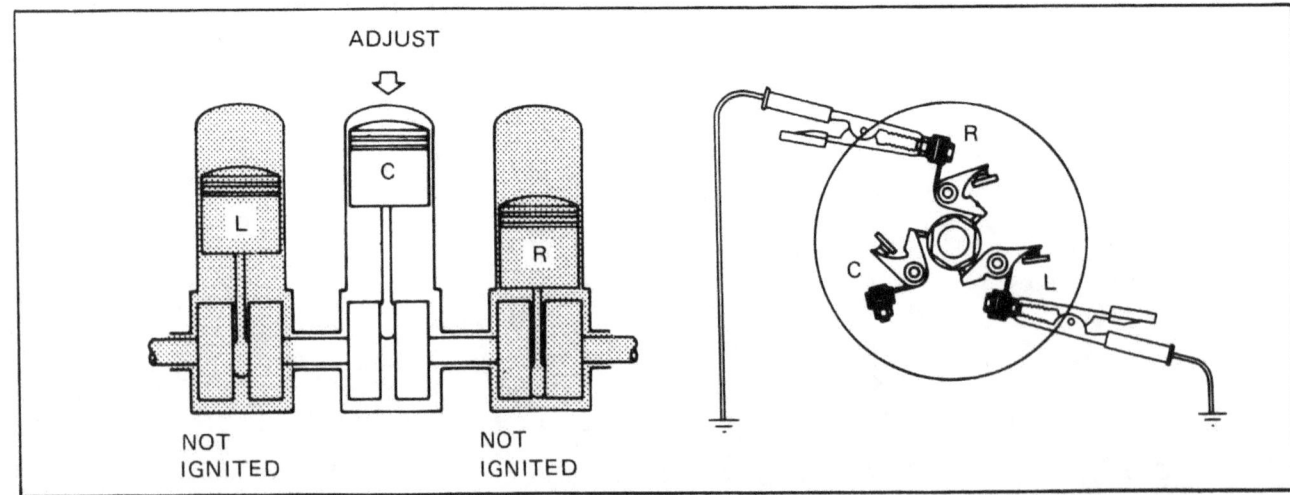

5. At this point, turn the throttle valve adjust screw at the left side carburetor as necessary. Stop turning the screw when the engine runs at 1,000 rpm.

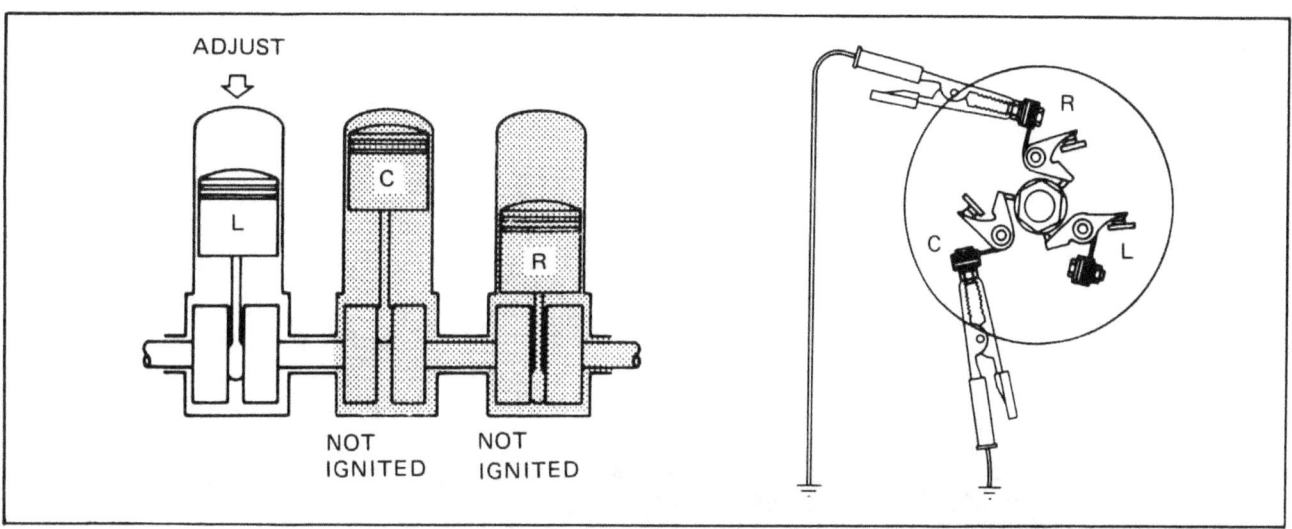

6. Finally, fire all cylinders. Turn out the throttle valve stop screw so that the engine will run at 1,000 rpm.

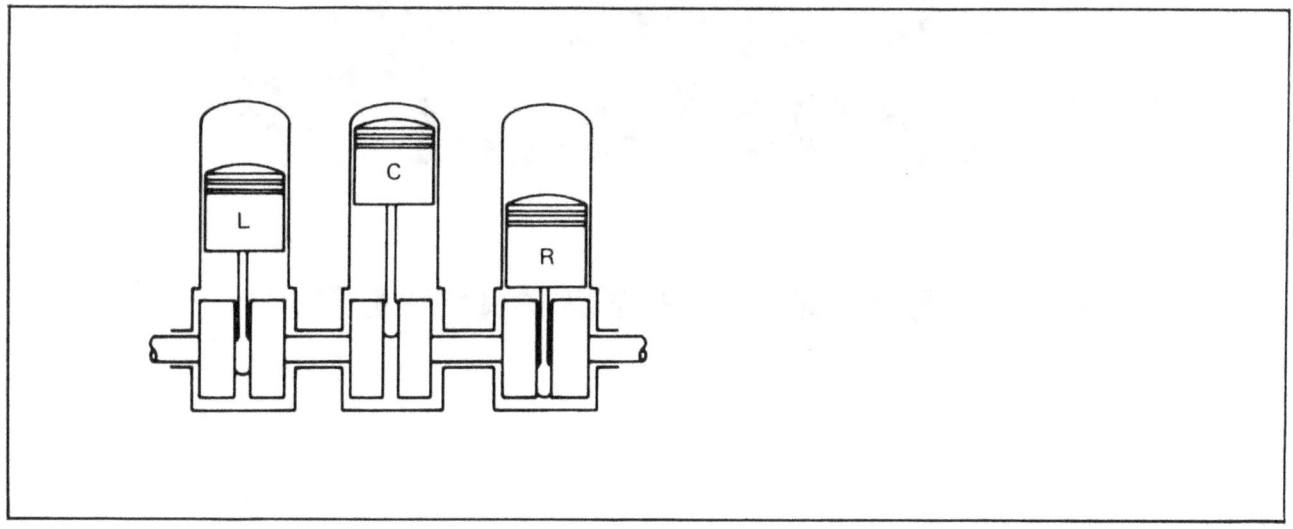

SUZUKI MOTOR CO., LTD.

VELOCEPRESS.com - MOTORCYCLE MANUALS BY MAKE

AJS 1932-1948 SINGLES & TWINS 250cc THRU 1000cc (BOOK OF)
AJS 1945-1956 SINGLES RIGID & SPTRING FACTORY WSM & PARTS
AJS 1945-1960 SINGLES MODELS 16 & 18 350cc & 500cc (BOOK OF)
AJS 1948-1956 TWINS MODELS 20 & 30 FACTORY WSM & PARTS
AJS 1955-1965 SINGLES MODELS 16 & 18 350cc & 500cc (BOOK OF)
AJS 1957-1966 SINGLES & TWINS (ALL) FACTORY WSM
AJS 1959-1969 G80CS G85CS & P11 OFF ROAD FACTORY WSM
AJS 1968-1974 STORMER FACTORY WSM & PARTS LIST
ARIEL UP TO 1932 (BOOK OF)
ARIEL 1932-1939 PREWAR MODELS (BOOK OF)
ARIEL 1933-1951 (WORKSHOP MANUAL)
ARIEL 1939-1960 4 STROKE SINGLES (BOOK OF)
ARIEL 1958-1964 LEADER & ARROW FACTORY WSM & PARTS LIST
ARIEL 1958-1964 LEADER & ARROW (BOOK OF)
BMW R26 R27 (1956-1967) FACTORY WORKSHOP MANUAL
BMW R50 R50S R60 R69S (1955-1969) FACTORY WORKSHOP MANUAL
BMW R50/5 R60/5 R75/5 (1969-1973) FACTORY WORKSHOP MANUAL
BRIDGESTONE 90 SERIES FACTORY WSM & PARTS CATALOGUE
BRIDGESTONE 175 SERIES FACTORY WSM & PARTS CATALOGUE
BRIDGESTONE 350 SERIES FACTORY WSM & PARTS CATALOGUES
BSA SERVICE SHEETS MASTER CATALOGUE ALL MODELS 1945-1967
BSA BANTAM D1 TO D7 1948-1966 FACTORY SERVICE SHEETS MANUAL
BSA BANTAM ALL MODELS FROM 1948 ONWARDS (BOOK OF)
BSA BANTAM D14 FACTORY SERVICE MANUAL
BSA DANDY FACTORY WORKSHOP MANUAL (COMPILATION)
BSA SINGLES & V-TWINS UP TO 1926 inc. 1927 SUPPLEMENT (BOOK OF)
BSA SINGLES & V-TWINS UP TO 1930 (BOOK OF)
BSA SINGLES & V-TWINS UP TO 1935 (BOOK OF)
BSA SINGLES & V-TWINS 1936-1939 (BOOK OF)
BSA C10, C11 & C12 1945-1958 FACTORY SERVICE SHEETS MANUAL
BSA OHV & SV SINGLES 250-600cc 1945-1959 (BOOK OF)
BSA C15 & B40 1958-1967 FACTORY SERVICE SHEETS MANUAL
BSA OHV & SV SINGLES 250cc (ONLY) 1954-1970 (BOOK OF)
BSA B31, B32, B33 & B34 1945-60 FACTORY SERVICE SHEETS MANUAL
BSA OHV SINGLES 350 & 500cc 1955-1967 (BOOK OF)
BSA M20, M21 & M33 1945-1963 FACTORY SERVICE SHEETS MANUAL
BSA TWINS A7 & A10 1948-1962 FACTORY SERVICE SHEETS MANUAL
BSA TWINS A7 & A10 1948-1962 (BOOK OF)
BSA TWINS A50 & A65 1962-1965 FACTORY WORKSHOP MANUAL
BSA TWINS A50 & A65 1962-1969 (SECOND BOOK OF)
BULTACO 125cc to 37cc SINGLES 1968-1979 WORKSHOP MANUAL
CZ 125cc to 380cc SINGLES 1967-1974 WORKSHOP MANUAL
DOUGLAS 1929-1939 PREWAR ALL MODELS (BOOK OF)
DOUGLAS 1948-1957 POSTWAR ALL MODELS FACTORY SHOP MANUAL
DUCATI 160cc, 250cc & 350cc OHC MODELS FACTORY SHOP MANUAL
HODAKA 90cc,100cc & 125cc SINGLES 1964-1978 WORKSHOP MANUAL
HONDA 50cc ALL MODELS UP TO 1970 INC MONKEY & TRAIL (BOOK OF)
HONDA 90cc ALL MODELS UP TO 1966 (BOOK OF)
HONDA TWINS & SINGLES 50cc THRU 305cc 1960-1966 (BOOK OF)
HONDA TWINS ALL MODELS 125cc THRU 450cc UP TO 1968 (BOOK OF)
HONDA C100 50cc SUPER CUB O.H.V. 1959-1962 FACTORY WSM
HONDA C110 50cc SPORT CUB O.H.C. 1960-1962 FACTORY WSM
HONDA 50-65-70-90cc O.H.C. SINGLES 1959-1983 WSM
HONDA 100-125cc SINGLES CB/CD/CL/SL/TL 1970-1984 FACTORY WSM
HONDA 150-125cc TWINS C/CS/CB/CA 1959-1966 FACTORY WSM
HONDA 125-160-175-200cc TWINS 1965-1978 WORKSHOP MANUAL
HONDA 250-305cc TWINS C/CS/CB 1961-1968 FACTORY WSM
HOHDA 250-350cc TWINS CB/CL/SL 1968-1973 FACTORY WSM
HONDA 250-360cc TWINS CB/CL/CJ 1974-1977 FACTORY WSM
HONDA 350F & 400F 4-CYLINDER 1972-1977 FACTORY WSM
HONDA 450cc TWINS CB/CL 1965-1974 K0 TO K7 WORKSHOP MANUAL
HONDA 500cc & 550cc 4-CYL 1971-1978 FACTORY WORKSHOP MANUAL
HONDA 750cc SHOC 4-CYL 1969-1978 K0~K8 WORKSHOP MANUAL
HUSQVARNA 125cc to 450cc SINGLES 1965-1975 WORKSHOP MANUAL
INDIAN PONYBIKE, BOY RACER & PAPOOSE ILL PARTS LIST & SALES LIT
J.A.P. ENGINES 1927-1952 & MOTORCYCLES 1934-1952 (BOOK OF)
KAWASAKI TRIPLES 1968-1980 ALL MODELS 250cc to 750cc WSM
MAICO 250cc to 501cc 1968-1978 WORKSHOP MANUAL

MATCHLESS 1931-1939 ALL MODELS 250cc THRU 990cc (BOOK OF)
MATCHLESS 1945-1956 RIGID & SPRING FACTORY WSM & PARTS
MATCHLESS 1945-1956 SINGLES G3 & G80 350cc & 500cc (BOOK OF)
MATCHLESS 1948-1956 TWINS G9 & G11 FACTORY WSM & PARTS
MATCHLESS 1955-1966 SINGLES G3 & G80 350cc & 500cc (BOOK OF)
MATCHLESS 1957-1966 SINGLES & TWINS (ALL) FACTORY WSM
MONTESA 1962-1978 125cc to 360cc ALL MODELS WORKSHOP MANUAL
NEW IMPERIAL ALL SV & OHV FROM 1935 ONWARDS (BOOK OF)
NORTON 1932-1939 PREWAR MODELS (BOOK OF)
NORTON 1932-1947 (BOOK OF)
NORTON 1938-1956 (BOOK OF)
NORTON 1945-1963 MODELS 16H, Big4, ES2, 19 & 50 WSM'S & PARTS
NORTON 1955-1963 MODELS 19, 50 & ES2 (BOOK OF)
NORTON 1948-1970 DOMINATOR TWINS FACTORY WSM'S & PARTS
NORTON 1955-1965 DOMINATOR TWINS (BOOK OF)
NORTON 1960-1970 TWIN CYLINDER FACTORY WORKSHOP MANUAL
NORTON 1970-1975 COMMANDO 850 & 750cc FACTORY WSM
NORTON 1975-1978 MK 3 COMMANDO 850 cc FACTORY WSM
OSSA 1971-1978 125cc, 175cc, 250cc, 310cc WSM
PANTHER 1932-1958 LIGHTWEIGHT MODELS 250 & 350cc (BOOK OF)
PANTHER 1938-1966 HEAVYWEIGHT MODELS 600 & 650cc (BOOK OF)
PENTON-KTM-SACHS 1968-1975 100cc & 125cc WORKSHOP MANUAL
PENTON-KTM 1972-1975 175cc, 250cc & 400cc WSM & PARTS MANUALS
PENTON-KTM 1972-1979 125cc to 400cc ENGINE WSM & PARTS MANUAL
RALEIGH MOTORCYCLES 1919-1933 (BOOK OF)
ROYAL ENFIELD 1934-1946 SINGLES & V TWINS (BOOK OF)
ROYAL ENFIELD 1937-1953 SINGLES & V TWINS (BOOK OF)
ROYAL ENFIELD 1946-1962 SINGLES (BOOK OF)
ROYAL ENFIELD 1948-1962 350cc & 500cc PRE-UNIT BULLET WSM
ROYAL ENFIELD 1948-1963 500cc TWINS FACTORY WORKSHOP MANUAL
ROYAL ENFIELD 1952-1963 700cc TWINS FACTORY WORKSHOP MANUAL
ROYAL ENFIELD 1956-1966 250cc CRUSADER & 350cc NEW BULLET WSM
ROYAL ENFIELD 1958-1966 250cc & 350cc SINGLES (SECOND BOOK OF)
ROYAL ENFIELD 1962-1970 INTERCEPTOR WSM'S & PARTS (Compilation)
RUDGE 1933-1939 (BOOK OF)
SACHS 1968-1975 100cc & 125cc ENGINES WSM & M/CYCLE PARTS LIST
SUNBEAM 1928-1939 (BOOK OF)
SUNBEAM 1946-1957 S7 & S8 (BOOK OF)
SUZUKI 50cc & 80cc UP TO 1966 (BOOK OF)
SUZUKI T10 1963-1967 FACTORY WORKSHOP MANUAL
SUZUKI T20 & T200 1965-1969 FACTORY WORKSHOP MANUAL
SUZUKI TWINS 1962 ONWARDS 125-500cc WORKSHOP MANUAL
SUZUKI GT750 1971-1977 A COMPILATION OF 4 FACTORY WSM's
TRIUMPH 1935-1949 SINGLES & TWINS (BOOK OF)
TRIUMPH 1937-1961 SINGLES SV & OHV 250cc-600cc + TERRIER & CUB
TRIUMPH 1945-1955 PRE-UNIT 350cc, 500cc & 650cc TWINS WSM No.11
TRIUMPH 1945-1959 TWINS (BOOK OF)
TRIUMPH 1956-1969 TWINS (BOOK OF)
TRIUMPH 1956-1962 PRE-UNIT 500cc & 650cc TWINS WSM No.17
TRIUMPH 1957-1963 UNIT CONSTRUCTION 350-500cc WSM No.4
TRIUMPH 1963-1974 UNIT CONSTRUCTION 350-500cc FACTORY WSM
TRIUMPH 1963-1970 UNIT CONSTRUCTION 650cc FACTORY WSM
TRIUMPH 1968-1974 TRIDENT T150 & T150V FACTORY WSM
TRIUMPH 1971-1973 650cc OIL-IN-FRAME FACTORY WSM
TRIUMPH 1973-1978 BONNEVILLE & TIGER FACTORY WSM
TRIUMPH 1979-1983 750cc T140, TR7 & TR65 FACTORY WSM
VELOCETTE 1925-1970 ALL SINGLES & TWINS (BOOK OF)
VELOCETTE 1933-1952 MOV-MAC-MSS RIGID FRAME FACTORY WSM
VELOCETTE 1953-1960 MAC SPRING FRAME WSM & ILL PARTS LIST
VELOCETTE 1954-1971 MSS-VENOM-THRUXTON-VIPER FACTORY WSM
VILLIERS ENGINE UP TO 1959 INC. 3 WHEELERS (BOOK OF)
VILLIERS ENGINE UP TO 1969 (BOOK OF)
VINCENT 1935-1955 (WORKSHOP MANUAL)
YAMAHA 1961-1967 YA5 & YA6 (WORKSHOP MANUAL & ILL PARTS LIST)
YAMAHA 1963-1976 50cc to 100cc ROTARY VALVE SINGLES WSM
YAMAHA 1968-1971 DT1 & MX SERIES Inc. GYT WORKSHOP MANUAL
YAMAHA 1971-1972 JT1& JT2 (WORKSHOP MANUAL & ILL PARTS LIST)

VELOCEPRESS.com – SCOOTER MANUALS

BSA SUNBEAM SCOOTER WORKSHOP MANUAL 1959-1965
BSA SUNBEAM SCOOTER 1959-1965 (BOOK OF)
LAMBRETTA 1947-1957 ALL 125 & 150cc MODELS (BOOK OF)
LAMBRETTA 1957-1970 LI & TV MODELS (SECOND BOOK OF)
NSU PRIMA 1956-1964 ALL MODELS (BOOK OF)
TRIUMPH TIGRESS SCOOTER WORKSHOP MANUAL 1959-1965
TRIUMPH TIGRESS SCOOTER (BOOK OF)
VESPA 1951-1961 (BOOK OF)
VESPA 1955-1963 125 & 150cc & GS MODELS (SECOND BOOK OF)
VESPA 1955-1968 GS & SS (BOOK OF)
VESPA 1963-1972 90, 125 & 150cc (THIRD BOOK OF)

VELOCEPRESS.com - MOPEDS & MOTORIZED BICYCLES MANUALS

CYCLEMOTOR (BOOK OF)
NSU QUICKLY 1953-1963 ALL MODELS (BOOK OF)
PUCH MAXI N & S MAINTENANCE & REPAIR (3 MANUAL COMPILATION)
RALEIGH MOPEDS 1960-1969 (BOOK OF)

VELOCEPRESS.com - THREE WHEELER MANUALS

BOND MINICAR THREE WHEELER 1948-1967 (BOOK OF)
BMW ISETTA FACTORY WORKSHOP MANUAL
BSA THREE WHEELER (BOOK OF)
RELIANT REGAL THREE WHEELER 1952-1973 (BOOK OF)
VINTAGE MORGAN THREE WHEELER (BOOK OF)

VELOCEPRESS.com – MOTORCYCLE TECHNICAL BOOKS

1930'S BRITISH MOTORCYCLE CARBS & ELEC COMPONENTS (BOOK OF)
1930'S BRITISH MOTORCYCLE ENGINES (OVERHAUL & MAINTENANCE)
1930'S BRITISH MOTORCYCLE GEARBOXES & CLUTCHES (BOOK OF)
CATALOG OF BRITISH MOTORCYCLES (1951 MODELS)
LUCAS ELECTRONICS BRITISH M/CYCLES REPAIR & PARTS (1950-1977)
MOTORCYCLE ENGINEERING (P.E. Irving)
MOTORCYCLE ROAD TESTS 1949-1953 (Motor Cycle Magazine UK)
SPEED AND HOW TO OBTAIN IT (Motor Cycle Magazine UK)
TUNING FOR SPEED (P.E. Irving)
WIPAC (COMBO) MANUAL NUMBER 3 + M/CYCLE & SCOOTER MANUAL

www.VelocePress.com

VELOCEPRESS.com - AUTOMOBILE MANUALS BY MAKE

ALFA ROMEO GIULIA WORKSHOP MANUAL 1300 TO 2000cc 1962-1975
ALFA ROMEO GIULIA TECH MANUAL CARBURETED CARS FROM 1962
ALFA ROMEO GIULIA TECH MANUAL FUEL INJECTED CARS FROM 1969
ALFA ROMEO GIULIETTA & GIULIA 750 & 101 SERIES 1955-1965 WSM
AUSTIN-HEALEY SPRITE & MG MIDGET WORKSHOP MANUAL 1958-1971
BMW 600 LIMOUSINE FACTORY WORKSHOP MANUAL
BMW 600 LIMOUSINE OWNERS HAND BOOK & SERVICE MANUAL
BMW 2000 & 2002 1966-1976 WORKSHOP MANUAL
BMW 2500, 2800, 3.0 & BARVARIA WORKSHOP MANUAL
CORVAIR 1960-1969 WORKSHOP MANUAL
CORVETTE V8 1955-1962 WORKSHOP MANUAL
FERRARI HANDBOOK ROAD & RACE CARS (SERVICE/SPECS) 1948-1958
FERRARI 250GT SERVICE & MAINTENANCE by JIM RIFF 1956-1965
FERRARI 250GT & 250GTE FACTORY PARTS AND REPAIR MANUALS
FIAT 500 FACTORY WORKSHOP MANUAL 1957-1973
FIAT 600, 600D & MULTIPLA FACTORY WORKSHOP MANUAL 1955-1969
FORD MUSTANG 1965-1973 TRANSMISSION WORKSHOP MANUAL
JAGUAR E-TYPE 3.8 & 4.2 SERIES 1 & 2 WORKSHOP MANUAL
JAGUAR MK 7, 8, 9 & XK120, 140, 150 WORKSHOP MANUAL 1948-1961
MERCEDES-BENZ 230 SERIES 1963-1968
MERCEDES-BENZ 280 SERIES 1968-1972
METROPOLITAN FACTORY WORKSHOP MANUAL
MGA & MGB OWNERS HANDBOOK & WORKSHOP MANUAL
MG MIDGET TC, TD, TF & TF1500 WORKSHOP MANUAL
PORSCHE 356 1948-1965 WORKSHOP MANUAL
PORSCHE 911 2.0, 2.2, 2.4 LITRE 1964-1973 WORKSHOP MANUAL
PORSCHE 911 2.7, 3.0, 3.2 LITRE 1973-1989 WORKSHOP MANUAL
PORSCHE 912 WORKSHOP MANUAL
PORSCHE 914/4 & 914/6 1.7, 1.8, 2.0 LITRE 1970-1976 WSM
TRIUMPH TR2, TR3, TR4 1953-1965 WORKSHOP MANUAL
VOLKSWAGEN TRANSPORTER, TRUCKS & WAGONS 1950-1979 WSM
VOLVO 1944-1968 ALL MODELS WORKSHOP MANUAL

VELOCEPRESS.com - AUTOMOBILE TECHNICAL BOOKS

HOW TO BUILD A FIBERGLASS CAR
HOW TO BUILD A RACING CAR
HOW TO RESTORE THE MODEL 'A' FORD
MASERATI OWNER'S HANDBOOK
PERFORMANCE TUNING THE SUNBEAM TIGER
SOUPING THE VOLKSWAGEN
SOLEX CARBURETORS (EMPHASIS ON UK & EU AUTOMOBILES)
SU CARBURETORS (EMPHASIS ON UK AUTOMOBILES)
WEBER CARBURETORS (EMPHASIS ON ALFA & FIAT)

VELOCEPRESS.com – AUTOMOBILE BOOKS & GUIDES

COMPLETE CATALOG OF JAPANESE MOTOR VEHICLES
FERRARI 308 SERIES BUYER'S AND OWNER'S GUIDE
FERRARI BROCHURES AND SALES LITERATURE 1968-1989
FERRARI SERIAL NUMBERS PART I - ODD NUMBERS TO 21399
FERRARI SERIAL NUMBERS PART II - EVEN NUMBERS TO 1050
HENRY'S FABULOUS MODEL "A" FORD
MASERATI BROCHURES AND SALES LITERATURE

VELOCEPRESS.com - AUTO RACING BOOKS

BOOK OF THE 1950 CARRERA PANAMERICANA - MEXICAN ROAD RACE
DIALED IN - THE JAN OPPERMAN STORY
VEDA ORR'S NEW REVISED HOT ROD PICTORIAL
LIFE OF TED HORN – AMERICAN RACING CHAMPION

www.VelocePress.com

www.ingramcontent.com/pod-product-compliance
Lightning Source LLC
Chambersburg PA
CBHW081153290426
44108CB00018B/2538